George Wallace

George Wallace. *Source:* Alabama Department of Archives and History, Montgomery, Alabama

George Wallace

Conservative Populist

LLOYD ROHLER

Great American Orators, Number 32
Bernard K. Duffy and Halford R. Ryan, Series Advisers

Westport, Connecticut
London

Library of Congress Cataloging-in-Publication Data

Rohler, Lloyd Earl, 1945–
    George Wallace : conservative populist / Lloyd Rohler.
        p.   cm. — (Great American orators, ISSN 0898–8277 ; no. 32)
    Includes bibliographical references and index.
    ISBN 0–313–31119–6 (hardcover : alk. paper)
1. Wallace, George C. (George Corley), 1919– 2. Governors—Alabama—Biography.
3. Presidential candidates—United States—Biography. 4. Conservatism—Alabama—
History—20th century. 5. Conservatism—United States—History—20th century.
6. Populism—Alabama—History—20th century. 7. Populism—United States—History—
20th century. 8. Alabama—Politics and government—1951– 9. Alabama—Politics and
government—1951—Sources. 10. United States—Politics and government—1945–1989—
Sources. I. Title. II. Series.
F330.3.W3R645   2004
976.1'063'092—dc22   2004014144

British Library Cataloguing in Publication Data is available.

Library of Congress Catalog Card Number: 2004014144
ISBN: 0–313–31119–6
ISSN: 0898–8277

First published in 2004

Praeger Publishers, 88 Post Road West, Westport, CT 06881
An imprint of Greenwood Publishing Group, Inc.
www.praeger.com

Printed in the United States of America

The paper used in this book complies with the
Permanent Paper Standard issued by the National
Information Standards Organization (Z39.48–1984).

10   9   8   7   6   5   4   3   2   1

Copyright Acknowledgments

The author and publisher gratefully acknowledge the following for permission to quote
from the texts of Wallace's speeches:

Mrs. Forrest Armstrong for the transcript made by her late husband of his tape of George
Wallace's speech at Memphis, Tennessee, June 11, 1968.

The Alabama Department of Archives and History in Montgomery, Alabama, for all other
speech texts.

This book is dedicated to my wife, Diana.

Contents

Preface

George Wallace deserves a place in a series of studies of important speakers in American history as an example of a demagogue and agitator whose power to arouse popular indignation was unequalled in his lifetime. His speeches would never be considered eloquent. They were not models of argument or style or organization. However, they were effective in reaching people who were afraid of the changes that the civil rights revolution was bringing to their neighborhoods, schools, jobs, and communities. Wallace expressed their resentment at their lack of power to resist or affect those changes and their anger at those outsiders who were the agents of change.

Wallace based his political career on the exploitation of fear: fear of blacks, fear of a powerful government, fear of communism. From his losing campaign for the governorship of Alabama in 1958, he drew the lesson that race would be the central issue in his political career, and he determined not to be seen as less extreme on the issue than any future opponent. This shaped his important speeches and actions, from his inaugural address with its proclamation of "segregation today, segregation tomorrow, segregation forever" to his confrontations with the federal government over school integration and voting rights. In doing so, he played an important role in the political scene of the 1960s and 1970s, participating in four presidential elections and acting as a catalyst for political change in the South as it moved from voting solidly Democratic to a competitive two-party region.

This is the first book-length study of Wallace's public speaking during these crucial years of political change. I have reprinted his standard campaign speech from each of his presidential campaigns from 1964 to 1976. I have also reprinted the speeches he made during his confrontations with the federal government over integration at the University of Alabama and his refusal to provide protection for the Selma march. I also provide both his first inaugural address as governor of Alabama and his retirement speech. Finally, I reprint his remarks on the 30th anniversary of the Selma march as an example of his efforts to make amends for his past actions. Most of these texts are not easily available elsewhere, either being found in old newspaper files or in doctoral theses.

This book takes Wallace's claim to be a populist seriously and subjects it to a critical analysis of its usefulness as a mask for his racism and its use in his campaign speeches. The book also examines Wallace's career as a whole by tracing his political development as a supporter of Jim Folsom, a progressive governor of Alabama, to his descent into the politics of racism and his final search for redemption and forgiveness from those he wronged. This is not a biography but an attempt to interpret the career of an important figure in American politics through an examination of his public speaking. This book provides the texts of those speeches so that others may study them and discover for themselves the powerful persuasion that George Wallace used to achieve political power.

Acknowledgments

I gratefully acknowledge the assistance of my editors, Bernard Duffy and Halford R. Ryan in the preparation of this manuscript. I thank Jo Ann Seiple, dean of the College of Arts and Sciences of the University of North Carolina at Wilmington, for a research leave that enabled me to do the research for this book. I could not have finished this book without the support of my wife, Diana, who encouraged me and supported my work.

PART I

Critical Analysis

CHAPTER 1

From Clio, Alabama, to Madison Square Garden: The Political Career of George Wallace

It is not recorded that the first words spoken by George Corley Wallace were "Vote for me," but they should have been, for his life was one long campaign for recognition and power. The main influences were family, community, and an intense ambition. All three motivated George Wallace to seek a political career. After service in World War II, Wallace won a seat in the Alabama General Assembly, where he allied himself with the progressive governor Jim Folsom and began his own quest for the governorship. Following a crushing defeat in 1958, Wallace turned his back on his progressive allies and embraced a politics of racial demagoguery. He would use his great skill at arousing the fears of the white working class to propel himself on to the national political scene and run for president of the United States four times. In the twilight of his political career, he would embark on another campaign for forgiveness from those he wronged and to influence his place in history. His story involves genuine tragedy and suffering, for Wallace himself, as well as for those who lived in Alabama and endured the terrible violence and social trauma involved in forcing the state and its citizens to live up to the constitutional guarantees of equal rights for all.

Family was an important element in shaping George Wallace's ambitions and his character. His grandfather, "Doc" Wallace, was a highly respected country doctor in Barbour County, Alabama. George's father, George Wallace Sr., could never equal the success of Doc Wallace because of poor judgment and poor health. He managed the three tenant farms that Doc Wallace owned before eventually buying them from him.

George Sr. married Mozelle Smith Wallace, a music teacher, in March 1918, and she gave birth to their first son, George C. Wallace, on August 25, 1919, in Clio, Alabama. They called their son George C., never Junior. Although he never ran for office, George's father never stopped talking politics to anyone who would listen, including his son. Barbour County was a very politically conscious part of the state and very proud that seven governors had been born there.

People noted that even as a youngster, George had a way with people. When visitors would come to Clio, George would approach them, introduce himself, and ask if there was anything he could do to help them. At age of 10, he accompanied his father to the courthouse in nearby Clayton to watch election officials hand count the ballots and tally the results. When he was 13, his father was the county campaign manager for Fred Gibson, a candidate for secretary of state, and young George passed out campaign leaflets door to door.

George Wallace's first personal political contest came at the age of 16 when he became a page in the Alabama State Senate.[1] His father drove him to the capitol, gave him a few dollars, and left him to make it on his own. George met every senator and asked each of them to support him for the job. He won election as page by a vote of 21 to 5.[2] Wallace made the most of his opportunity by cultivating the influential senators and even making friends with the representative from his district, Chauncey Sparks. It was at this point in his life that Wallace recognized what his lifelong dream would be. While standing on steps of the State Capitol Building near the very spot where Jefferson Davis had taken the oath as president of the Confederacy, Wallace "knew I would return to that spot. I knew I would be governor."[3]

The following year, 1936, while attending Barbour County High School, George won the state Golden Gloves bantamweight championship. In 1937 his father died, leaving the family almost destitute. That same year, George enrolled in the University of Alabama, supporting himself by boxing professionally and waiting on tables in a boardinghouse. He took an active part in campus politics, becoming president of the freshman class by beating the fraternity-supported candidate. Wallace played to his advantage the role of the poor country boy working his way through college. He soon had a large number of friends who could be depended on for a meal or a few dollars or a place to stay. He graduated from law school in 1942 and promptly enlisted in the U.S. Army Air Corps.[4]

Before being sent overseas, Wallace met and married Lurleen Burns. In the South Pacific, he served as the flight engineer on a B-29 flying from the Mariana Islands bombing missions to Japan. He was released before V-J Day for medical reasons and found employment as an assistant attorney general for the state of Alabama. In 1947 he successfully launched his political career by running for the state legislature from Barbour County.

He won by a huge margin, polling 618 more votes than the combined total of his two opponents.[5]

Wallace served two terms in the state legislature and was recognized by political observers as a progressive who could be counted on to support and sponsor many good bills in the public interest. Wallace fought for vocational and trade schools and for scholarships for children and widows of servicemen who lost their lives in the war. He was an ally of Jim Folsom, a progressive governor who tried to pass programs to help poor Alabamians, both black and white. Wallace got Folsom to appoint him a trustee of Tuskegee Institute. In 1948 Wallace was elected as an alternate delegate to the Democratic Convention in Philadelphia. He became the delegate and remained in his seat while other members of the Alabama delegation walked out of the convention. At that same convention, Wallace seconded the nomination of Senator Richard Russell for president. At this stage in his political career, he saw promise in remaining loyal to the national Democratic Party. Wallace was elected circuit judge of the Third Judicial Circuit, which included Barbour County, in 1953.[6]

In 1958 Wallace ran for the governorship in a state that had become obsessed with the issue of race. Reaction to the 1954 Supreme Court decision ordering integration of the public schools and the use of federal troops in Little Rock led to the creation of White Citizens' Councils and to public outrage over the possible desegregation of the pubic school system. Wallace was hampered by the public perception that he was not as ardent a segregationist as John Patterson, the attorney general, who accepted the support of the Ku Klux Klan. Patterson's father had been murdered because he campaigned for attorney general of the state of Alabama on a pledge to clean up Phenix City, Alabama, across the river from nearby Fort Benning, Georgia, and a notorious hotbed of gambling and prostitution. After his father's assassination, under pressure from his father's allies, John Patterson ran unopposed in the special election to replace his father as state attorney general of Alabama.

The story was soon used as the basis for a B-grade movie, *Phenix City Story*, that exploited the emotional appeal of the case by portraying John Patterson as a son who dutifully sought justice for his father's killers. This strong law-and-order appeal was combined with another strong appeal as an effective opponent of civil rights. Patterson had discovered that the National Association for the Advancement of Colored People (NAACP) had never registered with the state of Alabama's secretary of state and was therefore in violation of Alabama law. Patterson sought and obtained an injunction enjoining the NAACP from operating in Alabama. Included in the injunction was an order that the organization turn over its membership list to Patterson's office. The organization spent the next four years fighting the legal battle, including two appeals to the U.S. Supreme Court. The time and money spent fighting the injunction effectively drained resources away from the fight to desegregate Alabama's public schools. Patterson clearly enjoyed the discomfort that his actions had created and reminded audiences in the campaign for governor that he had successfully fought against the organization that was spearheading the attack on segregation.

In a crowed field, Wallace finished second to John Patterson. In the runoff election, Wallace attacked the Klan and defended his record as a judge. He had come under attack for sentencing a young black man involved in an accident and charged with reckless driving to a $25 fine and probation. In an election eve television address, he said, "And I want to tell the good people of this state, as a judge of the third judicial circuit, if I didn't have what it took to treat a man fair, regardless of his color, then I don't have what it takes be the Governor of your great state." Wallace went on to propose new initiatives in education, state old age pensions, conservation, highway construction, and the tourism industry, making sure to reassure the voters that "[t]here will be no race mixing socially or educationally while I'm the Governor of your state."[7] The speech is evidence that before he lost the election and turned to racial demagoguery, Wallace was seriously concerned with dealing with the problems of the state. When he discussed education, instead of vowing to fight integration, he promised to raise teacher's salaries and to propose a bond issue to finance new school construction. He also proposed to raise old age pensions to the maximum amount provided for in the federal-state matching program. He spoke of the need to reapportion the state legislature to allow more representation by the larger counties. He was running on his record and on his reputation as a legislator who tried to do good for the people of the state, but in a dirty campaign that featured anonymous leaflets accusing Wallace of being a draft dodger and a member of the Communist Party, he was overwhelmed. In the runoff election, Wallace lost to Patterson by over 64,000 votes. In analyzing the reason for this devastating loss, Wallace concluded, "John Patterson out-nigguhed me. And boys, I'm not goin' to be out-nigguhed again."[8]

In the waning days of his judgeship, Wallace seized upon an opportunity to force a confrontation with the federal government and lay the basis for his next campaign for governor. On January 9, 1959, federal judge Frank Johnson, an old law school classmate of Wallace, ordered Wallace to make the registration books for Bullock and Barbour counties available to the staff of the Civil Rights Commission, which was investigating black voter registration in Alabama. Wallace had earlier attacked the commission hearings as a "Roman Holiday" and vowed to "stand up and defend the rights of the people of Alabama." Knowing he faced contempt of court if he did not turn over the records, Wallace sought a face-saving compromise. According to eye-witness accounts, Wallace arranged a meeting with Judge Johnson in which he worked out a deal to turn the records over to a grand jury, which would then turn the records over to the Civil Rights Commission. Wallace could claim that he stood up to the federal government, the federal government would get the records, and all would be satisfied. Wallace then called a press conference and proclaimed victory.[9]

For the next four years, Wallace conducted a small law practice with his brother and spent every spare moment speaking to anyone or any group around the state that would listen to him. His campaign officially opened on March 10, 1962, in the city of Montgomery's auditorium, with country music stars headlined by Minnie Pearl. Viewers throughout the state watched on fourteen television stations as "Alabama's Fighting Judge" attacked the "integrating, scallawagging, carpetbaggin" federal judiciary and vowed to "refuse any illegal federal court order" to integrate Alabama's public schools "even to the point of standing at the schoolhouse door."[10] That was the biggest applause line of the entire speech and clearly signaled that George Wallace was going to focus this campaign on the single issue of race. In contrast with his 1958 campaign, the 1962 campaign was better financed; Wallace had the money to hire an effective campaign staff, including an energetic speech writer, Asa Carter. Carter was no stranger to racial politics, having been an organizer for the Alabama White Citizens' Council and later his own Klan organization. He gave Wallace's speeches the applause lines that brought the crowds to their feet. Wallace also relied on print ads and radio commercials, including one that urged Alabama voters to "Vote right—Vote White—Vote for the Fighting Judge."[11]

Although Wallace campaigned throughout the state and wowed growing crowds with his attacks on the federal judiciary, he did not win an outright majority of the votes and was forced into a runoff with Ryan de Graffenried, scion of an old and wealthy Alabama family. Wallace redoubled his efforts and won a convincing victory, carrying 56 of Alabama's 67 counties and 56 percent of the vote. He had achieved his boyhood dream of being elected governor of the state of Alabama but at the price of ransoming the future of his administration and his place in history. Wallace turned his back on his populist instincts and his concern with helping people and cast his lot with those who, fearful of change, were stirring up racial hatred.

In his inaugural address, Wallace's proclamation of "segregation today ... segregation tomorrow ... segregation forever" was a warning to all that he intended to make race central to the politics of his administration. Wallace carried out his campaign pledge by "standing in the door" to prevent the integration of the University of Alabama. In just a few months, Wallace had gone from being a relatively unknown governor to being a national figure challenging the Kennedy administration. He began to get invitations to speak at college campuses in the East and Midwest. It was on one of these speaking engagements, at the University of Wisconsin, that he encountered supporters who encouraged him to run in the presidential Democratic primary in that state. Surprised by the support he found at speaking engagements in Wisconsin, he decided to enter Democratic primaries in Wisconsin, Indiana, and Maryland. In all three primaries, he did surprisingly well. In Maryland he gained 43 percent of the vote.[12] For an ambitious man, the large crowds, the newspaper reporters, and the vote totals were a strong stimulus. Wallace had discovered that his message would play on the national scene, and although 1964 was not the best time for his campaign, 1968 would be another opportunity to run again.

Wallace faced one problem: his term as governor would expire in 1966 and he could not succeed himself. He tried to get the legislature to change the Alabama Constitution to permit him to run again, suffering a rare political defeat when his proposal was defeated. He promptly enlisted his wife, Lurleen, as a surrogate candidate, and with his help she was overwhelmingly elected. Now George Wallace was free to run for president of the United States in 1968. He chose an unconventional means to do so, organizing the American Independent Party and avoiding the Democratic primaries. Despite legal obstacles, the party got onto the ballot in all 50 states. Wallace carried five states, mostly in the Deep South, and won nearly 10 million votes, about 13.5 percent of the popular vote. He came close to his goal of winning enough electoral votes to throw the election into the House of Representatives.

Unfortunately, in May 1968, Lurleen died from cancer. Wallace lost control of the state government to the lieutenant governor, Albert Brewster, who ran for election as governor in his own right in 1970. In a bitter campaign, Wallace again won the governorship in 1970 and prepared for yet another presidential campaign. In 1972 he seemed stronger than ever and, abandoning the American Independent Party, won the Democratic primaries in Florida, Tennessee, North Carolina, and Maryland. While campaigning in Maryland on May 15, 1972, he was shot at point-blank range by Arthur Bremer. Paralyzed from the waist down, Wallace recuperated in a hospital bed while the 1972 Democratic Convention nominated George McGovern. After his hospital stay, Wallace returned to his duties as governor. In the Democratic primaries of May 1974, Wallace easily won the gubernatorial nomination for a third term without a runoff election—a move allowed by an Alabama constitutional amendment, approved in November 1968.

In 1982, following a four-year political hiatus, Wallace returned to the state political scene. He won the Democratic nomination for governor after a runoff and easily defeated Montgomery mayor Emory Folmar, the Republican challenger, in the general election. Wallace won the gubernatorial conquest with the unprecedented support of black voters. For the man who had made his political reputation as an outspoken advocate of segregation, this marked a complete turnabout in his political career. In his last term as governor, Wallace appointed a large number of blacks to state boards and commissions and made a genuine effort to reach out to interest groups that had been excluded from state government during his earlier terms, including black political organizations. He retired from active political life at the end of his fourth term in 1987, but he continued to actively campaign for forgiveness from his enemies and for recognition of his place in history.

In July 1987, Jesse Jackson called on Wallace, and the two men acted out a symbolic scene of forgiveness and redemption. Wallace, who was almost deaf at that point in his life, tried to understand what Jackson was saying to him but failing, looked up at Jackson and asked him to pray for him. The two men clasped hands and joined a circle that included Wallace's son, several ministers who accompanied Jackson, and Wallace's aide. According to Stephan Lesher, who was present as well, Jackson spoke as follows: "We know you're the God of redemption and the God of mercy. In this hour; be with Governor Wallace. . . . Let us be present on this new day when lions and lambs will lie down together, and none will be afraid and all of us can realize the joy in each other and the joy in thee." All who were present joined in a resounding "Amen!"[13]

NOTES

1. Stephan Lesher, *George Wallace: American Populist* (Reading, Mass.: Addison-Wesley, 1994), 20–24. I have relied on this full-length biography for many details.

2. Marshall Frady, *Wallace* (New York: Random House, 1996), 78. Frady's book is the best interpretation of George Wallace available. Although not footnoted, it was written by the *Newsweek* reporter who covered Wallace for most of Wallace's career.

3. Wayne Greenhaw, *Watch Out for George Wallace* (Englewood Cliffs, N.J.: Prentice-Hall, 1976), 94.

4. Lesher, *George Wallace*, 38–46.

5. Frady, *Wallace*, 95.

6. Lesher, *George Wallace*, 89–102.

7. The complete text of this speech by Wallace is reproduced in part 2 of this volume, in "1958 Gubernatorial Campaign Election Eve Appeal."

8. Frady, *Wallace*, 131.

9. Lesher, *George Wallace*, 132–140.

10. Dan T. Carter, *The Politics of Rage: George Wallace, the Origins of the New Conservatism, and the Transformation of American Politics* (New York: Simon & Schuster, 1995), 105.

11. *Montgomery Advertiser*, April 23, 1962.

12. Lesher, *George Wallace*, 303.

13. Lesher, *George Wallace*, 505–506.

CHAPTER 2

Throwing Down the Gauntlet: George Wallace's First Inaugural Speech

On January 14, 1963, George Wallace finally achieved his dream of becoming governor of the state of Alabama. Standing on a special platform near the bronze star that marked the spot on the Capitol's step where Jefferson Davis took the oath as president of the Confederacy, Wallace put his hand on a Bible held by his wife and took the oath administered by his brother, Circuit Judge Jack Wallace.[1] George Wallace and his son were dressed in identical morning coats and silk top hats, but the overcoats that the cold weather forced them to wear muted the effect. After taking the oath, Wallace opened his manuscript on the rostrum and began his inaugural speech with a formal welcome to the visiting dignitaries, which included Ross Barnet, the governor of Mississippi, whose university had been the scene of rioting when James Meredith, a young black man, attempted to integrate it. Asa Carter, a longtime member of the Ku Klux Klan, wrote the speech with the help of Grover Hall, an editor at the *Montgomery Advertiser*.[2] At the conclusion of his welcome, Wallace asks for "a few minutes patience" while he thanks "those home folks of my county who first gave an anxious country boy his opportunity to serve in State politics."[3] After mentioning by name several of the crossroads and small towns of Barbour County, he focuses on Blue Springs, where "the vote was 304 for Wallace and 1 for the opposition . . . and the dear little lady whom I heard had made that one vote against me . . . by mistake . . . because she couldn't see too well . . . and she had pulled the wrong lever."

Wallace begins the body of the speech by invoking the name of Robert E. Lee, quoting Lee's statement that " 'duty' is the sublimest word in the

English language," and claiming that he will follow in Lee's footsteps by doing his duty to "every man, to every woman, . . . yes, and to every child in this state" by eliminating the liquor agents—the paid middlemen who act on behalf of the State Alcoholic Beverage Commission. He further emphasizes, "Let me say one more time . . . no more liquor drinking in your governor's mansion." This is a not-so-thinly veiled attack on previous governor, and one of his former mentors, Jim Folsom, who was notorious for entertaining visitors with plenty of whiskey, including Congressman Adam Clayton Powell, the leading black politician of the time. In this way, Wallace fulfilled a campaign pledge that he "would eliminate the liquor agents in this state and that the money saved would be returned to our citizens." By connecting his action with a larger body of heroic myths and a heroic figure, Wallace tries to turn a bureaucratic housecleaning into a dramatic event. Next comes the most controversial part of the speech, designed to gain Wallace national attention:

Today I have stood, where once Jefferson Davis stood, and took an oath to my people. It is very appropriate then that from this Cradle of the Confederacy, this very Heart of the Great Anglo-Saxon Southland, that today we sound the drum for freedom as have our generations of forebears before us done, time and time again through history. Let us rise to the call of freedom-loving blood that is in us and send our answer to the tyranny that clanks its chains upon the South. In the name of the greatest people that have ever trod this earth, I draw the line in the dust and toss the gauntlet before the feet of tyranny . . . and I say . . . segregation today . . . segregation tomorrow . . . segregation forever.

It is a truism of rhetorical criticism that speakers make choices and that once those are announced, alternatives are closed to them or made more difficult to attain. In this crucial passage, George Wallace sets in motion a confrontation with federal authority over integration of the schools of Alabama. By invoking the sacred memory of the lost cause and framing the choice as a "duty," Wallace makes any effort at compromise difficult if not impossible to achieve. In this paragraph, Wallace joins with other intractable opponents of the civil rights struggle such as Governor Ross Barnet of Mississippi and Governor Marvin Griffin of South Carolina. This statement got him the notoriety that he desired, but it also made him into a symbol of the worst tendencies in the South that looked to the past, not to the future. Asa Carter used consonance and anaphora as well as hyperbole to construct this passage, but its overwrought imagery could only appeal to the true believers ("tyranny that clanks its chains upon the South"), and even they might find it overripe.

Wallace took thirty-five minutes to deliver this disjointed speech, which contains many diverse elements that are typically found in inaugural speeches, such as promises to recruit new industry and praise for the beauty of the state and its abundant natural resources, including forests, waterways, and mineral deposits. The forty-five paragraphs that follow the long, formal introduction contain two paragraphs of only one line and one long paragraph of fifty-seven lines. Eighteen of the forty-five paragraphs contain a reference to "God" or to "faith." Religion is the unifying device for the many themes of the speech, which allows Wallace to use God-Devil terms to polarize the audience by dividing the world into two opposing groups. One consists of God-fearing Alabamians and kindred folk who represent "the very heart of the great Anglo-Saxon Southland" and who share "freedom-loving blood." The other group threatens these native sons and daughters with "an idea [of] a centralized government" that "encourages our fears and destroys our faith. . . . It is therefore a basically ungodly government and its appeal to the pseudo-intellectual and the politician is to change their status from servant of the people to master of the people." In dividing the world into two opposed camps, Wallace identifies himself strongly with the God-fearing people of Alabama. This allows him to project himself as the man who can "assume the leadership of the fight and carry our leadership across the nation." He therefore can proudly repeat his pledge to "stand up for Alabama" and call upon his followers to "stand with me . . . and we together can give courageous leadership to millions of people."

Perhaps the best way to understand this speech is to see it as an example of the rhetorical strategy of polarization—"the process by which an extremely diversified public is coalesced into two or more highly contrasting mutually exclusive groups showing a high degree of internal solidarity in those beliefs which the persuader considers salient."[4] This is accomplished by the use of two complementary tactics: affirmation and subversion. Affirmation consists of the "judicious selection of those images which will provide a strong sense of group identity" and subversion by the likewise "careful selection of those images that will undermine the ethos of competing groups, ideologies of institutions."[5] A strategy of confrontation in which the in-group defines itself through conflict with an out-group heightens the polarization effect. And this is precisely what Wallace is doing with the God-Devil terms he employs to describe true Alabamians and true Americans and their foes.

Richard Raum and James Measell have identified message variables of argument and style that are characteristics of polarization rhetoric. The first is the use of concrete description devices such as "God-and devil-terms, *reductio ad absurdum*, and exaggeration to portray people and events in such vivid, forceful language that the auditor is forced to respond."[6] Copula tactics involve language choice that emphasizes the speaker's perception of reality. These include such tactics as "artificial dichotomies, we/they distinctions, monolithic opposition, motive disparagement, and self-assertion," which "substitute Wallace's claims of what is (or will be) reality for what should (or should be)."[7] An examination of the text of Wallace's speech reveals the use of these tactics to polarize the audience.

A clear example of the use of the we/they distinction occurs in the next section of the speech. Recognizing that several of the state's congressmen were in attendance, Wallace urges them to "send this message back to Washington . . . that we intend to take the offensive and carry our fight for freedom across the nation." With these words, Wallace signals his intention to become a symbol of resistance to the federal government's attempt to dismantle the legally mandated system of segregation in the South. He makes clear the nature of his challenge by proclaiming, "[L]et those certain judges put that in their opium pipes of power and smoke it for what it is worth." He follows this attack on the federal judiciary with an appeal to his fellow Southerners "who have moved north and west throughout this nation . . . to join with us in national support and vote" for politicians who support this point of view. He also appeals to like-minded people in New England, the Midwest, and the West to "come and be with us . . . for you are of the Southern spirit . . . and the Southern philosophy . . . you are Southerners too and brothers with us in our fight." In this obvious attempt to reach beyond the borders of Alabama and appeal for sympathy and support, Wallace is saying that being southern is not necessarily a geographical designation but a belief in limited government and states' rights. He clearly does not want to consider all Americans residing in areas outside of the South as irredeemably in the enemy camp. This is an appeal for them to heed his warning about the growing tyranny of the federal government and to join in his efforts to stop it.

Wallace makes this goal apparent in the later passages of the speech, with a strong attack on the growing power of the federal government and a corresponding loss of power by the states. Using the tactic of artificial dichotomies, he denounces as "utopian" the belief that a centralized government with powerful authority is necessary to produce good. For Wallace all arguments are in the form of either/or. He does not recognize the possibility of complementary states that combine or share the best characteristics of both. For example, he states that "governments do not produce wealth . . . people produce wealth," without taking into consideration the many ways that government, both state and federal, aids in wealth creation through such programs as building highways, maintaining educational institutions, investing in research and development, and so on. Wallace claims that government restricts, penalizes, and taxes incentive and endeavor and thus destroys incentive and confiscates wealth. As a result, government assumes more and more power, and "we are becoming government-fearing people . . . not God-fearing people." He charges that "pseudo-liberal spokesmen and some Harvard advocates" have substituted "human rights" for individual rights and overlooked the "spiritual responsibility of preserving freedom." This "strong, simple faith and sane reasoning of our founding fathers has long since been forgotten."

Wallace next draws a parallel between Hitler's Germany, Caesar's Rome, and the "new," "liberal," "changing world" of his day. "As the *national* racism of Hitler's Germany persecuted a *national* minority to the whim of a *national* majority . . . so the *international* racism of the liberal seeks to persecute the *international* white minority to the whim of the *international* colored majority. . . . But the Belgian survivors of the Congo cannot present their case to a war crimes commission . . . nor the Portuguese of Angola . . . nor the survivors of Castro . . . nor the citizens of Oxford, Mississippi." The best that can be said about this passage is that it is a far-fetched argument that strains at the bounds of credulity. To include the people of Oxford in the same category as the victims of Castro or the Belgians of the Congo or the Portuguese of Angola is to violate all the logical rules of comparing like cases.

Next, Wallace attacks the 1954 Brown v. Board of Education ruling by the Supreme Court because it was based on sociological theory and not legal precedent. He charges that this same reliance on "theory" led to the court ruling on school prayers. He traces these actions to a thirst for power by those in government in Washington, D.C. He uses the technique of motive disparagement as a polarization device to criticize actions taken by President Kennedy, including signing an executive order forbidding federal loan guarantees to those buying or selling segregated property and the sending of troops to integrate the University of Mississippi. Wallace concludes this section of his speech by saying, "We reject such acts as free men. We do not defy, for there is nothing to defy . . . since as free men we do not recognize any government right to give freedom or deny freedom."

As if to underscore his defiance of the Supreme Court, Wallace notes that he had ordered erected on the grounds of the Capitol a sign stating, "In God We Trust." He states that he did this "with the clear and solemn knowledge that such physical evidence is evidently a direct violation of the logic of that Supreme Court in Washington, D.C., and if they or their spokesmen in this state wish to term this defiance . . . I say . . . then let them make the most of it." He then develops his argument for local control and for states' rights. "This nation was never meant to be a unit of one . . . but a united of the many . . . that is the exact reason our freedom loving forefathers established the states, so as to divide the rights and powers among the states, insuring that no central power could gain master government control."

After outlining the differences among the various religious organizations and political parties in the United States, Wallace draws a parallel between religious and political differences and racial ones:

And so it was meant in our racial lives . . . each race, within its own framework has the freedom to teach . . . to instruct . . . to develop . . . to ask for and receive deserved help from others of separate racial stations. This is the great freedom of our American founding fathers . . . but if we amalgamate into the one unit as advocated by the communist philosopher . . . then the enrichment of our lives . . . the freedom for our development . . . is gone forever. We become, therefore, a mongrel unit of one under a single all powerful government.

Here and elsewhere in the speech, Wallace assumes that all opposition to segregation can be traced back to the monolithic source of communism. Again, the lack of logic in the arguments is astounding. To argue that religious denominations need to stay separate to maintain their identity or that political parties need to do so for the same reason is to establish that doctrinal differences need different places or structures in which to nurture themselves, develop, and grow. There is no connection between doctrinal differences and differences between human beings. People of all races and colors can associate with one another without amalgamating into one mongrel unit. Racial differences will be preserved because people usually associate with others of their own background. As the history of the years since Wallace spoke has demonstrated, we are still two separate races. Again, Wallace gratuitously uses the language of racism, "mongrel," to describe what will happen if racial barriers are removed and attributes the idea to a Communist philosopher who is not mentioned by name.

Toward the end of an address that features a strong defense of segregation, and repeated standard racist attacks on what would be the effect of better race relations—mongrelization of the races—Wallace condescends to address the concerns of Alabama's black citizens. "We invite the Negro citizens of Alabama to work with us from his separate racial station . . . as we will work with him . . . to develop, to grow in individual freedom and enrichment. We want jobs and a good future for BOTH races. We want to help the physically and mentally sick of both races, the tubercular and the infirm. This is the basic heritage of my religion, of which I make full practice . . . for we are all the handiwork of God."

Having addressed the black citizens of Alabama, Wallace turns to a standard topos of Southern oratory, the noble cause. He reminds his audience of the desolation wrought upon the South by the Civil War and how the South had to look to its own resources to survive: "There were no government handouts, no Marshall Plan aid, no coddling to make sure that our people would not suffer; instead the South was set upon by the vulturous carpetbagger and federal troops, all loyal Southerners were denied the vote at the point of bayonet, so that the infamous, illegal 14th Amendment might be passed. There was no money, no food and no hope of either. But our grandfathers bent their knee only in church and bowed their head only to God." Wallace draws another historical comparison between the actions of those southerners in the days following the Civil War and the actions of his fellow southerners: "They fought. . . . [T]hey knew what they wanted . . . and they fought for freedom! . . . [A]nd they won!" He concludes that those who say that the cause of segregation is lost are "whimperers. . . . I am ashamed of them . . . and I am ashamed for them. They do not represent the people of the Southland."

Nearing the end of the speech, Wallace lists the southerners who had been instrumental in the founding of the nation: Jefferson, Washington, Madison, George Mason, and Patrick Henry. He then vows: "Southerners played a most magnificent part in erecting this great divinely inspired system of freedom . . . and as God is our witness, Southerners will save it." In that spirit, he states: "My pledge to you . . . to 'Stand up for Alabama,' is a stronger pledge today than it was the first day I made that pledge. I shall 'Stand up for Alabama,' as Governor of our State . . . you stand with me . . . and we, together, can give courageous leadership to millions of people throughout this nation who look to the South for their hope in this fight to win and preserve our freedoms and liberties." Thus, in the conclusion of his speech, having polarized the audience into two competing groups, Wallace uses the tactic of self-assertion to offer himself as the leader of a movement to preserve the values of his fellow citizens both in Alabama and throughout the nation.

Wallace ends the speech with a prayer: "And my prayer is that the Father who reigns above us will bless all the people of this great sovereign State and nation, both white and black."

Bill Jones, Wallace's press secretary, probably best summed up the reaction to the speech: "He threw the gauntlet in the dust and dared the federals to tramp on him. The final defense of the social and educational order in Alabama was under way."[8] If Wallace wanted to set off alarm bells in Washington, this speech was designed to do so. It is uncompromising in its defiance of federal authority. There are several explanations for this. One is that Wallace wanted to secure his home state as a political base. The state constitution did not allow governors to serve two consecutive terms. In four years, Wallace would have to vacate the mansion and look elsewhere for a political base. He could either run for the Senate from Alabama or run for president. Without his home state securely in his pocket, Wallace could not run for either office. Another explanation is that Wallace came under the influence of the more extreme members of his inner circle. Asa Carter, Al Lingo—Wallace's choice to head the state troopers—Seymour Trammel, and John Kohn were all avowed segregationists and hard-liners in their recommendations that Wallace do all he could to resist the federal effort to integrate Alabama's schools.[9]

Editorial reaction to the speech included a *mea culpa* from Grover Hall, editor of the *Montgomery Advertiser*, who advised Wallace on the speech: "The only campaign commitment [we] ever sought from Gov. Wallace was disallowed by his very first act as governor. He promised that his speech would not exceed 15 minutes, but he went 35 minutes. To the frozen and weary we can but say we done our best."[10]

Other editorials were wary of the implications of Wallace's stand for the future of the state. The *Huntsville Times* reminded its readers that "[b]ravery and foolhardiness are not the same thing." The editor continued: "As much as we disagree with federal administration of state school systems, we still should remember what happened in those two states (Mississippi and Arkansas). Much was lost in each. Nothing was gained. Alabama wants no Little Rocks or Oxfords."[11]

Wallace got the attention that he craved from the national press. In a survey of southern gubernatorial speeches headed "New Note in Dixie," *Time* magazine praised the new governors of Georgia and South Carolina for "in a pleasant departure from the past they weren't just whistling Dixie." *Time* observed that "only in Alabama was the usual segregationist tirade heard, . . . where Wallace threatened a Dixiecrat rebellion."[12] *Newsweek*, which published a picture of George and George, Jr., in formal wear standing beside Lurleen, wrote that "while many Southerners looked in the future, Alabama's new governor, George C. Wallace, took a firm fix on the past." The magazine continued: "Wallace invoked the shades of the Old Confederacy—and oratory of the same vintage—to reaffirm the racist policy that won him the governorship.[13] The *New York Times* also featured a picture of Wallace standing before the microphone and addressing the crowd. After quoting the most outrageous portions of the speech, the newspaper provided context for it by noting that "the new Governor faces a racial showdown almost certainly within months" as the applications of three "Negroes" to the white University of Alabama will force a test of the segregated system.[14]

Wallace showed that he was a master of the technique of polarization in this speech, but by its very nature, that technique appeals only to true believers. Wallace's defense of states' rights had little appeal outside the South. The gratuitous use of such racial code terms as "amalgamation" to describe the results of integration could only offend those who did not share his racist outlook. The invocation of the lost cause was a staple of southern oratory, but it, too, was going out of fashion. Blaming communists for the movement for racial equality was still popular in the South, but it had limited appeal elsewhere. There is not much in the speech but the famous quotation of defiance. That quotation has defined the speech.

Perhaps the best critique of the speech was delivered by Martin Luther King, Jr., over a year later in his speech given at the March on Washington. The only person identified in that speech is Wallace:

I have a dream that one day, down in Alabama, with its vicious racists, with its governor having his lips dripping with the words of interposition and nullification, one day, right there in Alabama, little black boys and black girls will be able to join hands with little white boys and white girls as sisters and brothers. I have a dream today![15]

King makes clear that the central failure of Wallace's speech and his policy of supporting segregation is that it belongs to the past and is based on the discarded notion of states' rights. Wallace may have proudly proclaimed that segregation will last forever, but even his most fervent followers knew that it was only a matter of time before it would end because it had no moral basis. In using the American dream as the unifying theme for his speech, King demonstrated that the American ideals of justice and freedom would only be realized when "justice is a reality for all of God's children"[16] Wallace was defending a discredited policy by invoking the hallowed idea of the lost cause and the hollow dream of states rights. King spoke for the future by envisioning a time when America would achieve its promise of equal rights for all Americans. In his oratorical contest with King, Wallace clearly lost.

NOTES

1. The *Montgomery Advertiser,* January 14 and January 15, contains complete coverage of the inauguration and its activities. The January 15 edition also reprints the text of the speech.

2. E. Culpepper Clark, *The Schoolhouse Door: Segregation's Last Stand at the University of Alabama* (New York: Oxford University Press, 1993), 168.

3. The text of the speech is reprinted in the second half of this volume, in "The 1963 Inaugural Address." It is available on the Web site for the Alabama Department of Archives and History (ADAH) in Montgomery, Alabama. I personally examined the reading copy of the speech in the ADAH files, and the only changes are in Wallace's handwriting of the men he wanted to recognize in his introduction. Unfortunately, no drafts of early versions of the speech are preserved in the files.

4. Andrew A. King and Floyd D. Anderson, "Nixon, Agnew, and the 'Silent Majority': A Case Study in the Rhetoric of Polarization," *Western Speech* 35 (1971): 244.

5. King and Anderson, "Nixon, Agnew, and the 'Silent Majority,'" 244.

6. Richard D. Raum and James S. Measell, "Wallace and His Ways: A Study of the Rhetorical Genre of Polarization," *Central States Speech Journal* 25 (1974): 30.

7. Raum and Measell, "Wallace and His Ways," 31.

8. Bill Jones, *The Wallace Story* (Northport, Ala.: American Southern, 1966), 68.

9. Stephan Lesher, *George Wallace: American Populist* (Reading, Mass.: Addison-Wesley, 1994), 167–168.

10. Grover Hall, "To the Frozen," *Montgomery Advertiser,* January 15, 1962.

11. Reprinted in *Montgomery Advertiser,* January 20, 1962.

12. "New Note in Dixie," *Time,* January 25, 1963, 15.

13. "Now . . . Forever," *Newsweek,* January 28, 1963, 34.

14. "North Denounced by Gov. Wallace," *New York Times,* January 15, 1963, 16.

15. The "I Have a Dream" speech given by Martin Luther King in Washington, D.C., on August 28, 1963, is reprinted in Lloyd Rohler and Roger Cook, *Great Speeches for Criticism and Analysis*, 4th ed. (Greenwood, Ind.: Alistair Press, 2001), 352.

16. Rohler and Cook, *Great Speeches*, 350.

CHAPTER 3

Standing in the Schoolhouse Door

In the opening speech for his 1962 gubernatorial campaign, George Wallace made the following pledge:

I shall ask the legislature to give me the right to assign pupils to schools which are threatened with integration, and when the court order comes, I am going to place myself, your Governor, in the position so that the federal court order must be directed against the Governor and not some lesser official. As your Governor, I shall refuse to abide by any illegal federal court order even to the point of standing at the schoolhouse door in person, if necessary.[1]

He repeated that pledge in every stump speech in the campaign because it always got the most applause. He predicted that the federal government "will likely back down because the people of this country will not stand for the jailing of the highest official within a state."[2] This pledge, in combination with his strong defense of segregation in his inaugural address, made a confrontation with the federal government over integration of the public schools inevitable. The integration of the University of Mississippi in 1962 served notice that the Justice Department and the federal courts would soon target the University of Alabama, the last state university to maintain a segregated system. On May 21, 1963, Judge H. H. Grooms delivered a verdict in several consolidated cases involving the University of Alabama that ordered the university to admit two applicants—James Hood and Vivian Malone—in the fall of 1963. The stage for a confrontation was now set. The only mystery was what part Wallace would play in the unfolding events.

The players in the drama included the Justice Department, the students and their supporters, the university, and Wallace. All were acutely aware that the integration of Ole Miss had been accomplished by a riot that left two people dead and many federal marshals wounded. None of the players wanted to see a repetition of that fiasco. Thus began a series of meetings designed to plan for the students' arrival, provide Wallace with a face-saving opportunity to play his role, permit the federal government to enforce the court order, and preserve the peace.

Throughout the process, Wallace insisted that by symbolically standing as the representative of the people of the state of Alabama in the schoolhouse door and defying federal authority, he made the presence of other Alabamians unnecessary. In so doing, he was acting to prevent violence by keeping potential troublemakers away.

University officials and trustees were determined not to repeat the mistakes that occurred in 1956 when mob violence thwarted Autherine Lucy, the first black student to attempt to integrate the university. The university leadership had changed since then; a new president, Frank A. Rose, took office on January 1, 1958. At first Rose and the trustees maintained silence on the issue of integration while doing their best to discourage any black applicants by making the application process longer, requiring more information from black applicants on the pretext that the university had no prior experience in dealing with their segregated schools and required more information to properly evaluate their applications. When it became obvious that cases moving through the courts would force the university to integrate, the trustees established a planning committee led by Winston Blount.[3] Blount and other trustees began contacting members of the business community to build support for a peaceful integration of the university. Wallace, an ex officio member of the board, attended their meetings and was well informed about their actions. Recognizing that time was running out for the university, Wallace called a special meeting of the board for March 18, 1963, to review the university's plans for dealing with the anticipated court ordered integration. At that time, Wallace explained to the board what actions he intended to take. After declaring his opposition to any integration of any public school, Wallace repeated his vow to stand in the schoolhouse door. He further reiterated his intention to take all steps necessary to prevent mob violence. He concluded by stating, "If the court orders admission, the board must comply."[4]

The following month, Robert Kennedy, attorney general of the United States and the man who would be in charge of integrating the university, arranged for a meeting with Wallace, on April 25, 1963. Kennedy wanted to meet Wallace in person and to discuss how Wallace would carry out his pledge. He hoped to work out a face-saving arrangement that would allow Wallace to claim that he had fulfilled his promise while the federal government could enforce the court order to admit black students. Wallace surprised Kennedy by announcing that the conversation would be taped. Kennedy immediately realized that this precluded the possibility of serious negotiation. A documentary crew also filmed the meeting. The film of the meeting is fascinating in that it reveals the great lack of understanding by both sides of the other's position. Toward the end of the conversation, Wallace tried to get Kennedy to admit that the federal government was prepared to use troops to integrate the campus. Kennedy, knowing southern sensitivities to the use of federal troops dating back to Reconstruction times and more recently in Little Rock, declined to do so.[5]

On May 24, Justice Department lawyers went to federal court to get an injunction preventing Wallace from carrying out his threat to stand in the schoolhouse door. Federal Judge Seybourne H. Lynne ordered the governor to appear in court in Birmingham for a hearing on the motion on June 3. Wallace did not appear in person but was represented by counsel. Burke Marshall appeared for the federal government and played a tape of Wallace's speech of May 21 in which he pledged to defy the court order. Marshall then framed the question he wished the court to answer: Did Wallace as governor of a state have the constitutional right to block the implementation of a federal court order as a means of challenging its validity? While admitting that Wallace had every right to raise legal questions, Marshall argued that he had no right to block officers enforcing a court order. Wallace's attorneys argued that he was merely talking about the possibility of standing in the schoolhouse door and the court's injunctive powers required an overt act before they could be used against him. On May 5 Judge Lynne issued his ruling. He dismissed Wallace's claim absolutely: "[T]he governor of a sovereign state has no authority to obstruct or prevent the execution of the lawful orders of a court of the United States." His ruling barred Wallace from obstructing the entrance of the students to the university but did not forbid him from being on the college campus.[6]

University officials continued to plan for the registration day. They updated the plan drawn up in 1956 when Autherine Lucy was registered. They planned to cordon off the campus on June 8 by establishing a series of checkpoints requiring identification cards. There would be a 10 P.M. to 6 A.M. curfew. The campus itself was swept for rocks and other large objects that could be thrown at authorities. Meetings were held with faculty, students, and staff to apprise them of the plans and to enlist their support in maintaining the peace. University officials reached out to city, county, and state officials, including Al Lingo, head of the state troopers. They even made certain that there would be facilities for the large contingent of reporters and news camera people who would cover the event. Everything was ready for the confrontation on Tuesday.

Wallace flew to Tuscaloosa on Monday and set up his headquarters at the Stafford Hotel. Later that night, at 8:00 P.M., he met with the trustees and repeated his pledge that there would be no violence. Nicholas Katzenbach, Robert Kennedy's deputy and the man who would face Wallace the next day, also arrived that day. He established his command post in the Army Reserve Building, where he talked to the marshals about their duty the next day. He continued to refine his plans for the confrontation and had the presence of mind to obtain keys to the students' dormitory rooms in case they were needed. He remained in contact with Robert Kennedy and Burke Marshall in Washington, and the three of them agreed that Katzenbach and his two assistants, Marshall Peyton Norville and U.S. Attorney Macon Weaver, would confront Wallace. This would spare the students any indignity and also technically mean that the federal government would not have to arrest Wallace for barring them from entering the university. All the participants were now on the scene. The stage was set for the drama that would unfold on Tuesday morning.[7]

At 10:48, Tuesday, June 11, 1963, in 95-degree heat and high humidity, a caravan of three cars carrying Vivian Malone, James Hood, Katzenbach, Norville, Weaver, and several other U.S. marshals arrived in front of Foster Hall, where registration was taking place. As the lead car pulled to a stop, Katzenbach, accompanied by Norville and Weaver, got out and strode toward the door. There behind a podium stood George Wallace, who held up his hand to stop them. Wallace stood silently. After identifying himself, Katzenbach said, "I have here President Kennedy's proclamation. I have come to ask you for unequivocal assurance that you or anyone under your control will not bar these students." Wallace replied with a resounding, "No!" Katzenbach then pushed the proclamation toward Wallace, who accepted it. Still, no words from Wallace broke the silence. Katzenbach repeated his early statement, adding the words "that you will permit these students who, after all, merely want an education in the great University." At this Wallace interrupted him, saying, "Now you make your statement because we don't need your speech." Katzenbach, with obvious impatience, protested that he was making his statement and repeated his demand that Wallace give his unequivocal assurance that he would do his constitutional duty. At this Wallace pulled out the statement he had prepared and began to read it. It took about five minutes. When he finished, Katzenbach asked him again, "I take it from the statement that you are going to stand in the door and that you are not going to carry out the orders of the court, and that you are going to resist us from doing so. Is that so?" Wallace answered, "I stand according to my statement." Katzenbach exclaimed in exasperation, "I am not interested in this show. I do not know what the purpose of this show is. It is a simple problem, scarcely worth this kind of attention. . . . From the outset Governor, all of us have known that the final chapter of this history will be the admission of these students. . . . I ask you once again to reconsider." Wallace continued to look straight ahead without saying anything. Finally, Katzenbach walked to the waiting cars.[8]

Wallace had his show of defiance, but the practical effect was nil. The students were on campus, and thanks to Katzenbach's foresight, they had keys to their dorm rooms. They had already been registered for their classes in advance. All that was necessary was for them to go to class the next day. While the students got settled in their dorm rooms, events moved quickly in Washington, D.C. At 1:35 P.M. Washington time, President Kennedy signed an order federalizing the Alabama National Guard. At 2:40 P.M. Washington time, General Henry V. Graham arrived by helicopter near campus and immediately proceeded to the Army Reserve Center, where five hundred Alabama National Guardsmen were on duty, having been called up by Governor Wallace the night before. Graham consulted with General Abrams, the regular Army officer who was now his commander, who gave him instructions for confronting Wallace that afternoon. While they were talking, a call came through from Taylor Hardin, a close friend of the governor who wanted to meet with General Graham. When they met a few minutes later, Hardin conveyed the message that Wallace would step aside if allowed to make another statement. After conferring with Katzenbach, a deal was struck. Shortly thereafter, General Graham sent three troop carriers with one hundred national guardsmen to Foster Hall. At 3:30 P.M. General Graham, dressed in combat fatigues, strode forward and saluted Wallace, who had resumed his position at the entrance to Foster Hall. Graham said to Wallace, "It is my sad duty to ask you to step aside, on order of the President of the United States." Wallace replied, "General, I want to make a statement." Graham said that he could. Following his short statement, Wallace and his entourage walked to waiting patrol cars and left the campus. The entire second confrontation had taken less than three minutes.[9]

Wallace's statement concerning integration of the University of Alabama gave him an opportunity to posture as an aggrieved governor defending the honor of a sovereign state that had been subjected to an "unwelcomed, unwanted, unwarranted and force-induced intrusion upon the campus of the University of Alabama today of the might of the Central Government." In the statement, Wallace contends that this "intrusion results solely from force, or threat of force, undignified by any reasonable application of the principle of law, reason and justice. It is important that the people of this State and nation understand that this action is in violation of rights reserved to the State by the Constitution of the United States and the Constitution of the State of Alabama." Why is this so? Wallace argues that "[o]nly the Congress makes the law of the United States. To this date no statutory authority can be cited to the people of this Country which authorizes the Central Government to ignore the sovereignty of this State in an attempt to subordinate the rights of Alabama and millions of Americans. There has been no legislative action by Congress justifying this intrusion." Wallace bases his actions on the theory that only certain limited powers were granted to the federal government. "When the Constitution of the United States was enacted, a government was formed upon the premise that people, as individuals are endowed with the rights of life, liberty and property, and with the right of local self-government. The people and their local self-government formed a Central Government and conferred upon it certain stated and limited powers. All other powers were reserved to the states and to the people." The foundation of his argument is the 10th Amendment to the Constitution: "The powers not delegated to the United States by the Constitution nor prohibited by it to the states, are reserved to the states respectively, or to the people." He contends that this "amendment sustains the rights of self-determination and grants the State of Alabama the right to enforce its laws and regulate its internal affairs." He claims that he is standing

here today, as Governor of this sovereign State, and refuse to willingly submit to illegal usurpation of power by the Central Government. I claim today for all the people of this State of Alabama those rights reserved to them under the Constitution of the United States. Among those powers so reserved and claimed is the right of state authority in the operation of the public schools, colleges and Universities. My action does not constitute disobedience to legislative and constitutional provisions. It is not defiance—for defiance sake, but for the purpose of raising basic and fundamental Constitutional questions. My action is a call for strict adherence to the Constitution of the United States as it was written—for a cessation of usurpation and abuses. My action seeks to avoid having state sovereignty sacrificed on the altar of political expediency.

Wallace's statement is a clear exposition of the doctrine of states' rights, which has a long and honored history in American politics. However, by the time Wallace invoked the doctrine, it had been indelibly associated with opposition to the campaign for equal rights for all Americans. The most generous evaluation of his argument is that it is one-sided as he conveniently ignores the history and development of constitutional issues that run counter to his interpretation. Central to his position is the issue that the Constitution is a limited compact among sovereign states that grants limited powers to the federal government. Only those powers that are expressly enumerated in the Constitution may be exercised by the federal government. All other powers are expressly reserved to the states themselves. Chief Justice John Marshall in McCollough v. Maryland disposed of that argument early in the nation's history with the doctrine of implied powers. The victory of the North in the Civil War and the subsequent passage of the 14th Amendment effectively nationalized the Bill of Rights by applying them to the individual sovereign states. These are constitutional developments that were studied at the University of Alabama Law School, where George Wallace took his degree.

Particularly troubling about Wallace's argument is that he treats the "Central Government" as if it were an alien force imposed from outside the society and unresponsive to it. He seems to regard it as a busybody intruding itself where it has no business. In point of fact, the government was responding to changes in the society and economy that were unleashed by World War II that contributed to the growing nationalization of the economy and culture. Corporations that did business nationally did not want to confront difficulties in training and relocating black employees. Black families that had migrated to the North attracted by jobs in defense plants wanted to be able to visit kin in the South without being subjected to humiliating treatment. Radio and television created a national popular culture, and television news brought developments from distant cities into the living rooms of all Americans. The competition with the Soviet Union made the quality of American education a top priority. No longer could the United States afford the luxury of wasting the talents of black children in inferior schools. Far from being a busybody constantly intruding itself where it was not wanted, the government often seemed to black Americans to be dragging its feet and temporizing on its promise of equal justice for all.

Wallace also conveniently ignores the role that native Alabamians played in the integration of the University of Alabama. From Judge Johnson, a classmate of Wallace at law school, to the federal marshals who enforced the court orders, almost all the leading actors, save Robert Kennedy and Nicholas Katzenbach, were native Alabamians who shared many of the same beliefs as Wallace. They mainly differed in that the marshals were determined to uphold the orders of the court, and Wallace was not.

The speech was the concluding act in the drama that unfolded before the television cameras. It was a script to be enacted before a state and national audience designed to gain Wallace the reputation as a governor willing to defy the power of the federal government (and the Kennedys) on a matter of principle. It allowed Wallace to play the role of the hero defending the way of life of the people of the state against outsiders who would defile and destroy it. Throughout the speech, Wallace uses the personal pronoun "I" to single himself out and to call attention to his act of defiance. "I stand here today, as Governor of this sovereign State, and refuse to willingly submit to illegal usurpation of power by the Central Government." He further asserts that he is acting to carry out the will of the people of the state who, if he were not present as their representative, would be there themselves: "I stand before you today in place of thousands of other Alabamians whose presence would have confronted you had I been derelict and neglected to fulfill the responsibilities of my office." This sentence contains Wallace's rationalization for the elaborate charade that he has enacted. If he were not there, other Alabamians, including those disposed to violence, would have been present, and the situation would have been fraught with danger. In making this claim, Wallace portrays himself as a hero in another sense. Not only has he stood up for Alabama, but in doing so, he has keep the peace. He has prevented another tragedy such as the one that occurred at the University of Mississippi when the federal government integrated that campus.

Wallace's actions and his statement at the University of Alabama demonstrate his remarkable ability to claim victory in the face of overwhelming defeat. He was outmaneuvered by the representatives of the Justice Department who were able to thwart Wallace's attempt to keep the students off campus. While he was still posturing before television cameras, the students were safely in their dormitories, registered for classes, and preparing for the beginning of classes the next day. All of his efforts did not prevent the integration of the university. More important, the crisis forced the Kennedy administration, which had not made a serious effort in the field of civil rights, to confront its responsibilities to ensure equal rights for all Americans. That night President Kennedy would address the nation and for the first time pronounce civil rights for all Americans a moral imperative:

We are confronted primarily with a moral issue. It is as old as the Scriptures and is as clear as the American Constitution.

The heart of the question is whether all Americans are to be afforded equal rights and equal opportunities, whether we are going to treat our fellow Americans as we want to be treated. If an American because his skin is dark, cannot eat lunch in a restaurant open to the public, if he cannot send his children to the best public school available, if he cannot vote for the public officials who will represent him, if, in short he cannot enjoy the full free life which all of us want, then who among us would be content to have the color of his skin changed and stand in his place? Who among us would then be content with the counsels of patience and delay?[10]

By framing the confrontation with Wallace over integration of the university system in moral terms, the president seized the high ground and made it clear to the nation that this time there would be no turning back from the constitutional duty to guarantee equal rights for all Americans. Wallace not only lost the legal battle to integrate the university, but he lost the oratorical battle with Kennedy and thus the war against integration itself. In forcing Kennedy to defend federal intervention to integrate the university, Wallace made the president commit the prestige of his office and of himself to the cause of civil rights. Kennedy's speech made it clear that the issue transcended legal issues and went to the very essence of the rights and obligations of a citizen of the United States.

NOTES

1. Quoted in Bill Jones, *The Wallace Story* (Northport, Ala.: American Southern, 1966), 79.

2. Jones, *Wallace Story*, 80.

3. E. Culpepper Clark, *The Schoolhouse Door: Segregation's Last Stand at the University of Alabama* (New York: Oxford University Press, 1993), 158.

4. Clark, *Schoolhouse Door*, 179.

5. *Crisis: Behind a Presidential Commitment*, 16 mm, 52 min., Drew Associates, Brooklyn, N.Y., June 1963. My account of the action involving the integration of the university is based on this film. Clark also quotes from the tape of the meeting.

6. Clark, *Schoolhouse Door*, 203.

7. Stephan Lesher, *George Wallace: American Populist* (Reading, Mass.: Addison-Wesley, 1994), 222.

8. Clark, *Schoolhouse Door*, 225 ff.

9. Clark, *Schoolhouse Door*, 228–231. The entire text from Wallace's proclamation is reproduced in the second part of this volume, "Statement and Proclamation, University of Alabama, June 11, 1963."

10. John Fitzgerald Kennedy, "Radio and Television Report to the American People on Civil Rights, The White House, June 11, 1963," in *Papers of the Presidents of the United States, John F. Kennedy: Containing the Messages, Speeches, and Statements of the President, 1961–1963* (Washington, D.C.: United States Printing Office, 1962), 468–471.

CHAPTER 4

Testing the Waters: The 1964 Campaign

Following his confrontation with the Kennedys, Wallace capitalized on his national recognition by accepting invitations to speak outside of the South. He received many invitations from universities throughout the United States, including such Ivy League institutions as Harvard and Dartmouth, and public universities such as the University of California–Los Angeles (UCLA), the Ohio State University, and the University of Wisconsin. While at the University of Wisconsin in Madison, a political activist who was a member of the John Birch Society met with Wallace and urged him to run in the Wisconsin Democratic Presidential Primary.[1] Wallace and his advisors at first thought this was impractical, but the more they discussed it, the more attractive the idea became. His stand at the University of Alabama brought him an enormous amount of mail expressing agreement with his position. His nationwide speaking tour attracted the attention of many Americans who were curious about what he had to say. Running in the Democratic primaries would demonstrate the extent of his support. Besides, he believed that there was a real possibility that the South could be in a position to be the deciding factor in the Electoral College in 1964. A strong campaign in the primaries would help him build support for a free elector movement in the South. So, with little practical experience in running a political campaign outside of Alabama, little money, and no support among his state's political leaders, Wallace announced that he would run.

The political situation did not look promising for Wallace. Lyndon B. Johnson, who succeeded the slain John F. Kennedy as president, had successfully guided Kennedy's legislative agenda through the Congress and was near passage of his priority legislation, the Civil Rights Act of 1964. He had led the nation through the mourning for Kennedy, rallied many of Kennedy's political lieutenants to his side, and faced no serious opposition for nomination to his own term as president. Indeed, public opinion polls showed that sympathy for the slain leader and admiration for Johnson's political leadership would ensure defeat of any Republican challenger. Yet this is precisely the situation that encourages voters to cast a protest vote. In a close race, when every vote counts, a protest vote will be seen as a wasted gesture. When the outcome is not in doubt, some voters may feel encouraged to cast a protest vote to show up the political establishment that took them for granted. In addition, Wallace knew that the national press would cover the primaries and thus give him and his views even more exposure. He would not win in 1964, but he could have fun trying, and he would gain practical experience that would be necessary if he were to run again in 1968. Wallace and his associates were like fraternity boys off on a prank. They were tweaking the political establishment's nose and having a good laugh while they did it.

Because of legal deadlines, everything about the campaign was rushed. The telephone call that initiated the serious thinking about entering the primary came on February 19, 1964. The deadline for entering the primary was March 6. By that date, delegates had to be selected to run from each congressional district and to run statewide, and they had to be qualified to be on the ballot. Relying on volunteers, many of whom were members of the John Birch Society, Wallace's team recruited sixty delegates and completed the necessary legal requirements to be on the ballot on April 7.[2] Wallace formally launched his campaign at Appleton, Wisconsin, the hometown of Senator Joseph McCarthy, on March 19, 1964, in a speech to the Appleton Rotary Club.

The speech that Wallace gave that day, he repeated throughout the campaign in Wisconsin and also with minor modifications in Indiana and Maryland.[3] It was adapted from the speech he had been giving on his college tours where he spoke against the proposed Civil Rights Act of 1964 and is not a carefully crafted campaign speech such as Wallace would devise for the 1968 campaign. It is more like a first draft, with many themes more suggested than fully developed. Wallace has not yet found a way to tie discontent with civil rights into a broader theme of powerlessness and rage at the lack of respect shown to traditional values. He is too legalistic in focusing on the provisions of the Civil Rights Act of 1964, and his use of hyperbole in describing it as the "ultimate in tyranny" is not believable. His attempts to demonize the federal government would be convincing only to the true believers in the audience. The speech lacks memorable lines—none of which lend themselves to slogans. More important, the speech lacks a rousing conclusion. The concluding line, "We must not allow ourselves to be emotionalized into giving up the last bastion of freedom," is limp and not designed to bring a crowd to its feet.

Wallace does effectively use the device of polarization in this speech. He begins by calling upon members of his audience to perform their patriotic duty of speaking the truth about what is happening in the United States and the world. This will not be an easy task. It will require "character, individualism and vitality" because the enemies of freedom are behind a "scheme to create national chaos" by falsely and maliciously calling "haters" those citizens who believe in the rights of the individual states, fiscal responsibility, and the checks-and-balances system of our government. More important, those who object to "a socialist ideology," including Wallace himself, have been denounced as haters, hatemongers, and demagogues. By calling his listeners patriotic and summoning them to their duty, Wallace enlists them into a great campaign to "exercise the heritage bequeathed to us" to "take stock of our values and fully investigate the questions which have been raised as to our political direction as a nation."

Wallace cleverly divides the world into two camps: those patriotic Americans who believe in constitutional government and those "of the leftist ideology" who use "the Big Lie" to "destroy all opposition to their program of venomous destruction of our American Republic." He proudly proclaims, "I am here to campaign today because I believe we can no longer comfortably contemplate that war from afar." Note how easily he finds common ground with his audience on patriotism and how clearly he identifies with their concerns that traditional values are being questioned and long-standing practices in race relations are changing.

Wallace clearly identifies the enemy: "There is an ideal that believes government can manage the people and . . . bring about a utopian life. This ideal has come to be a predominant aim in Washington, D.C." What has been the result of this? "[W]e find the nation's Capitol becomes a jungle where citizens fear to walk the streets at night. . . . We are subjected to roving bands of irresponsible street rioters who are encouraged to break the laws by the irresponsible power gathers in Washington." This has resulted in "the astounding spectacle . . . of high officials calling for the passage of a so-called civil rights bill for fear of threat of mob violence. A mob movement which includes at least several communist indoctrinated leaders."

Wallace uses fear of the communist menace and fear of crime to denounce the political leaders of the nation. Although Wallace ritualistically says in the speech, "I have never spoken one word of evil or demagoguery against any race, or any religion, or any culture," the language he uses promotes racial fears. If the nation's Capitol has become a jungle, then one might easily conclude that savages—black savages—are stalking the streets at night. Accusing the leaders of the civil rights movement of being communists or communist dupes is a standard topos of those who resisted the movement.

Wallace is not surprised that "the official Communist Party of the United States is an enthusiastic supporter" of the Civil Rights Act because it transfers "private property to public domain under a central government. It is this way in Russia." He predicts the bill "will create a dictatorship the like of which we or our fathers have not witnessed." One can be charitable and say that such statements are part of the political persona that he has adopted of speaking truths that others fear to say. However, that brings up the question of whether he really believes these extravagant claims. One sometimes get the impression that Wallace is not concerned about the truth or falsity of the statements he is making but what their effect will be on his opponents. How can one rationally debate such arguments? The inferential leap from "the Communist Party supports this bill" to "this bill will make private property rights the way they are in Russia" defies rational analysis. Just because the Communist Party supports an idea does not necessarily make it bad. If the Communist Party supported clean air and water, would Wallace endorse dirty air and dirty water as a matter of public duty?

Wallace reserves his strongest denunciation for the news media, which he accuses of "grotesque distortion." He links racial violence and the way it is reported in the United States with newspaper accounts of China and Cuba that conveyed the impression that Mao and Castro were agrarian reformers with democratic aims. He concludes that this is part of a conspiracy by "the leaders of world communism . . . to destroy our political system." The news media subject Americans to "oceans of emotional propaganda that justifies the breaking of the law and a flagrant violation of the Constitution." He prophesies that "if victory for freedom is impossible, then surrender to communism is inevitable."

Anticommunism is the glue that holds together the divergent themes of the speech. For Wallace, the civil rights movement is communist led and directed, as is the press that does not inform the public but pushes communist propaganda. The federal judiciary, "basing its decision upon the twilight zone of psychology, psychiatry and sociology . . . [where] the communist rules supreme in these fields of double talk," has been breached. The executive branch has "made law without constitutional sanction," which the "communist applauds." The record of the past few years reveals that "we negotiated away a third of Europe, half of Germany and all of the Balkans." The future does not look bright; some analysts are "predicting that the whole of South American will be next." Interestingly, Wallace in the beginning of his speech discusses the way language can be manipulated to distort the truth. He warns against a movement "to vanquish freedom in the name of freedom, to destroy human rights and dignity in the name of civil rights, to inspire hatred and chaos in the name of love and peace." Yet in his speech, he practices the same techniques that he warns against.

The speech is predicated on the truth of a proposition that Wallace asserts without offering any evidence: "We have witnessed a scheme to create national chaos in recent months." Presumably, Wallace is referring to the rising tide of demonstrations for civil rights, including the demonstrations in Birmingham and other southern cities. To call those demonstrations "national" is a gross distortion of fact. Legal segregation was a regional phenomenon confined to the states of the old Confederacy and some bordering states such as Kentucky and Tennessee and Maryland. There were no demonstrations in the state of Wisconsin where he was campaigning because there were already civil rights laws comparable to the one before Congress on the books and there were few black Americans who resided in the state. There were vast areas of the United States, such as the West and the Rocky Mountain states and the Plains and the Northeast, where no civil rights demonstrations took place. The only way to demonstrate that such a national scheme existed would be to argue that television carried news of the demonstrations into every part of the United States. This is a possible interpretation of his meaning since he later attacks the news media in the speech, but it further begs the question of just how viewing television news, which is a passive activity, creates national chaos.

The rest of Wallace's charges are based on the fundamental truth of this assertion that the creation of chaos has led to bitter division in the society and produced claims that some individuals are haters: "Much has been written and said about the 'hate' that is purportedly prevalent in our society. Much has been written and said regarding the 'haters.'" He then lists the people who have been branded haters:

Those who believe in the rights of the individual states.
Those who believe in fiscal responsibility.
Those who object to amendment of the Constitution of the United States without regard to the basic precepts of the Founding Fathers.
Those who stand firm for the retention of the checks and balances system of government.
Those who object to a socialist ideology under which a few men in the executive and judicial branches of our government make decisions and laws without regard to our elected representatives who reflect the decisions of the people.

Wallace turns differences of opinion into differences of principle—principles that are antithetical to one another and admit no compromise, only unrelenting opposition. He further inflames the audience by charging that any "public official or an individual citizen, who attempts to stand in some manner of opposition to this express train of liberal revolution can be virtually destroyed by a flailing thresher of propaganda that smears him with a wide range of deprecating adjectives which can deceive and mislead the American public." Presumably, he includes himself in this group.

This speech lacks the simple colloquial style he will adopt in the 1968 campaign speech. In 1964, Wallace had been speaking on college campuses before entering the Democratic primaries. He was concerned that those audiences would see him as a stereotypical southern redneck. He was aware that he did not have the cultural background that students at Harvard, Brown, UCLA, or Wisconsin had, and so he tried to impress them with a more literary style than was typical in his usual campaign speaking. He is still doing so in this campaign speech. He uses longer words that are more appropriate to a formal presentation rather than the short colloquial expressions of a campaign speech. For example, consider the following paragraph:

We know by way of actual declaration that the leaders of world communism intend to attempt to destroy our political system. We know that our system under the Constitution, guaranteeing the dissemination of power among the 50 states, preventing a concentration of central authority, is a frustrating road block to communism and its liberal forerunners. Hence, we have witnessed a venomous attack on all who believe in states sovereignty. We have witnessed a propaganda barrage of emotionalism that creates a climate of hysteria in promoting and justifying deliberate violations of those rights by judicial edict and by physical force.

There are four sentences in this paragraph, consisting of 99 words. The first sentence is 21 words long; the second, 34; the third, 14; and the last, 30 words. Of these words, 18 are two syllables; 16 are three syllables; 11 are four syllables; and 1 is five syllables. These sentences do not roll easily off the tongue, nor do they have the power to move a crowd. Wallace is clearly trying to sound respectable in this speech. The best thing that can be said for this paragraph is that Wallace effectively uses the device of parallel construction: "We know . . . We know . . . we have witnessed . . . We have witnessed . . . "

The speech is more tightly organized than the 1968 speech, with more subordination. Because he is making an argument that moves from premises to a conclusion, the order in which the ideas are presented matters. Wallace in this speech lacks the freedom he will have in 1968 to move back and forth from one idea to another in response to audience reaction or to his own associative reasoning. Nonetheless, the speech was enthusiastically received, especially in the Polish section of Milwaukee, where Wallace spoke to an overflow crowd at Serbian Memorial Hall.[4]

In his 1964 campaign, George Wallace gained the support of many voters threatened by the social changes that were developing in the early part of the decade and that would accelerate throughout the 1960s. With his plain-folks appeal, he spoke to the fears of the factory worker worried about loss of seniority, the quality of schooling for his children, the safety of his neighborhood, and the loss of respect for traditional values of hard work, religion, and patriotism. Wallace's rhetoric drew upon concern for the loss of local control to large organizations far removed from the people themselves. Wallace played on the feeling of many of his supporters that they were powerless and that decisions affecting their lives were being made by people far distant from them and their experiences. The Wallace campaign consisted of two closely related strategies: (1) demonize the federal government and (2) sharpen class and racial antagonism by arguing that the political economy is a zero-sum game in which gains by one group come at the expense of others.

From his first emergence on the national scene in his defiant inaugural address, Wallace consistently portrayed himself as a defender of states' rights against the unlawful usurpation of the federal government. He depicted the federal government as the other—almost as an alien force—an occupier that was unresponsive to the needs of the people and manipulated by special interest groups. In attacking the federal government, he discredited the legacy of the New Deal in the eyes of many who directly benefited from its expansion of government programs. Wallace succeeding in shifting the focus from the economic benefits of government to the real and imagined costs of government inspired social change. To do so, Wallace demonized the federal government as an evil force serving not the people but an elite who were duped by left-wingers following the communist line.

Wallace charged that "government referees all rights and the individual is subject to the caprice and whim of an autocratic, all-powerful governmental structure."[5] He claimed his opposition to the Civil Rights Bill of 1964 was based on his fear that "Washington is planning an additional invasion of the lawful prerogatives of the state. It is reaching into homes, schools, businesses, farms and labor."[6]

Wallace accused federal officials of being "hypocrites who preach one thing and practice another."[7] He noted that "[w]hen Washington integrated the proportion of white in the schools was high. Now the proportion of Negroes there is high and all the whites are taking children to Virginia and Maryland."[8] He charged that the "attempt is being made to destroy the neighborhood-school policy in order to satisfy the whims of some social engineers."[9]

Wallace also recognized that many white workers felt resentment and even envy of the gains that black workers were making as a result of passage of the Civil Rights Act. He returned time and again to his claim that the Civil Rights Act directly threatened the seniority system:

They will tell an employer who he's got to employ. If a man's got 100 Japanese Lutherans working for him and there's 100 Chinese-Baptists unemployed he's got to let some of the Japanese-Lutherans go so he can make room for some of the Chinese-Baptists. And of course what does that do for your seniority rights? It destroys them because some men got to come off the top so they can make room for others at the bottom.[10]

Using such far-fetched examples allowed Wallace to deny he was talking about black workers taking white workers' jobs. He had not even mentioned the word *black*. But everyone in the audience knew precisely what he was talking about.

A consummate campaigner, Wallace understood the price that the social changes of the 1960s exacted on the political system, and he gave voice to those who felt threatened by it. Once dismissed as a regional phenomenon, Wallace demonstrated that white working-class audiences in northern cities would respond to the same appeals as southerners.

When the votes were counted on April 7, 1964, Wallace surprised his staff and every political observer in the state of Wisconsin by winning 266,136 votes or 33.7 percent of the Democratic primary vote.[11] He repeated his success in Indiana, where he received 170,146 votes, or 29.81 percent of the Democratic primary votes, and in Maryland, where he astounded everyone by carrying 15 out of 23 counties and gaining 212,068 votes, or 42.7 percent of the Democratic primary vote.[12]

Wallace concluded his 1964 campaign with an appearance at a Fourth of July celebration at the Southeast Fairgrounds in Atlanta, Georgia. He had been invited to speak by one of the organizers of the celebration, Lester Maddox, who won attention and political influence by passing out ax handles to symbolize his opposition to serving blacks who might try to integrate his restaurant. On July 3, after President Johnson signed the Civil Rights Act of 1964, which outlawed discrimination in public accommodations, Maddox swung an ax handle at a black minister who was trying to integrate the restaurant and also threatened him with a pistol. Wallace was joined on the platform by Calvin Craig, the Wizard of the Georgia Ku Klux Klan, and was enthusiastically received by a screaming and shouting crowd. The long speech that Wallace delivered was written by Asa Carter, a member of the Ku Klux Klan. Wayne Greenhaw, who covered the event for the *Alabama Journal*, noted that "Wallace was at his speech-making best. He would later repeat the style and form countless times, but he would never be better. He had his audience humming with him like the best brush-arbor revivalist in south Alabama."[13]

Greenhaw saw that Wallace was the perfect mimetic orator, reflecting back to the crowd their own thoughts. "They had thought the same thing, they had cursed the Supreme Court in the privacy of their homes since the Brown vs. Board decision in 1954, and now somebody had stepped up there on that red, white and blue-papered wooden platform and was saying it to them loud and clear."[14] Not only was Wallace expressing aloud their own private thoughts, he was also working with their emotions. He knew how powerless they felt to change the world that seemed so threatening to them.

Wallace shrewdly focused on the Supreme Court as the archenemy of democracy because, of the three branches of the federal government, it is the least subject to popular control. The nine justices are identifiable persons who Wallace can denounce as "omnipotent black-robed despots."[15] He attributes to them not only evil intentions but actions that threaten the very basis of our democracy: "I consider the Federal Judiciary system to be the greatest single threat to individual freedom and liberty in the United States today." He charges that "[t]he court today, just as in 1776, is deaf to the voices of the people and their repeated entreaties: they have become arrogant, contemptuous, highhanded, and literal despots."

According to Murray Edelman, the construction of political enemies is vital to political communication because enemies "arouse passions, fears and hopes"[16] as "identifiable persons or stereotypes to whom evil traits, intentions or actions can be attributed."[17] Wallace knew instinctively how effective this technique could be, especially with an institution so remote from popular control and whose decisions seemed to ignore the social mores of the people of the South. Wallace links the court and the executive branch of the government with the hated memory of federal occupation of the South following the Civil War: "The only reason it is the Supreme Law of the Land today is because we have a President who cares so little for freedom that he would send the armed forces into the states to enforce the dictatorial decree." He links enforcement of the court decision to integrate the University of Alabama to the stationing of British troops in the colonies. Going back to the Declaration of Independence, he reminds his audience, "Our colonial forefathers had something to say about that too. The Declaration of Independence cited as an act of tyranny the fact that, ' . . . Kept among us in times of peace standing armies without the consent of the legislature.' "

After this long exposition, Wallace finally asserts: "A politician must stand on his record. Let the Court stand on its record. The record reveals, for the past number of years, that the chief, if not the only beneficiaries of the present Court's rulings, have been duly and lawfully convicted criminals, Communists, atheists, and clients of vociferous left-wing minority groups." Wallace makes clear the nature of the enemy: "A left-wing monster has risen up in this nation. It has invaded the government. . . . [I]t is a drive to destroy the rights of private property, to destroy the freedom and liberty of you and me." This attack on the court follows the line of many right-wing organizations such as the Christian Anti-Communism Crusade and the John Birch Society, who sponsored billboards throughout the South calling for the impeachment of Earl Warren, the chief justice of the Supreme Court. It was a popular argument that would resonate with his audience of true believers but be unconvincing to others.

By scapegoating the institution that promoted black advancement, Wallace achieved his purpose without even mentioning the word *black*. He could claim that he was merely standing up for constitutional rights, not talking about race. But as one of reporter Marshall Frady's informants stated, "He can use all the other issues—law and order, running your own schools, protecting property rights—and never mention race. But people will still know he's telling them, 'a nigger's trying to get your job, trying to move into your neighborhood.' What Wallace is doing is talking to them in a kind of shorthand, a kind of code."[18]

The strong showing that Wallace made in the primaries encouraged him to dream of running in the November election as an independent, but soon he had to face reality. He had no organization and little of the money needed to gather the signatures necessary to get on the ballots in sufficient states to have an impact on the election. Also, Barry Goldwater's nomination by the Republicans made a Wallace's run for the White House seem superfluous. Goldwater was even more conservative than Wallace, and he would present the voters with a clear choice for a change. Goldwater also voted against the Civil Rights Act of 1964. When his supporters began to endorse Goldwater, Wallace faced reality and in an appearance on *Face the Nation* on July 19, 1964, announced that he was ending his campaign. However, he did not endorse Goldwater.

Although he withdrew from the race and his name was not even placed in nomination, the short campaign was a success in the eyes of Wallace and his staff. Running for the nomination against the man who took office after the assassination of President Kennedy and who enjoyed overwhelming support in the public opinion polls, Wallace managed to gain a respectable number of votes in three primaries. He even claimed that he would have won in Maryland had not the Democratic machine counted him out. This was gratifying to him because most political observers gave him little chance for success, believing that his political stance and his southern style would not translate well across the Mason-Dixon Line. He demonstrated that many people were discontented with the Civil Rights legislation making its way through Congress and that racial politics was not confined to the South. He gained precious television exposure outside the South. He obviously enjoyed the chance to perform on *Meet the Press* and to joust with northern reporters. He also collected valuable signatures in his campaign to get on the ballot, and he would use these as the basis for highly effective direct-mail fund-raising for his next campaign. More important, he and his staff, who had never ventured far from Alabama, gained much-needed experience in running a political campaign far from home and far from the familiar faces and family ties that constituted Alabama politics. He got his feet wet testing the waters, and the experience convinced him that he would do far better next time in the deeper waters of a genuine national campaign. From his perspective, national politics was ready for Wallace, and he was ready to campaign seriously for the presidency.

NOTES

1. Jody Carlson, *George C. Wallace and the Politics of Powerlessness: The Wallace Campaigns for the Presidency, 1964–1976* (New Brunswick, N.J.: Transaction Books, 1981), 28.

2. Bill Jones, *The Wallace Story* (Northport, Ala.: American Southern, 1966), 175.

3. The entire text to this speech is reprinted in the second part of this volume, in "Wallace for President: The 1964 Campaign Speech."

4. Jones, *Wallace Story*, 216–218.

5. Wallace speech, University of Cincinnati, February 11, 1964, excerpt printed in George Wallace, *Hear Me Out* (Anderson, S.C.: Droke House, 1968), 12.

6. News Conference, Terre Haute, Indiana, 1964 Presidential Primary, in Wallace, *Hear Me Out*, 13.

7. Statement at Oshkosh, Wisconsin, March 20, 1964, in Wallace, *Hear Me Out*, 74–75.

8. Speech at the University of Notre Dame, Notre Dame, Indiana, April 29, 1964, in Wallace, *Hear Me Out*, 74–75.

9. Interview, *U.S. News & World Report*, June 1, 1964, 63.

10. John J. Makay, "The Rhetorical Strategies of Governor George Wallace in the 1964 Maryland Primary," *Southern Speech Journal* 36 (1970): 173.

11. Carlson, *George C. Wallace*, 30.

12. Carlson, *George C. Wallace*, 33, 36.

13. Wayne Greenhaw, *Watch Out for George Wallace* (Englewood Cliffs, N.J.: Prentice-Hall, 1976), 151.

14. Greenhaw, *Watch Out*, 152.

15. Wallace, speech given in Atlanta on July 4, 1964. All subsequent references are to this speech text, reprinted in the second part of this volume, in "The Civil Rights Movement: Fraud, Sham, and Hoax, July 4, 1964."

16. Murray Edelman, *Constructing the Political Spectacle* (Chicago: University of Chicago Press, 1988), 66.

17. Edelman, *Constructing the Political Spectacle*, 87.

18. Marshall Frady, *Wallace* (New York: Random House, 1996), 275.

CHAPTER 5

Confrontation at Selma

Dan T. Carter has called George Wallace the "most influential loser" in American politics because all his efforts to prevent racial justice only hastened it.[1] He stood in the schoolhouse door to prevent integration of the public schools in Alabama to no avail. His campaign against the Civil Rights Bill of 1964 only seemed to accelerate its passage. His order to troopers to stop a march for voting rights in Selma awakened the moral conscience of the nation and moved voting rights to the top of the legislative agenda. Wallace was very good at using each of these situations to gain publicity for himself while ending up on the losing side of the issue. This was particularly true of the issue of voting rights. President Johnson had announced in his State of the Union Address that "elimination of barriers to the right to vote" would be a priority, but these were empty words that were not backed up by any significant action.[2] The Justice Department had not drawn up a bill to submit to Congress because the Justice Department was itself divided over what strategy to pursue. Some members believed that only a constitutional amendment could effectively deal with the issue. Others believed that federal supervision of local officials would be not only legal but effective in solving the problem.

While discussions were going on within the administration about how to deal with voting rights, Martin Luther King, Jr., set in motion events in Alabama that would rapidly escalate into a crisis and force the issue by addressing a mass meeting in Selma on January 2, 1965. Selma, in Dallas County, was one of the so-called black belt counties that had huge black majorities but few registered black voters. The statistics are striking: 67

percent of Selma's 14,000 prospective white voters were registered, but barely 2 percent of its 15,000 prospective black voters (325 people) were.[3] Selma was also the first Alabama city to form a White Citizens Council. Located about 45 miles from the state capital, Selma was the ideal location to dramatize the issue of voting rights for black Americans. It had the right mix of ingredients that could potentially explode into a violent confrontation that would attract media attention and force the administration's hand. The new mayor, Joseph Smitherman, a politically inexperienced appliance salesman, ran on a platform that stressed attracting new industry to Selma. Racial peace would be a necessity if his plans were to succeed. Unfortunately, others were not committed to these goals. Chief among them was Sheriff Jim Clark, who dressed in a military uniform, complete with an officer's billed hat, and showed open disregard for the rights of anyone who disagreed with his point of view. As head of a posse of men who traveled across the state upholding segregation, he led his men as they attacked demonstrators in the streets of Birmingham. Mayor Smitherman had appointed Wilson Baker to the post of public safety director and instructed him to assume control of law enforcement within the city boundaries. The flash point of contention between Baker and Clark was the County Court House. Obviously, the sheriff had authority within the building, but what about the sidewalks leading into the building? Baker insisted that they were under his jurisdiction, but Clark with equal conviction insisted they were not.

Although Dr. King's organization, the Southern Christian Leadership Council (SCLC), planned the January 2 mass meeting, it did so at the request of the Dallas County Voters League, a coalition of black organizations supporting the voting registration project in Dallas County. King always worked with local leaders and organization in his campaigns, but in this case he had to be especially careful not to alienate the members of the Student Nonviolent Coordinating Committee (SNCC), who had been on the scene in Selma for the past two years. Although their efforts had not made an appreciable difference in the number of black voters registered, they had begun the process of organizing the black population by arousing discontent with their low status. Had it not been for the SNCC, the turnout for the rally would have been far smaller than it was. In his speech, King made it clear that Selma was the beginning of an organized campaign to get the vote for black people not only in Alabama but throughout the South.

After his speech, King left town. Baker managed to maintain an uneasy peace in Selma itself, but in neighboring Marion, violence broke out following a nighttime march on February 18, 1965. SCLC staffers C. T. Vivian and Willie Bolden had not planned for a march following a meeting at Zion Methodist Church that night, but Bolden's speech so inflamed the crowd that at its conclusion, when he asked how many would march, they all stood in unison and began to file out of the church toward the Perry County Courthouse less than a block away. Police Chief T. O. Harris faced the marchers with over two hundred men, including state troopers, town policemen, sheriff's deputies, and Sheriff Jim Clark and his posse from neighboring Selma. When the marchers were about halfway to the court house, Chief Harris, using a megaphone, ordered them to disperse. Without further warning, the forces of law and order charged the marchers. Television cameras tried to cover the scene of violence, but locals spray painted the lenses of the cameras black. ABC television reported Richard Valeriani was hit on the back of the head by an ax handle, drawing blood. In the resulting melee, Jimmy Lee Jackson, a young black man, was shot at point-blank range in the stomach. Seven days later he died.[4]

The death of Jimmy Lee Jackson not only symbolized the repression that black Americans experienced in their daily struggle for existence, but it provided a martyr for the cause of black voting rights. The Reverend James Bevel, a staff member of the SCLC and in charge of their workers in Selma, had been struggling to find an appropriate way not only to memorialize Jimmy Lee Jackson but to make the story of the struggle for voting rights vivid to the rest of the nation. Suddenly, he had an inspiration. A march from Selma to Montgomery would focus the attention of the news media on the issues involved and put pressure on the administration to act. Dr. King and other leaders of the SCLC embraced the idea, which King announced on Monday, March 1, following the funeral for Jackson. The march would begin on Sunday, March 7 in Selma, cross the Edmund Pettus Bridge, and proceed down Highway 80 to Montgomery.[5]

A march of this magnitude required extensive preparation: places had to be secured for the evening rest; sanitary facilities needed to be identified and made available; preparations for feeding the marchers and for dealing with their medical needs had to be arranged; and in addition, security for the marchers had to be in place. In the short period of time between the announcement and the day of the march itself, not much had been done. An SNCC organizer on the scene observed that "preparations made for it during the latter part of the week were scanty, haphazard."[6]

The announcement of the march touched off a flurry of activity involving Governor Wallace, Al Lingo, the head of the state troopers, Sheriff Clark, and Wilson Baker. Although initially persuaded by his press secretary, Bill Jones, to allow the march on the grounds that the demonstrators were not prepared to travel the 50 miles between Selma and Montgomery, Governor Wallace later changed his mind because of fears that Klan-inspired whites would shoot or bomb the marchers in Lowndes County. He determined to stop the march and met with Al Lingo, John Cloud, and William R. Jones of the state troopers.[7] According to Wallace's press secretary, who was also present at the meeting, Wallace insisted and the officers agreed that troopers would do everything possible to prevent a violent confrontation. When the marchers approached the line of troopers stretched across the bridge, Major John Cloud would order them to halt and to turn back. The troopers were to stand in place with their nightsticks in a protective position. If the marchers persisted, the troopers were to raise their nightsticks. If the marchers pushed the troopers, tear gas was to be used to disperse them. There was to be no charging of the marchers and no attempt to beat them. According to Jones, that was the plan that was agreed to by Wallace, and Al Lingo, the commander of the Alabama state troopers. This plan was communicated to Mayor Smitherman, who pledged the full cooperation of the city police, and to Sheriff James Clark, who seemed to be in agreement.

When Wilson Baker, who was out of town for a few days of much-needed rest, returned to the city and learned of the plan, he was incredulous. He could not believe that the state troopers had enough discipline to follow the agreed-upon procedure. He believed that they were waiting to get their hands on the demonstrators, which Baker had prevented by keeping them from leaving the perimeters of the housing project. Baker wanted to arrest the marchers using his own policemen as soon as they started the march to prevent them from getting into the troopers' hands. But Smitherman, assured by Wallace aides that everything would go according to plan, told Baker to play his part in it. Baker refused, believing that it would result in a bloody confrontation, and threatened to resign. Following a long, heated debate, Baker agreed to post two policemen across the bridge in a patrol car, but that was as much of a commitment as he would make.

On Sunday morning, March 7, Baker met with Major John Cloud, who would be in command of the troopers, and again was assured that there would be no violence and, they hoped, no arrests. City police were to monitor the march until it reached the bridge and were to do so again once it had turned around and headed back to the city. At Brown Chapel, the assembly point for the march, the crowd was determined to march but sensed the tension in the air. Dr. King, who had planned to lead the march, stayed in Atlanta to preach to his own congregation. Hosea Williams of the SCLC took King's place at the head of the line, accompanied by John Lewis of the SNCC. Williams and Lewis led six hundred people out of the church in columns of two, followed by four ambulances carrying medical teams toward the Edmund Pettus Bridge. When they reached the bridge, they saw a long line of troopers standing shoulder to shoulder across the four lanes of the highway with billy clubs held in front of them and gas masks hanging at their waists. Major Cloud, standing in front of the line, called out to them to stop and to disperse. Williams asked if they could have a word with him, and he answered by ordering his troopers to advance. The troopers reached Williams and Lewis first, knocked them down, and began beating them. At that point, all discipline disappeared. Troopers broke ranks and began running after the retreating marchers, swinging clubs at whomever they could find. After a moment, Lingo got them to reform their line. He ordered them to put on their gas masks and spray the marchers with tear gas. Almost on signal, Sheriff James Clark's posse mounted on horseback and, armed with whips and ropes, rode into the crowd and began beating them. By now any semblance of order had vanished. People choking on tear gas ran toward the downtown area seeking any refuge from the posse and the pursuing troopers.[8]

The melee continued as the demonstrators retreated to the safety of Brown Chapel Church, where Wilson Baker finally asserted his authority by ordering Clark and his posse to leave. Baker posted his policemen around the church and allowed the ambulances to cross the bridge and pick up the wounded. Inside the parsonage adjoining the church, the leaders of the march telephoned Dr. King in Atlanta with a report of the event. Shocked by what he heard, King asked if he should immediately return to Selma and lead another march the next day. After a heated discussion of the alternatives, the group decided that King should send out telegrams that night to his supporters throughout the nation asking them to come to Selma to participate in another march. On Monday, lawyers for the SCLC would seek a restraining order in federal court barring Al Lingo, Jim Clark, and Wilson Baker from interfering with the next march. The march would not take place until Tuesday, to give outside supporters time to arrive in Selma. Even as these plans were being discussed, television reporters who were present during the march and had captured it on film were making certain that the nation knew of the brutal assault. ABC news interrupted the Sunday Night Movie to show a long sequence of images of blacks being attacked by white troopers with billy clubs. The movie that was being shown was *Judgment at Nuremberg*.

That night and the next day, opinion leaders throughout the nation reacted angrily to the beatings at the bridge. From Attorney General Nicholas Katzenbach, congressmen, senators, and religious leaders came strong denunciations of the action. Perhaps Senator Ralph Yarborough summed up the consensus most succinctly: "This is not the American Way."[9] Demonstrators took to the streets in Chicago, Los Angeles, and Washington, D.C. Sit-ins were staged at the White House and the Justice Department. In Detroit, Governor Romney joined with Mayor Cavanagh to lead over 10,000 demonstrators in a mile-long protest march.[10] *Newsweek's* lead article called the event "An American Tragedy" and proclaimed that "Selma's name was forever linked with those of Little Rock, Oxford, Birmingham—the great battlegrounds of the American Negro revolt."[11]

On Monday, lawyers for the SCLC appeared in Judge Frank M. Johnson's court seeking a restraining order to prevent Wallace, Lingo, Clark, and Baker from interfering with the planned march on Tuesday. Judge Johnson refused to issue the requested order until he could hold a hearing and on Tuesday issued an order forbidding the march until a hearing could be held and his decision made. On both Monday and Tuesday, hundreds of white supporters arrived in Selma, including such notables as Methodist Bishop John Wesley Lord, the Rev. Malcolm Boyd, Mrs. Charles Tobey, the widow of a New Hampshire Senator, and Mrs. Harold Ickes, the widow of a former secretary of the interior.[12] King now faced a dilemma. Judge Johnson had ordered him not to march, but the pressure from the more militant members of his staff and from SNCC leaders to go ahead and march was intense. Complicating matters was the presence of the outside supporters who had been invited to appear in Selma for a march and who did not anticipate having to sit and wait for several days. At 10:30 A.M. on Tuesday, King arrived at Brown Chapel Church and addressed the assembled crowd, telling them that "we will not be turned around." The march would go on. It took several more hours before the milling throng could be organized for the march. Before they set out, King proclaimed, "I have no alternative but to lead a march from this spot to carry our grievances to the seat of government. I have made my choice. I have got to march."[13]

What King did not announce to his supporters was an agreement that had been worked out by former Florida governor Leroy Collins, now head of the Community Relations Service of the U.S. Department of Justice, with Clark and Lingo not to attack the marchers if they stopped when ordered to do so and turned around and went back across the bridge toward Brown Chapel.[14] When the marchers reached the foot of the bridge, U.S. marshal H. Stanley Fountain was waiting for them with a copy of Judge Johnson's order, which he read to them. King replied that he was aware of the order but was going ahead anyway. Fountain stepped aside, and the marchers proceeded to cross the bridge, where a line of state troopers awaited them on the other side. Major John Cloud, again in command of the state troopers, using his bullhorn ordered King and the marchers to stop. King asked if the group could kneel and pray. Cloud agreed, providing that they then returned to the church. The Rev. Ralph Abernathy, a close associate of King's, offered a fervent prayer, followed by prayers from Bishop Lord and Rabbi Richard Hirsch of the Union of American Hebrew Congregations. At the conclusion of the prayers, King turned the line around and marched back across the bridge to Brown Chapel. At a mass meeting that night, he explained his actions and pledged that a march from Selma to Montgomery would take place.[15]

After the meeting broke up, three white clergymen went for dinner at a black restaurant downtown. After dinner, the three men, Clark Olsen, Orloff Miller, and James Reeb, left the restaurant and headed back to Brown Chapel. Unfamiliar with the town and confused by the darkness, they made a wrong turn that took them past the Silver Moon Cafe, a notorious hangout for racists and opponents of the demonstrators. Four white men approached them with clubs and attacked them. Reeb took the worst blow. Stunned by the attack and unable to get up by himself, he could barely speak and had difficulty in seeing. His companions helped him up and made their way to the SCLC office on Franklin Street, where they sent for an ambulance. When he arrived at the Burwell Infirmary, Reeb fell into a coma. He was transferred to University Hospital in Birmingham, where the examining surgeon saw that he had a massive skull fracture, a blood clot, and pneumonia. He died two days later, on Thursday, March 11, 1965.[16]

While the public was mourning the death of James Reeb, two other events were unfolding in Washington that would bring the crisis to a conclusion. Attorney General Katzenbach, whose staff had been working all that week on drafting a voting rights bill, arranged a meeting with Senator Dirksen, the minority leader of the Senate to seek his support for the legislation.[17] This was a crucial move. Dirksen's support would be necessary to break the expected filibuster by southern Senators against the bill. With his endorsement, the bill would move easily through the Senate. Second, on Friday, March 12, Governor Wallace sent a telegram to the White House requesting a meeting with President Johnson, who readily agreed to a personal meeting in the White House on Saturday. This meeting not only gave the two men a chance to meet and to attempt to establish a personal relationship, but it put in motion the convoluted moves by which Wallace would have to admit that he and the state of Alabama could not protect the marchers and that federal help would be needed.

On Sunday, March 14, Johnson met with the leadership of Congress to discuss the general outline of the voting rights bill and the best means of presenting it to Congress. House Speaker McCormack invited the president to make an address before a joint session of Congress to present the bill, and Johnson readily agreed. Johnson's speech to Congress the next day is widely regarded as his most eloquent speech.[18] In it he made a strong case for the voting rights act. The next day, Tuesday, March 16, Judge Johnson issued his ruling, allowing the march to proceed with certain restrictions on the number of marchers allowed on the public highways. His order noted that the primary responsibility for protecting the safety of the marchers rested with the state of Alabama, but if the state could not do so, he directed the federal government to protect them. Judge Johnson's order provided the immediate impetus for Wallace's speech to the legislature on Thursday, March 18, in which he admitted that Alabama did not have the resources to protect the marchers and requested help from the federal government.

Wallace addressed a joint session of the Alabama Legislature at 6:30 in the evening of March 18 in a hastily prepared speech.[19] He was scheduled to speak to the Alabama Education Association at 11:00 that morning in Birmingham and did not arrive back in Montgomery until 3:00, giving him about three hours to put together the speech. This speech shares with Wallace's speech in the schoolhouse door (see chapter 2) the same blustery pose of defiance while conceding defeat. Broadcast statewide, it is designed to reassure Wallace's supporters that he has done all he could to resist the outside forces that are threatening to change the social and political culture of Alabama. Wallace makes no effort to reach beyond his core supporters. He does not even deign to acknowledge the death of the Reverend James Reeb nor to express any sympathy to Reeb's family. He merely recycles the old arguments that the demonstrations are communist led and attacks the federal courts for encouraging anarchy in the streets.

Wallace begins the speech with the claim that the first march in Selma was stopped because it would be impossible to provide safety and security to the marchers that numbered about six hundred people. He states that "we understood ourselves that at that time what a colossal undertaking it would be to provide safety and security" for the marchers. He then claims that "[t]o show you that we understood when others did not, and evidently the Federal Courts did not, I have a telegram in my hand from one of the leaders of the march that says we expect you to meet the health and safety needs of 5,000 marchers." He next reads a telegram requesting protection for the 5,000 people who will be at the march scheduled for the next Sunday. This is a bit disingenuous. There is a big difference between the original 600 people who marched and the projected 5,000 for the upcoming one. Wallace does not acknowledge his responsibility in creating the larger number of marchers. Had he followed his press secretary's advice and allowed the original march to proceed with the protection of state troopers, it is entirely possible that the march would have ended in failure. It was the attack on the marchers at the Edmund Pettus Bridge that escalated the incident and attracted the large number of outsiders who now wanted to march from Selma to Montgomery.

Next Wallace attacks the federal courts and especially Judge Frank Johnson, calling him a hypocrite who "prostitutes our law in favor of that of mob rule." Wallace gives examples of the actions of "peaceful demonstrators" to show that they have abused their rights to use the public streets and sidewalks. He concludes from this catalogue of abuses that the demonstrators are "employing the street warfare tactics of the Communists." This is a key devil term in Wallace's vocabulary that he uses to denounce anyone or any action with which he disagrees. He does this in all the speeches discussed in this book. It was standard topos for southerners opposed to integration because it allowed them to dismiss the movement for racial equality without considering the justice of the argument. If the communists were behind the movement, then there were no grounds for considering whether segregation was legally or morally justified or not.

Communism represents evil; everything they are for is evil; therefore. . . . Wallace used this topos so frequently that he must have believed it, and he found that it was effective with his southern audiences.

Next Wallace tries to estimate what it would cost to carry out Judge Johnson's order to protect the marchers from Selma to Montgomery by detailing what it cost the federal government to protect the marchers who took part in the one-day March on Washington in August 1962. Again, his comparison is not fair. There were over 100,000 people in Washington on that day. These marchers will be limited to no more than 5,000. However, he adds up all the costs and gets a figure of $805,000 for a one-day demonstration in Washington.

Wallace then claims that "[t]he call has gone out . . . for every left-wing, pro-Communist, Fellow Traveler and Communist in the country to be here." He declares that this march is "going to be much more difficult to control than was the one-day march in Washington." He estimates that it will cost between "$350,000 to $400,000 of state funds to handle this march completely by ourselves." He argues that this "financial burden" would take monies from "the care of our sick and infirm, both white and Negro," who need them. Having made the point that protecting the marchers would be a burden, Wallace next moves on to a denunciation of a "foreign philosophy" that encourages people to "demonstrate and cause chaos" to create conditions that will enable the transfer of "all police powers unto the central government." Wallace in this passage hints at but does not develop his standard topos of states' rights versus the federal government. He hastens on to denounce yet again "communist-trained" demonstrators and charges that the "Negroes used as tools in this traditional type of communist street warfare have no conception of the misery and slavery they are bringing to their children." Wallace next uses another of his standard topos, that what is happening in the streets of Selma happened in the past in Czechoslovakia, Cuba, Vietnam, and China and cost them their freedom as a result.

Having attacked the federal courts, communists, left-wingers, fellow travelers, federal judges, and alien philosophies, and having shouted his defiance of those who would threaten "our heritage," Wallace in the end agrees to "obey—we will do our duty. We will not abdicate our responsibilities to provide protection in as best as we can." However, he asks the legislature to "call on the President of the United States to provide sufficient federal civil authorities" to provide for "the safety and welfare of" the demonstrators. He also asks his fellow citizens to "see that this march is peaceful." He ends the speech with his standard prayer that God "will bless all the people of this great and sovereign state, both white and black." He calls on the legislature and the people of the state to "stand with me in this crisis that we face here in Alabama."

The speech was put together hastily by Wallace and his staffers. There was not time to type up a complete text. He read the speech from note cards. The lack of time to write a coherent text is evident in the number of topics brought up in the speech that are not completely developed and in the use of commonplace arguments used in previous speeches. Wallace uses figures to give credence to his argument that the state cannot afford to provide protection for the marchers, but his failure to compare equivalent situations lessens the impact of his argument. The comparison of the March on Washington to the Selma to Montgomery March is to compare a massive one-day event involving over 100,000 people with a much smaller event involving at most 5,000 people.

A more telling criticism is that Wallace is only addressing his own base of true believers. He does not make any effort to reach out to others. Some recognition that a mistake had been made in beating the demonstrators at the bridge or some expression of sympathy for the death of the Reverend James Reeb would have at least begun the process of reaching out to those who suffered through this ordeal. To continue to refer to those who demonstrate for the basic rights of citizenship for black Americans as communists or communist dupes is not only insulting but rhetorically insensitive. Again this topos ensured that Wallace's speech would be persuasive only to those who already agreed with him.

This time, Wallace lost a major rhetorical encounter with the president of the United States, Lyndon B. Johnson. In his speech, Johnson defined the situation:

I speak tonight for the dignity of man and the destiny of democracy. I urge every member of both parties, Americans of all religions and of all colors, from every section of this country to join me in that cause. . . . The issue of equal rights for American Negroes. . . .

This was the first nation in the history of the world to be founded with a purpose. The great phrases of that purpose still sound in every American heart, North and South: "All men are created equal." "Government by consent of the governed." "Give me liberty or give me death." And those are not just clever words, and those are not just empty theories. In their name Americans have fought and died for two centuries and tonight, around the world, they stand there as guardians of our liberty risking their lives. . . .

Our fathers believed that if this noble view of the rights of man was to flourish it must be rooted in democracy. The most basic right of all was the right to choose your own leaders. . . . [A]bout this there can and should be no argument: every American citizen must have an equal right to vote.[20]

In seizing the high ground and defining the issue as a fundamental test of America's dedication to the democratic ideals that were the basis of its founding and the inspiration for its highest achievements, Johnson indicated that Wallace was acting outside of the mainstream of American values. As Johnson stated, "There is no reason which can excuse the denial of that right" to vote.

Because Wallace spoke after President Johnson's televised address, he could have more effectively argued for state control of the electoral laws within his philosophical position defending states' rights. Instead, he gave a petulant speech that did not address the larger issues raised by the president. Johnson was not an accomplished public speaker, but Richard Godwin, who wrote the speech for him, used strong appeals to American values to overcome the objections of conservative southern politicians to hasten the passage of the bill. It was a great moment for President Johnson and another public humiliation for Wallace.

Johnson was not the only speaker to confront Wallace during the Selma demonstrations for voting rights. Martin Luther King, Jr., at the conclusion of the march made an eloquent speech that clearly enunciated the need for voting rights legislation:

The Civil Rights Act of 1964 gave Negroes some part of their rightful dignity, but without the vote it was dignity without strength. . . . Our whole campaign in Alabama has been centered around the right to vote. In focusing the attention of the nation and the world today on the flagrant denial of the right to vote we are exposing the very origin, the root cause, of segregation in the Southland. . . . Today I want to say to the people of America and the nations of the world: We are not about to turn around. We are on the move now. Yes, we are on the move and no wave of racism can stop us.

Let us march on ballot boxes, march on ballot boxes until race baiters disappear from the political arena. Let us march on ballot boxes until the Wallaces of our nation tremble away in silence. . . . Our aim must never be to defeat or humiliate the white man but to win his friendship and understanding. We must come to see that the end we seek is a society at peace with itself, a society that can live with its conscience. That will be a day not of the white man, not of the black man. That will be the day of man as man.[21]

NOTES

1. Dan T. Carter, *The Politics of Rage: George Wallace, the Origins of the New Conservatism, and the Transformation of American Politics* (New York: Simon and Schuster, 1995), 468.

2. Lyndon B. Johnson, "State of the Union, January 4, 1965," in *Public Papers of the Presidents of the United States, Lyndon B. Johnson*, vol. 1 (Washington, D.C.: United States Government Printing Office, 1965), 6.

3. Stephan Lesher, *George Wallace: American Populist* (Reading, Mass.: Addison-Wesley, 1994), 316.

4. Lesher, *George Wallace*, 318–319.

5. Charles E. Fager, *Selma, 1965: The March That Changed the South*, 2nd ed. (Boston: Beacon Press, 1985), 82–83.

6. Fager, *Selma, 1965*, 86.

7. Bill Jones, *The Wallace Story* (Northport, Ala.: American Southern, 1966), 357.

8. *Bridge to Freedom*, vol. 6 of *Eyes on the Prize* (Alexandria, Va.: PBS Video,

1986), videocassette. This video has graphic images of the attack on the marchers. I have relied on it as well as accounts in "An American Tragedy," *Newsweek*, March 22, 1965, 18–22; and Fager, *Selma, 1965*, to recount the story of the march and its aftermath.

9. *Bridge to Freedom*.

10. "An American Tragedy," 21.

11. "An American Tragedy," 18.

12. Fager, *Selma, 1965*, 100.

13. Fager, *Selma, 1965*, 103.

14. Fager, *Selma, 1965*, 102.

15. Fager, *Selma, 1965*, 105.

16. Fager, *Selma, 1965*, 107–109.

17. David J. Garrow, *Protest at Selma: Martin Luther King, Jr., and the Voting Rights Act of 1965* (New Haven, Conn.: Yale University Press, 1978), 91–92, 99.

18. Kurt Ritter and William Forrest Harlow, "Lyndon B. Johnson's Voting Rights Address of March 15, 1965: Civil Rights Rhetoric in the Jeremiad Tradition," in *Great Speeches for Criticism and Analysis*, 4th ed., ed. Lloyd Rohler and Roger Cook (Greenwood, Ind.: Alistair Press, 2001), 198–219.

19. The entire text of this speech is reproduced in the second part of this volume, in "Speech to the Joint Session of the Alabama Legislature, March 18, 1965."

20. Lyndon B. Johnson, "Special Message to Congress, March 15, 1965," in *Public Papers of the Presidents of the United States, Lyndon B. Johnson*, vol. 1 (Washington, D.C.: United States Government Printing Office, 1965), 281–287.

21. "Excerpts from Dr. King's Montgomery Speech," *New York Times*, March 26, 1965, 22.

CHAPTER 6

The American Independent Party: The 1968 Campaign

Wallace's amateurish campaign in 1964 demonstrated not only that he could win votes outside the South but also the extent of discontent with the political establishment and its policies. When Wallace and his aides began to plan for the 1968 campaign, Lyndon Johnson was riding high in the public opinion polls, following his triumphant win in the 1964 election. Wallace did not believe that it would be possible to challenge Johnson successfully in the primaries in 1968. His idea of unpledged electors had not gained sufficient support in 1965, mainly due to Strom Thurmond's vigorous campaigning for Barry Goldwater. This left as the only alternative open to Wallace a third-party challenge to both the Democrats and the Republicans.

Third-party campaigns are not easy in American politics. Both the Democratic and Republican parties benefit from the two-party monopoly, and officials from those parties write the legislative rules that govern access to the ballot in each of the 50 states. Rules differ from state to state and are enforced by officials, such as the secretary of state, who are likely to be very literal in interpreting the requirements and more likely to try to keep a third party off the ballot than allow it access. Some states such as Colorado required relatively few signatures on a petition to list a new party on the ballot—three hundred—while Ohio required half a million. California required that 1 percent of voters sign an affidavit changing their party registration to the new party for it to be granted access to the ballot. In 1968 that meant that almost 66,000 voters in California needed to be contacted and persuaded to change their registration. The Wallace campaign had to spend precious time and money to get on the ballot in all 50 states. Without the help of Alabama state officials, who according to the governor's office were working on their vacation time, this would not have been possible. Ohio proved too formidable a task, and so the Wallace campaign got the U.S. Supreme Court to order Ohio officials to list the party on the ballot. The irony of using the hated Supreme Court to order a state to change its laws governing voting procedures was lost on Wallace's aides.

The American Independent Party was not a grassroots affair. It was a vehicle for George Wallace's run for the presidency in 1968, and Wallace kept close control of it. In his history of the party, Marshall Frady characterizes it as "a haphazard assortment of small, fractious, strident groups from the more obscure reaches of the American right, along with a motley company of ideological outriders, radio gospel patriots and such antediluvian southern politicians as Louisiana's Leander Perez and Georgia's Roy Harris and Lester Maddox."[1] The authors of *An American Melodrama,* who did extensive research on the backgrounds of Wallace electors and committee members in the various states, report that "the list of Wallace backers, managers, and electors in many states reads like a national directory of extremists, a political bestiary."[2] Wallace refused to hold a convention on the somewhat sensible grounds that "You get a big bunch of folks together like that, there'll always be a few who'll try to take the thing over."[3]

There was a more pressing problem. Like it or not, to meet ballot requirements and eventually electoral college requirements, the party needed a vice presidential nominee. At first, Wallace came up with Georgia's former governor Marvin Griffin as a stand-in, but having two avowed segregationists both from the Deep South did not give the ticket either geographic or ideological balance. Few mainstream politicians were willing to run with Wallace, which severely limited his choices. Finally, he sent his advisors to Los Angeles to approach retired Air Force General Curtis LeMay about running on the ticket with him. LeMay, who had been retired for three years, was growing tired of golf and socializing and was ready for something new. Following his advisors' upbeat report on their meeting, Wallace met LeMay in Chicago on September 27, 1968, where LeMay agreed to become Wallace's running mate.

The news conference to announce the ticket was scheduled for 10 A.M. on October 3 in Pittsburgh. It was broadcast live by all three networks. At first things went well. LeMay read a statement written for him by Wallace's staffers and exuded the confidence of someone who had been through press briefings many times before. Then it was time for questions from the assembled reporters. One of the first came from Jack Nelson of the *Los Angeles Times,* who asked if it would be necessary to use nuclear weapons to win the war in Vietnam. While LeMay admitted that it would be possible to win the war in Vietnam without using nuclear weapons, he could not avoid an opportunity to talk about one of his pet subjects—the American public's phobia about the use of nuclear weapons. What followed was one of the strangest press conferences since Richard Nixon's celebrated ranting against the press following his loss of the California governorship in 1962. LeMay revealed that he had seen movies of the Bikini Atoll in the South Pacific, which had been the site of nuclear tests in the 1950s that showed that both the fish and the birds were back and the coconut trees were bearing fruit. He did admit that the land crabs are "a little hot," but he noted that the rats are "bigger, fatter, and healthier than they ever were before."[4] An aghast Wallace tried to edge LeMay away from the microphones, but the retired general continued to talk. Finally, Wallace ended the press conference with a blunt command to LeMay, "General, we got to go."

This was not the end of LeMay's controversial statements. Following a speech two weeks later to an audience at Yale University's School of Forestry, LeMay was asked about the relationship between population growth and excessive use of natural resources. He gave a good, thorough answer to the question and then endorsed the use of abortion as a method of population control. Since Wallace's campaign was targeting blue-collar workers in northern cities, many of whom were Catholic, this was too much for even Wallace to tolerate. LeMay was unceremoniously sent to Vietnam for a fact-finding tour, where he would miss most of the crucial last weeks of the campaign.

With access to the ballot in all 50 states and a running mate in place, Wallace was ready for a national campaign. And the times were ready for Wallace. For many Americans in 1968, it was the worst of times. The passage of the Civil Rights Act of 1964 and the Voting Rights Act of 1965 had not brought racial harmony but racial riots and increased tension between whites and blacks. The issue of law and order moved to the top of the agenda as increased crime and violence swept the nation's cities. The counterculture's lack of respect for traditional values sometimes expressed itself as outright contempt for the working class and the middle class. The war in Vietnam divided the nation, with many college students openly calling for a Viet Cong victory and burning draft cards. The assassinations of Martin Luther King, Jr., and Robert Kennedy dramatized the social conflicts tearing the nation apart. Those troubled times were ripe for an agitator of Wallace's skills.

In his 1968 campaign, George Wallace offered himself as the champion of the white working class who would stand up for America. "Send them a message!" he cried, and through his campaign rallies he showed ordinary Americans that he was willing to defend their values of neighborhood, family, church, and flag. He was an agitator who used mimetic oratory to tell people what they wanted to hear: that patriotism and love for country was still important; that neighbors and family were anchors for decency and respect; that hard work still counted; and that religion was the basis for morality.[5] Twenty years before Wallace appeared on the scene, Leo Lowenthal and Norbert Guterman drew a portrait of the agitator that was remarkably prescient:

The agitator appeals to predispositions which are still in flux; his function is to bring to flame the smoldering resentments of his listeners, to express loudly and brazenly what they whisper timidly. . . . He works, as it were, from inside the audience, stirring up what lies dormant there.[6]

This theoretical description of the agitator and his audience finds support in survey research of the Wallace voter. Jody Carlson did extensive analysis of the polling data from the 1968 campaign and found: "The data show that Wallace supporters are politically alienated and feel powerless in relation to the American political system. In demanding power, they are also demanding that the system operate in a legitimate fashion, rewarding effort and faithfulness, distributing goods and services equitably."[7]

In 1968 the Wallace campaign went back to its roots in Alabama politics by taking to the North and West the campaign rally that worked so well in southern politics, complete with a country music band but lacking the plates of barbecue. Usually held in large outdoor baseball fields or county fair grounds, the rallies attracted huge crowds numbering in the thousands. As the people gathered, Sam Smith and His American Independent Party Band would play country music, and the Taylor Sisters, Mona and Lisa, would lead them in song or clap hands to the music. Usually, there were demonstrators outside the arena and frequently inside, too. Sometimes shouting matches would occur, accompanied by shoving, which the police would be quick to stop. When most of the crowd had been seated, the band would shift to "God Bless America" and a local minister would take the podium to offer a prayer. Next, the band would play "The Star Spangled Banner," and a Wallace aide, Dick Smith, would come on stage to lead the audience in the Pledge of Allegiance. He would next introduce local dignitaries and instruct the "Wallace Girls" to pass through the crowd with plastic buckets to accept contributions for the campaign. After some good-natured banter about the necessity of supporting the campaign, Smith would introduce some local celebrity whose task it was to introduce Wallace who would stride down the aisle and up the stage steps. Wallace would be greeted by shouts, rebel yells, thunderous applause, and a few boos and loudly yelled obscenities.[8]

As expected, the rally attracted hecklers and demonstrators, who played a role in the script. Wallace turned their presence to his own advantage by portraying them as the "other"—as representatives of the very forces undermining the traditional values of his faithful supporters. The confrontation with the hecklers became a highly stylized feature of every Wallace rally. Violence seemed always to be lurking in the background, and it frequently burst forth when college students heckled him. When they did, they played into Wallace's hands as he would direct the wrath of the crowd toward them, taunting them: "You young people seem to know a lot of four letter words. But I have two four-letter words you don't know: S-O-A-P and W-O-R-K."[9]

A Wallace speech enacted before his supporters their own attitudes and reactions to people and forces they could not understand. Wallace's show of power was particularly effective with audiences whose daily experience convinced them that they lacked the power to affect their own lives. As Lurleen Wallace said of another context when Wallace confronted his critics in the press, "When he's on Meet the Press they can listen to George and think, 'That's what I would say if I were up there.'"[10] Of course, it made for good television. Invariably, the segments of the speech that made the local news showed Wallace standing up to the hecklers and sending a message.

Wallace also broadened his appeal in 1968 to include more issues than the narrow focus on the Civil Rights Act, which was his main issue in 1964. He did so by adapting the pose of a populist champion of the white working class. The nationally televised confrontation over integration at the University of Alabama and the police attack on the marchers in Selma had solidified his standing as the leading opponent of integration. He did not need to do anything to carry those voters. He and his political advisers thought that Wallace would carry the South in the election for a solid electoral base of 128 electoral votes. The problem was to move beyond that base and pick up the border states with 49 electoral votes or perhaps an industrial state such as Ohio or Pennsylvania. If he were to do so, he would have real bargaining power in the electoral college. The populist pose also provided a convenient cover for his racist past. He could argue that his opposition to the Civil Rights Act was motivated by his concern for majority rule. If the majority in a community did not want to integrate their schools, then integration should not be forced upon them.

Because it is the pattern of the arguments and not their content that defines the populist persuasion, populist arguments can be used to support conservative political programs as well as progressive ones. As Michael Kazin argues, "The most basic and telling definition of populism [is] a language whose speakers conceive of ordinary people as a noble assemblage not bound narrowly by class, view their elite opponents as self-serving and undemocratic and seek to mobilize the former against the latter."[11] This basic pattern of populist rhetoric—an attack on elites for victimizing the people—can be adapted to progressive or conservative political ends depending on what or who is being scapegoated. One reason for the effectiveness of this pattern is that contemporary institutions, either governmental or corporate, rely on impersonal bureaucratic means of control that are not amenable to the preferences of local communities. Thus, by targeting an unresponsive big government in the place of unresponsive big business, Wallace could use the same form of arguments that the orators of the Peoples Party used to attack big-business practices to attack big government.

Because the populist pose was so ambiguous and could be used as a justification for conservative goals, it allowed Wallace to forge a coalition between two disaffected groups that were the core of his campaign. The most active members of his campaign organization were members of the John Birch Society, Liberty Lobbyists, Christian Anti-Communist Crusaders, and other right-wing groups.[12] These were people who feared and actively supported a crusade against the growing power of the federal government. They distrusted the growing power of trade unions, loathed the expansion of the welfare state, and worried that the economic and social costs imposed by government programs on ordinary Americans were leading to economic and moral bankruptcy. They supported Wallace primarily because they believed that he would return power to the states and localities, where it belonged. They had organizational muscle in the campaign, but the mass appeal of their policies was severely limited. Wallace also had to appeal to the white working class, who had benefited from governmental programs but were threatened by integration of their neighborhoods, schools, and workplaces and who strongly disapproved of the changing moral values involving drugs, sexual behavior, and antiwar protest advocated by college students. Wallace united both these groups with his attack on an elite establishment comprised of the leadership of both political parties that supported civil rights legislation, seemed to condone rioting and violence in the streets, and was more concerned about poor black Americans than their more numerous white counterparts.

In his study of populism, Kazin identifies four themes that characterize its appeal:

1. Americanism defined as majority rule—"understanding and obeying the will of the people."[13] This is not restricted solely to the rule of law but also means that the social and moral preferences of the majority should be respected and obeyed by the community.
2. The producer ethic, which holds that "only those who create wealth in tangible, material ways (on and under the land, in workshops, on the sea) could be trusted to guard the nation's piety and liberties."[14]
3. An opposition to the elite, "the perpetual antithesis and exploiter of 'the people'"[15]
4. The call for a strong movement to vanquish the enemy and restore "the ideals of the nation and protect the welfare of the common folk."[16]

These themes will be used to analyze the appeal of Wallace's 1968 campaign speech based on the text of his speech given at the Mid-South Coliseum on June 11, 1968, in Memphis, Tennessee.

In his speech in Memphis, Wallace uses the first of these populist themes, majority rule, to portray himself as the representative of "millions of people in this country who think exactly as you do."[17] Wallace focuses on the issue of majority rule to argue that the "right of people to determine the policies of democratic domestic institutions" had been "taken away" by the leadership of the National Democratic Party and the National Republican Party. He charges that they had taken away the right of the people to "control the policies of their schools, the education of their children, to run their own hospitals, the seniority and apprenticeship list of their own labor unions, or their businesses."

For Wallace and his supporters, majority rule meant that the will of the majority should prevail over minority rights. Although Wallace makes the case for majority rule without regard to race, the issue is always there. For example, his attacks on the Supreme Court remind his followers that the Court has been in the forefront of the protection of minority rights:

In California, they voted on the matter of housin' not too long ago, in 1966, and the people of that state voted 4½ million to 2 million that they wanted to dispose of their property in the manner they saw fit. And the Supreme Court of your country said, "You cain't vote that way." And they struck it down. And the people of Oklahoma voted on the matter of apportionment of their legislature. And the Supreme Court said, 'The people of Oklahoma cain't vote that way.' Well, why cain't the people of California and Oklahoma and Tennessee vote to dispose of their property in the manner they see fit or apportion their legislature in the manner they see fit? It never has been unconstitutional for them to do that and its not unconstitutional now, just because the Supreme Court of our country said so. . . . [W]hen they can change the law at their own whim, I say they go beyond the law and I'm gonna appoint some different sorts of judges when attrition takes its toll.

Demonizing the federal judiciary because it thwarted the will of the people not only reflected populist themes but gave Wallace an identifiable enemy. As Murray Edelman observed, the construction of political enemies is vital to political communication because enemies "arouse passions, fears and hopes" as "identifiable persons or stereotypes to whom evil traits, intentions or actions can be attributed."[18] Wallace shrewdly focused on the Supreme Court as the archenemy of democracy because, of the three branches of the federal government, it is the least subject to popular control. By scapegoating the institution that promoted black advancement, Wallace achieved his purpose without even mentioning the word *black*. He could claim that he was merely standing up for constitutional rights not talking about race. But as one of reporter Marshall Frady's informants noted, "He can use all the other issues—law and order, running your own schools, protecting property rights—and never mention race. But people will still know he's telling them, 'a nigger's trying to get your job, trying to move into your neighborhood.' What Wallace is doing is talking to them in a kind of shorthand, a kind of code."[19]

In addition to protecting the rights of minorities, the Court was insisting that the rights of the accused be respected and was applying the protection of the Bill of Rights to those accused in state criminal courts. That this judicial activism coincided with a rise in crime provided the Court's opponents with the potent issue of law and order. This legitimate concern for the rising incidence of crime in the society became in Wallace's speeches a code word for "black crime." Wallace made no distinction between legitimate peaceful protest and criminal activity, arguing that the breakdown in law and order began with judicial decisions encouraging civil rights demonstrations. For him the relationship of the early civil rights movement to the violent riots of the mid-1960s was a direct one. He linked court decisions enforcing the rights of the accused to the larger spectacle of rioting and looting: "The Supreme Court . . . has made it impossible to convict a criminal and if you walk out of this buildin' tonight, and someone knocks you in the haid, the person who knocked you in the haid will be out of jail before you get in the hospital, and on Monday they'll try the policeman."

According to Wallace, the permissive attitude encouraged by the Supreme Court has infected the whole society. Social scientists are consulted to find out the causes of urban riots when the real answer is obvious to everyone: "Do you know who's responsible for the breakdown of law and order in this country? It's those who want to lose the war in Viet Nam. It's militants, activists, revolutionaries, anarchists and communists, that's who." Wallace believes that tolerating dissent has led to lack of respect for political leaders and that this has brought on the crisis in law enforcement. He also attributes it to "people in high places [saying] that you've got a right to obey the laws you wanna obey and to disobey those you don't wanna obey. And if that prevails we'll have anarchy." For Wallace, the situation has gotten so bad that when the president of the United States last visited California, a group of "anarchists lay down in front of his automobile." In one of the great applause lines of the speech, Wallace vows:

I want to tell you as I said on television the other night, you elect me the president, and I go to California, or I come to Tennessee, and a group of anarchists lay down in front of my automobile, it's gonna be the last one they ever gonna wanna lay down in front of.

The second and third themes identified by Kazin are central to Wallace's persuasion, which contrasts the decent, hard-working people who are the producers of the wealth of the nation with the parasitic elite composed of bureaucrats who live off of their taxes and write onerous regulations that go contrary to custom and common sense. He regularly listed the occupations of the ordinary Americans who were being exploited by the bureaucrats who wrote guidelines: "the bus driver, the truck driver, the beautician, the fireman, the policeman, and the steelworker, the plumber, and the communication worker and the oil worker and the little businessman." All these are hard-working Americans who perform a valuable service (policeman, truck driver) or produce something of value (steelworker, oil worker). They share the work ethic of the producer class, in contrast to the "pseudo-theoreticians, and these pseudo-social engineers that we find on some college campuses. . . . [S]ome of 'em have pointed heads and cain't even park a bicycle straight." The glorification of the common people has as its complementary argument a virulent strain of anti-intellectualism. Wallace, who liked to mention that he was a former cab driver, says that we ought to use "some old cab-drivin' logic, . . . which would be just as good or better than some of the pseudo-theoreticians logic" because their "fierce contact with life teaches them some things that some of our pseudo-social-engineers never learn." Part of his animus has to do with opposition on college campuses to the war in Vietnam. He criticizes the extreme forms of dissent found on some campuses and vows "that a few of them ought to be dragged by the hair on their heads and stuck under a good jail and that would stop that and that's what we are gonna do when I get to be president."

Wallace clearly supports the war, but he talks around the issue, arguing that the United States should never have become involved alone but insisted that our European allies should have helped us. His choice of General LeMay as running mate clearly signals his intention to pursue a strong anticommunist foreign policy, but recognizing the controversy surrounding the issue, he does not make it a major issue in his campaign.

Wallace returns to the attack on elites who look down their noses at the common people and their values, mentioning a professor who "made a speech derogatory of Alabamians in which they referred to us as rednecks—and I said, 'Yes, our necks are red from workin' in the sun.'" Hard-working ordinary people represent what is decent and good in the United States, and they deserve respect, not the condescension of the liberal elite. Wallace is angry that the elite say that "our people are sick." He insists:

The people of our nation are as good and fine a people as ever populated the United States and I'm tired—I tell you who's sick. It's some of the leadership in this country that's sick. When the newspapers, the *Washington Post* and the *New York Times* and the *Milwaukee Journal* and the other large newspapers when they write an editorial about you and me you remember that the editorial writer's one man and you are one man and you one woman and your attitude and mine it is just as good about these matters or better as theirs.

The last characteristic of Kazin's populist persuasion—the call for a strong movement to vanquish the enemy—is exemplified in Wallace's conclusion, in which he calls on his supporters to in the South to "place this nation back on the road to sanity." Mindful that he is addressing an audience in Memphis, Tennessee, he says:

[T]here are millions of people who are as good as we in other parts of the country but their leadership has let them down. And they lookin' to us. And if you don't believe it you go with me to Milwaukee or to Escanaha, Michigan, to Macomb, Ohio, to Tacoma, Washington, to Fontana, California, you can see that they dependin' on you.

He promises his supporters in Memphis that "if you'll go out and work for us from now on till this campaign's over, I'll come back to Tennessee prior to the election and you and me together will continue to shake the eyeteeth of the liberals in both national parties." Wallace presents his candidacy and the American Independent Party as the vehicle for change because, as he said elsewhere in the campaign, there is not "a dime's worth of difference" between the two national parties.[20] In this speech, he asks, "[I]f Mr. Nixon and Mr. Rockefeller stand for the same things that Mr. McCarthy and Mr. Humphrey stand for, what difference does it make?" He predicts that "if you elect the National Republican party in November, one week after they are inaugurated you'll want to put them out and you'll have to wait four years to do it. Let's put 'em both out in November."

Wallace's speech at Memphis successfully used the four themes of populist rhetoric, and Wallace repeated the speech during the rest of the campaign. A reporter for *Newsweek* observed that aside from minor tinkering, the speech "does not really change."[21] To his supporters, this was a strength of the Wallace campaign. *The Florence Times and Tri-Cities Daily* dismissed criticism that Wallace makes the same speech wherever he goes by, expressing their belief that "he has it down pretty good" and promised to "laud his continuing to say the same thing."[22] In this speech, Wallace is finally using a more colloquial style that speaks directly to his listeners. Unlike the 1964 campaign, when Wallace felt the need to convince people that he was not a redneck who could not use proper English, Wallace is now an experienced performer on the political stage who is comfortable with his own persona. This speech uses a more "open" organizational pattern, with little subordination of ideas, which allows him to adapt to crowd response and to hecklers. The transitions in the speech are evidence that Wallace was simply moving from one issue to another in no particular order. At the beginning of the speech, he asks the rhetorical question, "Now what are we talkin' about and what are some of the issues in this country that confront people in Memphis?" as a transition between his greeting and the body of the speech. His next transition is characteristic of the shopping-list organization of the speech: "Another great issue that faces the American people is the breakdown of law and order." Later in the speech he says, "And another issue, and there are many issues in the campaign that we'll develop as we go along is our involvement in Southeast Asia."

Whatever its shortcomings as a formal oration, the speech did target the middle-class and lower middle-class whites that Wallace needed to attract to his campaign. It was pitched to their resentment about crime, inflation, taxes, and the growing lack of respect for traditional values. In particular, it tapped their resentment that national leaders seemed more attentive to black Americans, who were perceived as welfare cheats and loafers, than the white working class. In adopting a populist persuasion, Wallace legitimized the complaints of his constituency into a larger critique of the lack of responsiveness of America's political institutions to the needs of its ordinary citizens. The populist rhetoric masked the hate and fear that fueled Wallace's movement. The veteran political reporter Teddy White, who traveled with Wallace as he campaigned in the Chicago suburbs, witnessed firsthand the hatred and the violence that surfaced in the crowds that attended Wallace rallies. After describing an assault on a young man carrying a McCarthy banner, White concluded, "The Wallace campaign . . . made decent people ashamed to stand with George Wallace . . . because it gave them no other cause but hate."[23]

The success of Wallace's campaign can be measured by his standing in the public opinion polls. In answer to the question, "If the Presidential election were held today, who would you vote for," Wallace started at 9 percent in May, moved to 16 percent in June, and rose to 21 percent by mid-September.[24] The Harris poll in September found that half of all those it surveyed agreed that George Wallace was right for "saying it the way it really is," and over 80 percent agreed with the statement that he had "the courage of his convictions." More than 53 percent agreed that "Wallace would handle law-and-order the way it ought to be handled, if elected President."[25] Had he been able to hold on to his supporters and attract new ones, George Wallace might have achieved his dream of an electoral college deadlock, with no candidate achieving a majority of the votes, leaving him in the bargaining seat able to deal for cabinet or Supreme Court appointments.

Wallace's rapid rise in the polls had alerted organized labor to the necessity of a counterattack, and attack they did. Their campaign developed on two fronts. First, they did everything to discredit the notion that Wallace was a friend of the working man by circulating 55 million pamphlets summarizing Wallace's record in Alabama. These pamphlets pointedly emphasized that Alabama was a "right-to-work" state that imposed restrictions on union organizing and noted that in all of Wallace's years as governor, the state still ranked among the lowest states in per-capita income and per-pupil expenditure for public schools and that it had one of the highest illiteracy rates in the nation.[26] Second, they registered 4.6 million new voters, many of them black.[27]

Nor were Republicans ignoring the Wallace threat. Concerned that conservatives would cast their vote for Wallace, the Republicans used their most potent argument: that a vote for Wallace would actually let Humphrey and the Democrats win the White House. Nixon had already appropriated Wallace's most potent issue of law and order by attacking the Democrats on that issue and promising to appoint a law-and-order attorney general. And Nixon also hinted to southern leaders that he would try to seat a southerner on the Supreme Court.

This effort paid off on election day. From his high of 21 percent in the public opinion polls, Wallace dropped to 13.5 percent in the actual election poll. Perhaps this was to be expected. In recent history, Americans have not rewarded third-party efforts with much success. It is one thing to tell a public opinion pollster in August or September that you favor a third-party candidate; it is another thing to actually vote for that candidate on election day. When all the votes were counted, Wallace carried five states—Arkansas, Alabama, Georgia, Louisiana, and Mississippi—for a total of 46 electoral votes.[28] Although some political reporters were ready to write Wallace's epitaph, Wallace had other ideas. He had over 2 million dollars in unspent campaign funds, and he was already planning to run for the governorship of Alabama to provide himself with a power base for another try at the White House. His campaign aide Charles Snider agreed to work full-time for Wallace and established a campaign headquarters in Montgomery that soon grew to 22 full-time staffers. George Wallace was not about to retire from his first love of politics.

NOTES

1. Marshall Frady, "The American Independent Party," in Arthur M. Schlesinger, Jr., *History of U.S. Political Parties* (New York: Chelsea House, 1973), 4:3429.

2. Lewis Chester, Godfrey Hodgson, and Bruce Page, *An American Melodrama: The Presidential Campaign of 1968* (New York: Viking Press, 1969), 703.

3. Frady, "American Independent Party," 4:3436.

4. Cited in Dan T. Carter, *The Politics of Rage: George Wallace, the Origins of the New Conservatism, and the Transformation of American Politics* (New York: Simon & Schuster, 1995), 359.

5. A mimetic orator speaks not to shape or change the beliefs of an audience but to reflect them. See Edwin Black, *Rhetorical Criticism: A Study in Method* (New York: Macmillan, 1965), 167.

6. Leo Lowenthal and Norbert Guterman, "Portrait of the American Agitator," in *Readings in Speech*, ed. Haig A. Bosmajian (New York: Harper & Row, 1965), 271.

7. Jody Carlson, *George C. Wallace and the Politics of Powerlessness: The Wallace Campaigns for the Presidency, 1964–1976* (New Brunswick, N.J.: Transaction Books, 1981), 6.

8. "Wallace's Army: The Coalition of Frustration," *Time*, October 18, 1968, 17.

9. Michael Kazin, *The Populist Persuasion* (New York: Basic Books, 1995), 240.

10. Carlson, *George C. Wallace*, 6.

11. Kazin, *Populist Persuasion*, 1.

12. Chester, Hodgson, and Page, *American Melodrama*, 703.

13. Kazin, *Populist Persuasion*, 12.

14. Kazin, *Populist Persuasion*, 13.

15. Kazin, *Populist Persuasion*, 15.

16. Kazin, *Populist Persuasion*, 16.

17. All quotations are to the text of the speech that Wallace delivered in Memphis, Tennessee, on June 11, 1968. The text, which appears in part 2 of this volume, in "Stand Up for America: The 1968 Campaign Speech," is transcribed from a tape recording made by Forrest Armstrong and is reproduced by permission of his wife, who owns the copyright. Armstrong transcribed Wallace's speech as it was delivered, to convey the folksy nature of his delivery.

18. Murray Edelman, *Constructing the Political Spectacle* (Chicago: University of Chicago Press, 1988), 66.

19. Marshall Frady, *Wallace* (New York: Random House, 1996), 275.

20. L. Dean Fadely, "*Dispositio* in the Rhetoric of a Former Debater: George Corley Wallace," in *Current Criticism: Essays from Speaker and Gavel*, ed. Robert O. Weiss and Bernard L. Brock (Lawrence, Kans.: Allen Press, 1971), 70.

21. "Wallace and His Folks," *Newsweek*, September 16, 1968, 26.

22. Quoted in "Another Opinion. Wallace for President," *New York Times*, October 20, 1968, E15.

23. Theodore H. White, *The Making of the President, 1968* (New York: Atheneum, 1969), 409.

24. White, *Making of the President*, 405.

25. White, *Making of the President*, 425.

26. Chester, Hodgson, and Page, *American Melodrama*, 708.

27. White, *Making of the President*, 426.

28. Stephan Lesher, *George Wallace: American Populist* (Reading, Mass.: Addison-Wesley, 1994), 428.

CHAPTER 7

Back in the Fold: The 1972 Democratic Party Primary Campaign

By 1972 George Wallace was an experienced campaigner ready for another try for the presidency. He was once again governor of Alabama, with the full resources of the office at his disposal. He had a new wife, Cornelia, a niece of Jim Folsom, the former governor of Alabama whom Wallace in his younger years admired. Cornelia convinced George to abandon his usual black suit and white shirt for double-knit suits with colored shirts and wide ties. His new image was the outward expression of his inward desire for recognition as a respectable and legitimate candidate for the Democratic Party nomination for president of the United States. To do so, he tried to make over his confrontational image by expanding the issues he discussed to include such concerns of the middle class as tax reform and preserving social security. But beneath this surface respectability, Wallace's basic appeal was to the lack of political power felt by his supporters. In almost all of his speeches and public statements, Wallace praised the ability of the common man to make wise choices concerning the policies and actions of the government. His statement on *Meet the Press* is typical: "[T]he average citizen feels that he has been ignored, that the leadership of the Democratic and the Republican Party have paid attention to the exotic and those who made the most noise. They have given their money away in foreign aid, they have given it away to welfare loaders, and they have skyrocketed administrative costs of government to the point that they have broken his back financially."[1]

Busing for racial integration as an issue fit very well into this framework. This one issue encompassed many of the themes that Wallace had made his own over the course of his career. It involved race, the role of the courts, and local control of the public schools. It developed as the courts sought some means to achieve integrated schools despite segregated housing patterns in the nation's cities. By the end of the 1960s, four cities—Gary, Washington, D.C., Newark, and Atlanta—had a majority of black residents, and 15 of the 51 largest school systems had a majority of nonwhite pupils in their elementary school systems. The immediate decision that thrust the issue of school busing into presidential politics was issued by Federal Judge Robert R. Merhige, Jr., involving the public schools of Richmond, Virginia. Because the Richmond school system was 70 percent black, and there was no way to adjust the racial imbalance within the confines of the city limits, Judge Merhige ruled that the surrounding counties must bus white pupils into the city to achieve racial balance. On June 6, the 4th U.S. Circuit Court of Appeals overturned Judge Merhige's decision by a vote of 5 to 1, but throughout the primary period the judge's decision stood as a hot-button issue that George Wallace pushed every chance he got. He could simultaneously praise the common sense of the people and decry the social planning schemes of "pseudo-intellectuals who can't park their bicycles straight." He could call for a return to local control of the schools without acknowledging that as long as residential segregation persisted, this policy would perpetuate school segregation. It was an issue that made clear to the people the lack of control over their lives that they experienced. Many had moved to suburbs to escape the crime and poor schools of the cities. Now the federal government was threatening to bus their children back to those same neighborhoods. No other issue so aroused passions as school busing for racial balance.[2]

Although school busing for racial balance was the heart of his campaign, Wallace used economic issues such as tax reform to broaden his appeal. He paints a picture of the middle class as caught in a tax squeeze between those "who refuse to work and the silk stocking crowd with their privately controlled tax free foundations." He declares that it is time to put "an end to these illegal activities and let every citizen pay his share of taxes."[3]

Wallace also benefited from the experience of the 1968 campaign. He had a mailing list of over 1 million names of people who were likely contributors. In June 1971, the campaign enlisted the help of Richard Viguerie, a conservative activist who knew how to exploit direct mail effectively. Wallace chose a young aide to manage the 1972 campaign, Charles Snider, who quickly assembled a staff of six to help him. By October 1971, Wallace had decided to run in the Democratic primaries, but he did not announce this until later. Before the official announcement, Wallace "appreciation" banquets were held in several cities to raise funds and to keep Wallace's name before the public. The campaign bought an old C-46 airplane and hired off-duty Delta pilots to fly it. Although the campaign had the appearance of being run by professionals, at the core of the campaign was George Wallace, who did not take advice easily from anyone. Running in the Democratic Party primaries required the Wallace campaign to play by the Democratic Party's rules, which were significantly changed following the disastrous 1968 Chicago Convention. Wallace and his advisors did not pay sufficient attention to the rule changes, which would hurt them later when Wallace's large vote pluralities did not translate into a large number of delegates.[4]

Wallace launched his campaign for the 1972 Democratic Party presidential nomination with a speech to a packed Florida State Senate chamber on January 13, 1972. After reading from the prepared text of his speech, he "warmed to his audience's applause and flashed signs of his old campaign style" by "jabbing the air with clenched fists." He told the audience, "If the people of Florida vote for me, Mr. Nixon in 30 to 60 days after this campaign is over will end busing himself." He drew the biggest applause from the crowd when he promised to return to Florida in two weeks to begin an "old fashioned stumping" campaign with three speeches a day for six days a week until election day.[5]

The 1972 campaign speech shares with its 1968 counterpart a lack of organizational unity. It is composed of a series of proposals that can be presented in any order without sacrificing the unity or the integrity of the speech. Wallace favors the use of this approach to organizing his campaign speeches for the freedom it gives him to improvise according to the mood of the audience as indicated by their applause. The speech covers a variety of topics, from such staples from his previous campaigns as law and order and a strong national defense to issues tailored to his Florida audience, such as the protection of the social security trust fund and no recognition of Castro Cuba. They are held together by the common theme of opposition to the "unnecessary control of big government." The centerpiece of the speech is a call for "the return to local control of public education," which involves a "complete halt to involuntary busing" to achieve racial balance in the schools. This issue is the hot button in the campaign, and Wallace pushes it every chance he gets. He reminds the voters that "those candidates in this race from the Senate either voted or supported, and it is a matter of record, to bus little children in Florida to achieve racial balance." He draws the conclusion that "[t]hey helped to bring about the ills we now suffer" and that they just as obviously do not need to be rewarded with votes.[6]

New in this speech is a stronger emphasis on populist themes, including taxing "the multi-billion and multi-million dollar foundations which are now virtually tax exempt" and "levying of taxes upon . . . church commercial property." He further promises to reduce "taxes for the individual and businesses" through the closing of tax loopholes and to restrict American industry from exporting jobs to low-wage countries.

Wallace's speeches "sound" better than they read. On a videotape or audiotape recording, one is carried along by his energetic delivery so that the lack of transitions is not so apparent. Reading the speech in manuscript, one notices the lack of organization, lack of internal summaries, lack of transitions, and the lack of an adequate preview of the body of the speech. On the platform, Wallace used his manuscript as a jazz musician would a musical score, as something to improvise upon. The listing of topics in no discernable order allowed him to respond to audience reaction by expanding on some topics and omitting others if time required it. He could also adapt to his audiences by telling stories of local interest.

As in 1968, Wallace relied on large rallies rather than the hand-shaking tours and small meetings used by the other candidates. As Teddy White observed, "The rally style was old-tub-thumping country music, this year led by Billy Grammer, star of the Grand Old Opry; the guitar-playing; the flags on either side of him as he spoke; the glowering state troopers watching the crowd for violence; the singing; the pails which were passed around among the audience and which returned full of coins and bills."[7] George Mangum, a white-haired Baptist minister, served as the master of ceremonies, introducing distinguished guests and musical acts and pleading for contributions. Finally, he would introduce Wallace, who would take the stage to prolonged applause. Part of Wallace's appeal was his identification with members of his audience. These were people who were looked down upon by the elite and who felt the hidden pain of class in a society where class was not supposed to exist. Wallace told them that they were better than the "so-called intellectual snobs who feel that big government should control the lives of American citizens from the cradle to the grave." In a speech at Bradenton, he declared that "the average citizen is fed up with much of this liberalism and this kowtowing to the exotic few."[8] He charged that the government was run by "bureaucrats, hypocrites, uninterested politicians" who can't even "park their bicycles straight." He reserved his greatest scorn for the Senators who were in the contest who sent their children to private schools but still supported busing: "Washington is the hypocrite capital of the world.[9]

Wallace enjoyed ending his speeches with a denunciation of busing and of the politicians who supported it:

Busing . . . is the most atrocious, callous, cruel, asinine thing you can do for little children. . . . [T]hese pluperfect hypocrites who live over in Maryland or Virginia and they've got their children in a private school. . . . [T]omorrow the chickens are coming home to roost. They gonna be sorry they bused your little children and had somthin' to do with it. So, my friends, you give 'em a good jolt tomorrow. You give 'em the St. Vitus Dance.[10]

On another occasion, Wallace spoke of his supporters in terms that the old Peoples Party leaders could have used:

This is a people's awakening. Those pluperfect hypocrites in Washington don't know what's coming over you. Well, if they'd gone out and asked a taxi driver, a little businessman or a beautician or a barber or a farmer, they'd have found out. But no, they don't ask those folks when they make their decisions. They ask some pointy-headed pseudo-intellectual who can't even park his bicycle straight when he gets to the campus, that's who they ask. But they're not ignoring you now. You're tops. You're the people.[11]

Gary Wills, who covered a Wallace appearance at a civic organization luncheon meeting in Miami Beach, noted the difference in Wallace's manner before such a small and sedate gathering: "Wallace . . . begins almost apologetically, telling people they do not need to worry, he's spoken to all kinds of gatherings. . . . 'and every single club has survived my visit.'" Wills observed that "the only variation in a Wallace speech are those of tone—less or more bellicose. Today is, mainly, less but he covers the same old territory as ever."[12] Wills noted that Wallace emphasized five major issues in his speech to the group: defense, taxes, foreign aid, law and order, and busing.[13] Wallace followed his set speech, complete with the same anecdotes and applause lines, only condensed to deal with the time constraints of a business lunch. When it was finished, Wills saw that Wallace was "anxious be off. The man so alive at the podium seems lost and disanimated when crowds move up to him as individuals."[14]

Michael Novak observed the same behavior when Wallace addressed the Orlando Jaycees organization:

Wallace was plainly nervous, too. His movements were jerky, his smile and self-assurance forced. "Now I'm not gonna let out all the stops," Wallace teased, nervously, not really looking at his audience, his eyes on the ceiling. . . . He was a little like the schoolboy, brushed and dressed, squeezed into uncomfortable collar and shiny shoes, and declaiming in the school play.[15]

To Novak, Wallace had "the manner of a man saying forbidden things, opening up people's eyes to injustices and lies and principalities and powers they already knew were plaguing them but didn't talk about."[16]

The contrast between the somewhat subdued individual who tried to be respectable before small crowds of business people and the man who strutted on the stage of a large auditorium before adoring crowds was evident to Wayne Greenhaw, a journalist who covered Wallace during his entire career: "With the applause breaking up his sentences, he became wound up. His delivery was fast, as powerful and enunciated as ever. He was sending them his message, saying that busing was 'the most atrocious, callous, cruel, asinine thing you can do for little children.'"[17]

Wallace tried to change his image in 1972. His new, stylish clothes and haircut made him appear more respectable—more moderate. However, he did not change his message. He was still the agitator who played with the emotions of his audience. He based his campaign on appealing to their feelings of alienation and lack of power to present himself as their champion whose election would send a powerful message to the establishment that things were going to change. A useful way of analyzing Wallace's stock speech in 1972 is to use the criteria that Lowenthal and Guterman employed in their classic study of the American agitator.[18] They argued that it was not the specific nature of the grievances that American agitators used as much as the emotions or emotional complexes that they aroused that accounted for their success. Lowenthal and Guterman identified five sets of emotions that characterized American agitators: distrust, dependence, exclusion, anxiety, and disillusionment.[19]

"*Distrust.* The agitator plays on his audience's suspicions of all social phenomena impinging on its life in ways it does not understand."[20] Wallace throughout his speech encourages his audience to *distrust* the leaders of the Democratic Party and the elected and appointed government leaders in Washington, D.C. They are the ones who are responsible for big government, high taxes, and intrusive government regulation. He states, "Too long this party has been controlled by the so-called intellectual snobs who feel that big government should control the lives of American citizens from the cradle to the grave." He expanded on this idea in another speech, "We're here tonight because the average citizen in this country—the man who pays his taxes and works for a living and holds this country together—the average citizen is fed up with much of this liberalism and this kowtowing to the exotic few."[21] Wallace emphasizes that the leaders are an elite with different values and do not understand the needs of the common people. As earlier noted, he charges that government leaders ignore "a taxi driver, a little businessman or a beautician or a barber or a farmer" when they want to know what is going on. Instead they "ask some pointy-headed pseudo-intellectual who can't even park his bicycle straight when he gets to the campus."[22] In a reference calculated to appeal to Floridians, he charges that "[t]hose in the Senate who are candidates voted against the nominee to the Supreme Court from Florida because, in my opinion, he thought and expressed himself as a average Floridian, and that is unthinkable, so they think. If a Floridian is not good enough for the Supreme Court, then maybe their thinking is not good enough for Floridians."[23]

"*Dependence.* The agitator seems to assume that he is addressing people who suffer from a sense of helplessness and passivity."[24] According to Wallace, the people feel themselves helpless to change this situation. They are victims who are being manipulated, but their lack of *independence* makes them weak. School busing for integration is to him a classic example of the lack of power of people to control their own neighborhoods and the lives of their children. In one speech, he told a story about President Nixon in China meeting with Mao Tse-tung: "I hear Mao Tse-tung told him, 'Well, over here in China, if we take a notion to bus 'em, we bus 'em, whether they like it or not.' Well, Mr. Nixon could have told him that we about do the same thing over here."[25] Wallace charges that judges of the Supreme Court "decree their own political, social and economic philosophy into court-made law." In another speech, Wallace spoke of the courts as follows:

The courts can redistrict, reapportion, put a tax on, take a tax off, tell you what to do with your child. Your union, your property, your business. These judges are appointed for life and have all that power over you and you wouldn't even recognize one of them if they came in here right now. You might be sitting next to one, but you'd never know it—yet he has all that power over your life, your child, your money, your property. They're despots, dictators.[26]

This point hit home. Many people in his audience moved to the suburbs to escape the problems of the cities, including crime and failing public schools. Now they felt that their control over their schools and by extension over their neighborhoods was being taken away by faceless bureaucrats and unelected federal judges located in distant places far from the scene of their problems. The implication was clear. The only way to change the situation is to vote for George Wallace. He will send them a message.

"*Exclusion.* The agitator suggests that there is an abundance of material and spiritual goods, but that we do not get what we are entitled to."[27] In developing his populist themes, Wallace argues that the ordinary citizen is *excluded* from the prosperity that he sees all around. His taxes are given away to help foreigners who are ungrateful. In his stock speech, Wallace charges that the other candidates in the race "have voted to give away our money by the billions to those who not only did not appreciate it, but who in many cases worked against the interests of the United States." What is worse, according to Wallace, is that "the average citizen is being taxed to death while these multibillionaires like the Rockefellers and the Fords and the Mellons and Carnegies go without paying taxes. They got billions of dollars in tax-shelter foundations and they don't pays as much tax as you do on a percentage basis."[28] Moreover, much of that money is wasted on welfare cheats: "There's people in New York get five checks of $700 a month."[29] This theme was a constant one in Wallace's campaigns. He consistently defended the honest working man who pays more than his fair share of taxes while the wealthy avoid their share and sees his hard-earned money wasted on foreign aid and welfare for those who are too lazy or irresponsible to work.

"*Anxiety.* This complex manifests itself in a general premonition of disasters to come, a prominent part of which seems to be the middle class fear of a dislocation of its life by revolutionary action and its suspicion that the moral mainstays of social life are being undermined."[30] The theme of law and order was one of Wallace's stock issues because it allowed him to invoke the anxiety of the white middle class about black street crime. He long accused the courts of coddling criminals and encouraging lawless behavior. In his standard speech, Wallace calls upon the states and the federal government "to make it safe to walk on the streets of the cities of our nation." One of his favorite lines—because it always got applause— was to claim that if someone got mugged leaving the rally that evening, the offender would be out on the street to commit another act of violence before the victim got released from the hospital. He also charges that his opponents in the Florida primary "served in the Congress while crime grew to run rampant in the Country and saw it rise every year in the Nation's Capital to the point where it is unsafe for even them to walk much less ride in the streets of Washington, D.C." He further charges that "more than half of the cities are so infested with crime that citizens cannot walk the streets unmolested at night. Law-abiding citizens are imprisoned behind the locked doors of their homes because criminals who should be locked up are in the streets."[31]

"*Disillusionment.* This complex, a tendency more than an actuality is seen in such remarks as the agitator's characterization of politics as 'make-believe, pretense, pretext, sham, fraud, deception, dishonesty, falsehood, hypocrisy.'"[32] Since he was a politician running in the Democratic Primary and asking people for their votes, Wallace used this complex of emotions to arouse anger and promote disenchantment with his rivals. In his standard speech, he attacks his opponents in the primary, most of whom were congressmen, as frauds who "helped to bring about the ills we now suffer. But now they tell us that they want to save us from their own deeds." He has a long catalogue of failures, including a weakened military, insufficient social security payments, foreign aid to Communist countries, and support of giveaway programs that have led to massive deficits. He attacked President Nixon as "a double dealer, a two-timer, and a man who tells folks one thing and does another."[33] Nixon was but one example of the national politicians who were the "pluperfect hypocrites who live over in Maryland or Virginia and they've got their children in a private school" who vote for busing for school integration.[34]

In 1972 Wallace is still the agitator, still the outsider trying to stir the emotions of the crowd, but offering no real analysis of the problems that beset them or any realistic proposals to solve them. In Jody Carlson's words, "He is still the loud complainer."[35] Carlson notes that he has broadened his appeal but contends that "he is not interested in either the problems or their solutions; no real remedies are offered. . . . The real Wallace hides powerless behind the symbol of his raised fist."[36]

When the votes were counted in the Florida primary, Wallace finished first with 42 percent, clearly outdistancing Hubert Humphrey, with 18.6 percent. Wallace carried every county in the state, from the rural panhandle to urbanized Dade County, which included Miami. He was not the only person reading the voting returns. Three days after the vote, Richard Nixon in a nationally televised address stated that people "do not want their children bused across the city to an inferior school just to meet some social planner's concept of what is considered to be the correct racial balance."[37] Wallace could not have said it better himself. He reminded reporters of his prediction that Nixon would embrace his position opposing busing for racial balance.

The primary campaign continued to the states of Wisconsin, where Wallace came in second with 22 percent of the vote; to Pennsylvania, where he finished second with 21.3 percent; to Indiana, with second place and 41.2 percent; Tennessee and North Carolina, which Wallace won outright; and ending for Wallace in Maryland, which he carried with 38.7 percent of the vote. In Laurel, Maryland, the day before that state's primary, Wallace was shot and seriously wounded by Arthur Bremer. The day after the Maryland primary, Wallace's total number of votes in all the primaries stood at 3,354,360. Humphrey was in second place with 2,647,676 votes, and George McGovern had 2,202,840. The delegate totals reveal a different order, with McGovern having 409.35; Wallace 323; and Humphrey 291.35. Wallace had 1,151,520 more votes than McGovern but trailed him in delegates by 86.[38]

Paralyzed from the waist down and in pain, Wallace lacked the energy to continue his campaign. George McGovern continued to collect delegates and came to the convention in firm control of its proceedings. Wallace addressed the convention during deliberations over a substitute plank for the party platform and received polite applause.

NOTES

1. Quoted in Jody Carlson, *George C. Wallace and the Politics of Powerlessness: The Wallace Campaigns for the Presidency, 1964–1976* (New Brunswick, N.J.: Transaction Books, 1981), 174.

2. Judith F. Buncher, ed., *The School Busing Controversy: 1970–75* (New York: Facts on File, 1975). This work is a useful compilation of court decisions and reactions from the local and national press to the issue.

3. Quoted in Carlson, *George C. Wallace,* 176.

4. Stephan Lesher, *George Wallace: American Populist* (Reading, Mass.: Addison-Wesley, 1994), 476 ff.

5. Jon Nordheimer, "Wallace Joins Florida Race as Democrat," *New York Times,* January 14, 1972, 1, 14.

6. The text of the speech is reprinted in part 2 of this volume, in "Send Them a Message: The 1972 Campaign Speech."

7. Theodore H. White, *The Making of the President, 1972* (New York: Atheneum, 1973), 96.

8. Quoted in Lesher, *George Wallace*, 471.

9. Quoted in White, *Making of the President*, 97.

10. Quoted in White, *Making of the President*, 98.

11. Quoted in Lesher, *George Wallace*, 475.

12. Garry Wills, "Can Wallace Be Made Respectable?" *New York*, April 8, 1972, 33–34.

13. Wills, "Can Wallace Be Made Respectable?" 34.

14. Wills, "Can Wallace Be Made Respectable?" 34.

15. Michael Novak, *Choosing Our King: Powerful Symbols in Presidential Politics* (New York: Macmillan, 1974), 182.

16. Novak, *Choosing Our King*, 183.

17. Wayne Greenhaw, *Watch Out for George Wallace* (Englewood Cliffs, N.J.: Prentice-Hall, 1976), 40.

18. Leo Lowenthal and Norbert Guterman, "Portrait of the American Agitator," in *Readings in Speech*, ed. Haig A Bosmajian (New York: Harper & Row, 1965), 274–275.

19. Lowenthal and Guterman, "Portrait," 274–275.

20. Lowenthal and Guterman, "Portrait," 274.

21. "They Have to Listen Now," *Newsweek*, March 27, 1972, 22–28.

22. "They Have to Listen Now," 24.

23. The reference is to Harold Carswell, a Nixon nominee for the Supreme Court who was rejected by the Senate.

24. Lowenthal and Guterman, "Portrait," 274.

25. "They Have to Listen Now," 24.

26. Wills, "Can Wallace Be Made Respectable?" 30.

27. Lowenthal and Guterman, "Portrait," 274.

28. "They Have to Listen Now," 23.

29. "They Have to Listen Now," 23.

30. Lowenthal and Guterman, "Portrait," 275.

31. Quoted in Carlson, *George C. Wallace*, 177.

32. Lowenthal and Guterman, "Portrait," 275.

33. Quoted in Greenhaw, *Watch Out*, 39.

34. Quoted in Greenhaw, *Watch Out*, 40.

35. Carlson, *George C. Wallace*, 179.

36. Carlson, *George C. Wallace*, 179.

37. Quoted in Lesher, *George Wallace*, 476.

38. Carlson, *George C. Wallace*, 148.

CHAPTER 8

The 1976 Campaign

In the early months of 1973, Wallace and his staff began to plan for his next presidential campaign in 1976. Some circumstances, such as the health of the candidate, were beyond their control. Wallace would be in and out of the hospital undergoing nearly a dozen operations in 1973 alone.[1] The staff had to trust that Wallace's doctors would succeed in making Wallace well enough to endure the rigors of a national campaign. A more pressing problem was dealing with the debt left over from the 1972 campaign that totaled more than a quarter-million dollars.[2] In the summer of 1973, Richard A. Viguerie of Falls Church, Virginia, a direct-mail wizard, was hired to raise money for the Wallace campaign. Viguerie combined the list of contributors to previous Wallace campaigns with his own list of conservative activists and began sending out letters on a regular basis. He sent out almost 4 million letters in 1973, grossing $1,410,033. After Viguerie's cut of 53 percent, this left the Wallace campaign with over $660,000.[3]

Before he could run for the presidency in 1976, Wallace needed to win re-election as governor of Alabama. Although his martyr status following the assassination attempt virtually assured him of reelection, Wallace and his staff saw this election as a means of making him more respectable and broadening his appeal. Wallace recognized that the main barrier to his being considered a serious candidate for the presidency was his reputation as a racist. He also knew, as a practical politician, that black Alabamians were registering to vote and now constituted almost 25 percent of the electorate. In 1973 he began in earnest to change his image. One of the most visible ways was his crowning of a black homecoming queen at the University of Alabama.[4] He also began to make public appearances before black groups and to appoint more blacks to the various boards and commissions that were an important part of state government. All these efforts resulted in endorsements by black officials. Johnny Ford, the black mayor of Tuskegee, Alabama, endorsed Wallace, as did the Southern Democratic Conference of Birmingham and William M. Branch, a black probate judge. The *Birmingham Times* endorsed his candidacy as well.[5] All this paid off. Wallace captured 64 percent of the votes in the Democratic primary for governor, of which 20 to 25 percent was estimated to be that of black Alabamians.[6] Tom Wicker, a respected political observer and columnist, noted that "the Alabama primary has gone a long way to give Mr. Wallace the political respectability he never quite had before."[7]

Wallace knew that a serious presidential candidate must make an effort to show that he is knowledgeable about foreign affairs and capable of making the decisions that involve war or peace. In a further effort to build credibility for his candidacy, Wallace arranged for a five-nation tour of Europe in early 1975. Wallace met with such leaders as Harold Wilson and Margaret Thatcher, as well as Belgian prime minister Tindemans, President Leone and Prime Minister Aldo Moro of Italy, West German foreign minister Genscher, and French minister of industry Michel d'Ornano. Wallace did not meet West German chancellor Helmut Schmidt, French president Valery Giscard d'Estaing, or Pope Paul VI. The trip achieved what Wallace hoped it would. He was seen as a serious candidate for the presidency. The *New York Times* acknowledged as much when it stated that he was now seen as "a potential President rather than just a protest candidate."[8]

With his base secure, Wallace now turned his attention to another run for the presidency. He announced his candidacy on November 12, 1975, at a press conference at the Governor's Mansion Motel in Montgomery.[9] The motel had an adjoining exhibition hall with an entry door that permitted trucks to enter with supplies to set up an exhibit. This allowed Wallace's car to drive within a few feet of the speaker's podium to minimize the distance he would have to be pushed in his wheelchair. As with most Wallace events, this one had a live band to bring the crowd to its feet before Wallace appeared. The event was televised live, and Wallace was to read a prepared statement, which he put aside as soon as he was on the air. Instead, he reverted to some of the popular lines from his past campaigns and attacked the "ultra-liberals" who had taken the Democratic Party away from "average Americans." He called on his followers to join him in a crusade at "the ballot box in the primaries of 1976 "to save" the "middle class."[10] Little of his prepared speech survived except the title, "Trust the People." Clearly, Wallace trusted the people to propel him to victory in the upcoming primaries, but he and his advisors were not naive enough to waste their resources on states where they did not think he had a chance. Thus they decided to skip the first primary in New Hampshire and concentrate their effort in Florida and Massachusetts, where they thought they had a better chance of winning. They chose Florida because of Wallace's past success there and Massachusetts because it was one of the few states where the busing issue was still salient.

The Massachusetts primary came first, and Wallace, over the objections of his campaign manager Charles Snider, decided to spend time and money there that Snider thought could be better spent in Florida. Wallace's reasoning was simple: "I'm not supposed to do well at all. But if my name's on the ballot there and I do just fairly good, that'll shake 'em up just fairly good. I ain't supposed to get no votes in Massachusetts. You know that."[11] He followed up this remark with another: "If I do go up there, I ain't gonna say a word about busing. 'Course all them folks in Massachusetts know that if I'm President, there ain't gonna be any."[12] Wallace enjoyed high-energy, confrontational politics, and he knew he could enflame the crowd with his antibusing rhetoric in Massachusetts. He was eager to try it. After all, as Snider recalled, "he felt if he could kick off with a win in Massachusetts he would be back where he was in '72. It was a bold move and if he could have won, maybe he would have caught on again."[13]

Billy Grammer, of the Grand Ole Opry, and his band accompanied Wallace on his trips throughout the state. Wallace drew big crowds, especially in Boston, where busing was still an important issue. But the campaign rallies lacked the energy of past campaigns. For one thing, increased security by both Secret Service agents and Alabama state troopers did not allow any direct contact with the candidate. Wallace, who in past campaigns had pranced around the platform giving salutes to people in the audience, now was seated in a wheelchair behind a bullet-proof lectern. For a high-energy performer such as Wallace had been in the past, this was a major letdown. The strong voice and the menacing facial and arm gestures that accompanied the biting humor were still there. And yet something was missing. Many reporters noticed that Wallace seemed to have lost his zeal for winning. He was like an aged tiger that had lost the killer instinct. One reporter noticed that in the midst of his best stories or patented attacks on opponents, Wallace's voice would trail off. The fire was gone.[14] When the votes were counted, it was clear that Wallace's hopes for an early breakthrough in Massachusetts were far from the mark. Senator Scoop Jackson took 23 percent, Mo Udall took 18, Wallace was one percentage point behind with 17, and Jimmy Carter took 14 percent.

Now the campaign moved to Florida, where Wallace expected to do well. He had handily won the primary there in 1972. He was from a neighboring state. North Florida was similar to Alabama, with small towns and good ole boys, where Wallace had his strength. South Florida might be more cosmopolitan, but with its large Cuban population, Wallace's strong anticommunism still commanded respect and votes. He did come into Florida with something of a handicap. He ran third in Massachusetts and spent a lot of money to do so. Campaigning for Wallace was now more expensive since he had to have a chartered jet that was fitted to handle his wheelchair. He had lost time and momentum on his quest for votes in Massachusetts, and he faced a disciplined opponent who also came from a neighboring state, Jimmy Carter from Georgia. Carter seemed to have the best chance of any of the other Democratic candidates to beat Wallace, and so Mo Udall and Birch Bayh both avoided Florida to avoid splitting the anti-Wallace vote. The contest for Florida would come down to a choice between Wallace and Carter and Jackson, the only non-Southerner in the race.

The 1976 race would not be a repeat of the 1972 primary. The times had changed. The end of fighting in Vietnam had removed one of the most divisive issues in American politics. Busing as an issue still remained, but as communities learned to live with it and as some of the more extreme judicial orders were overturned or modified, it lost its salience. The Watergate scandal and the subsequent resignation of President Nixon had moved public trust in elected leaders to the forefront of the national dialogue. Wallace recognized these changes and attempted to change as well. His attempts to reach out to black voters and to moderates have already been detailed. His trip to Europe was part of this attempt to show people that he was knowledgeable about the problems, foreign as well as domestic, facing the United States. More important, in 1976 Wallace softened his image. He relied less on attack and invective. The hecklers were gone and with them the confrontations that marred his rallies in the past. In trying for middle-class acceptability, Wallace focused on their concerns for a decent life for themselves and their children in a new stump speech centered on the theme of "Trust the People."[15]

Wallace begins the speech by focusing on the fear that America's future will not live up to its past achievements—that there will be a "gap between promises and performance." He uses several geographical images to make the point that we are "surrounded on all sides by great mountains of accumulated troubles." We are on "a road that seems to lead us only to dead ends and blind passageways." We need "to get America on the right road" if we are to achieve greatness. The only way out of this confusion is to elect "strong, honest and unblinking leaders . . . to guide our dreams into reality." By implication, Wallace is one of these leaders.

The rest of the speech is a recycling of old themes that had worked well for Wallace in the past, but in 1976 these issues no longer resonate with the voters, nor does Wallace himself. In his attempt to become respectable, the fire has gone out of his performance. His lines lack the power to enrage or to denounce enemies, real or imagined. Although he uses the stand topos of the powerful few exploiting the powerless many, he cannot sustain the indignation and rage necessary to inflame the passions of the audience. Instead, the speech is a list of complaints that individually lack the power to move the audience and collectively do not build to a climax.

Wallace denounces (not by name) Nixon's foreign policy and calls for leaders who will "not go kowtowing off to our enemies in a show of spineless weakness." However, he quickly drops that issue and moves on to the totally unrelated issue of "bureaucratic" bungling. The quick shift in issues, failing to develop any one issue, is the major weakness of the speech.

Wallace next disposes of busing in a one-line comment about "federally appointed judges" determining the future of children. In 1972 he could always manage to rant about the "pluperfect hypocrisy" of judges and bureaucrats who enforced busing but sent their own children to private schools. Those lines, which always brought the crowd to its feet, are gone. He devotes one line to high taxes and another to the United Nations before going on to discuss his major issue of a loss of control over the individual person's everyday life. He links this to "a never-ending storm of permissiveness, inflation, crime, social disturbances, economic problems and despair." Again, the effect is underwhelming to say the least. In past campaigns, Wallace would have denounced malevolent federal bureaucrats or black-robed judges who lacked common sense for their role in perpetuating a permissive climate that encouraged violent crime and lack of respect for law and order. He is willing to sacrifice this effective way to move an audience for a bland respectability.

There are some good lines in the speech. His speech writer uses alliteration well. For example, the phrase "dead-end roads of doubt, disaster, drift, despair and defeat at home and abroad" effectively expresses Wallace's critique of the American political system. And one of the concluding lines of the speech, "America will be saved by decent men and women who dare to dream the decent dream of a decent America" certainly emphasizes the concept of decency through repetition.

Worried that concerns about Wallace's health might influence some voters into not voting for him, the staff scheduled as many appearances as possible during the campaign to make the point that Wallace was physically strong enough to endure a punishing schedule. When an early rally in Orlando failed to fill the 3,000-seat auditorium, the staff began to spend money on advertising and produced overflow crowds. They also began to schedule smaller halls that would produce overflow crowds that would be dutifully noted in the stories filed by the reporters covering the campaign.

The question before the voters in the primaries was posed by Wallace himself. Did George Wallace have the wisdom and the deliberation to lead the American people into a new day? More important, did he have the physical strength and bodily health to do so? In the past campaigns, Wallace had motivated his supporters and overwhelmed his opponents with his sheer energy and determination. He was a dynamo who out-talked, out-campaigned, and out-lasted his opponents. Now confined to a wheelchair, he could not physically "stand up" for what he believed in. His wife reminded reporters covering Wallace that Franklin Delano Roosevelt won four elections while confined to a wheelchair, but that was before the television age. Everywhere Wallace went, television cameras showed him being carried by aides on and off of planes, out of cars, and into halls and convention centers. Most disastrous, at the airport in Pensacola, Florida, as Wallace was being carried aboard his plane by two Alabama state troopers, one caught his foot on the carpet and fell, letting Wallace fall on top of him. The second trooper fell on top of Wallace, breaking Wallace's leg.[16]

One of his campaign workers realized that this incident was the end of the Wallace campaign: "Wallace started being perceived by the American public as a disabled person when he broke his leg and didn't know it." In addition, the worker noted, "All of a sudden it gave everybody the excuse to go out and say, 'You see what I told you, Wallace isn't capable of . . . ' "[17] In Florida, where Wallace trounced all his rivals in 1972 to win by a big margin, he now came in second, with 31 percent of the vote to Jimmy Carter's 34 percent.[18] In North Carolina, a must-win state that Wallace had won handily in the 1972 primary, he lost to Carter by 54 percent to 35 percent.[19] The end for Wallace was near. A *CBS News/New York Times* nationwide poll taken after the North Carolina primary showed that Wallace had half the support that he had just six weeks earlier. In interpreting the results, Robert Reinhold noted that "the collapse of support for Mr. Wallace can be traced both to his crippled condition and to the relative unimportance of racial matters as issues. The governor's health seems to be the more important factor."[20] Although Wallace did not end his campaign, money problems forced him to severely curtail spending, and in the end he did not permit himself to be nominated at the convention.

On the final night of the convention, following the acceptance speeches, Wallace joined the other defeated rivals for the nomination—Mo Udall and Scoop Jackson—on the platform with Jimmy Carter in a show of unity. In a surprise to the watching television audience, Martin Luther King, Sr., gave the closing benediction. In doing so, he took the opportunity to preach unity to the assembled Democratic congregation. When he closed his prayer, he was accompanied by a thunderous "Amen" from the assembled delegates. King embraced his daughter-in-law, and the assembled throng joined hands and sang "We Shall Overcome." Although Wallace did not join in the singing, he did shake hands with King. Their symbolic embrace in front of a smiling Jimmy Carter was dramatic evidence of the change that was taking place in the political life of the South.

Wallace represented the old politics of resistance and confrontation; Carter represented the new politics of conciliation and change. This was Wallace's last appearance as a major player on the stage of American politics. He did not play an active role in Carter's campaign. His days as a national political figure were over.

THE FINAL CAMPAIGN

Although his days as an important figure on the political stage were over, Wallace still had one last campaign to wage. It was a fight for forgiveness from those he wronged; a battle for redemption and reconciliation. It was ultimately a campaign to influence how he would be viewed by history—to cleanse his name of the stigma of racism and hatred. It also had a practical effect. Wallace wanted to be elected governor again in 1982. The passage of the Voting Rights Act of 1965 had profoundly altered Alabama politics. Black Alabamians now held the balance of power in statewide elections. Wallace could not afford to ignore or alienate this powerful bloc of voters. So Wallace responded to both practical political considerations and deeper personal reasons to convince black Alabamians and their white allies in the struggle for civil rights that he was a changed person who deserved a chance to show that he was capable of doing good to make up for the terrible wrongs he had perhaps inadvertently helped to inflict upon them.

He began this effort in the 1974 campaign for governor, when he gained the endorsement of black politicians such as Johnny Ford, the mayor of Tuskegee, a black judge, a black newspaper, and several black political organizations.[21] These efforts continued in 1976 when in October of that year, Wallace ordered that the Confederate flag be removed from flying atop the state capitol and that the United States flag be restored to the place of honor.[22] A few weeks later, Wallace pardoned Clarence Norris, the last surviving member of the Scottsboro Boys, who were convicted in a sensational case in the 1930s of raping two white women.[23] Shortly after his reelection, Wallace addressed the Progressive Baptist Mission and Education convention at a meeting at the Dexter Avenue Baptist Church in Montgomery, the same church where Martin Luther King, Jr., rose to prominence during the bus boycott.[24]

Wallace returned to Dexter Avenue Baptist Church in late 1979, a year after he had left office and almost two years before he would decide to run again. An aide pushed him to the front of the congregation, and Wallace asked for their forgiveness: "I have learned what suffering means. In a way that was impossible before. I think I can understand something of the pain that black people have come to endure. I know I contributed to that pain, and I can only ask for your forgiveness."[25]

In 1982, while running for governor for the last time, Wallace accepted an invitation to speak at the Southern Christian Leadership Conference's (SCLC) annual convention. In his speech, Wallace told the group, "I, too, see the mistakes all of us made in years past."[26] No text of that speech exists, but the leader of SCLC, the Reverend Joseph Lowery, in a newspaper interview described his "mixed feelings" at seeing Wallace address the group. He said, "When they put him up to the pulpit in the wheelchair, it made me sad. As he began to speak, I began to feel anger as I remembered him standing in the schoolhouse door trying to block black children from attending public schools. Then when he began to confess his mistakes and ask, almost beg, for votes, both the sadness and anger left."[27] While accepting Wallace's confession of past errors, Lowery could not bring himself to endorse Wallace's candidacy. He said, "I can't support a candidate who represents the shadows of the past not the light of today."[28]

Perhaps the most dramatic of Wallace's attempts to reach out to those he wronged came at the 30th anniversary celebration of the Selma to Montgomery March on March 10, 1995. Wallace asked the organizers of the event for an opportunity to appear and to read a statement greeting the marchers. The symbolism of the event was obvious to everyone. Thirty years before, the marchers had been beaten by Alabama state troopers who had been ordered to prevent the march by Wallace. When they eventually reached Montgomery, Wallace initially refused to meet with their representatives and only changed his mind after the intervention of the Methodist bishop of Alabama. Now the man who was once their enemy sat in his wheelchair surrounded by marchers who came to shake his hand and to greet him. An aged and nearly deaf Wallace had a statement read for him. The statement is brief. It does not contain the words "apology" or "sorry" or even "regret." It does acknowledge that the times have changed and that those changes are reflected in the lives of the people present there. Wallace states, "We have learned hard and important lessons in the 30 years that have passed between us since the days surrounding your first walk along Highway 80." He welcomed them to Montgomery and concluded with these words: "May your message be heard. May your lessons never be forgotten. May our history be always remembered " As an apology, it is indirect. Wallace does use the technique identified as "transcendence" as he takes a long view by stating, "Much has transpired since those days. A great deal has been lost and a great deal has been gained, and here we are."[29] The Reverend Joseph Lowery, who was president of the Southern Christian Leadership Conference, warmly responded to Wallace in a statement released to the news media:

By car, it is less than three hours from the university in Tuscaloosa to St. Jude High School. But it is more than 30 years by way of the heart—the tortured distance Mr. Wallace has traveled between the time he stood in the schoolhouse door and the time he welcomed many of the same marchers his troops had brutalized 30 years earlier. The arc of the universe bends toward justice. I thanked George Wallace for his act of courtesy. Marchers applauded his welcome. We could not, would not, deny him an act of repentance. We serve a God who makes the crooked places straight, makes the desert bloom and makes the lion to lie down with the lamb. There was an air of regeneration and caring in those moments! Isn't that what the world needs now? I think so![30]

John Lewis, who as leader of the Student Non-Violent Coordinating Committee led the first Selma to Montgomery March and who was beaten by Alabama state troopers, also testified to Wallace's change of heart. Recalling meeting with Wallace in 1979, he said, "I could tell that he was a changed man; he was engaged in a campaign to seek forgiveness from the same African-Americans he had oppressed. He acknowledged his bigotry and assumed responsibility for the harm he had caused. He wanted to be forgiven."[31]

Did Wallace undergo a dramatic conversion in his last few years? Certainly, scenes such as the one described here have led some observers to conclude that this is so. However, when one looks at the larger picture of Wallace's life, it becomes more accurate to say that he simply returned to the values that he had when he started his political career. When Wallace burst onto the national political stage in 1963, he did so as a strong champion of segregation. Since his early political career in Alabama was mostly unknown to observers outside the state, that image of an implacable segregationist defined him to the national audience. However, Wallace began his political career in 1946 as a state representative from Barbour County, where his hometown of Clio was located. In his first term in the state legislature, he strongly identified with the Folsom wing of the Democratic Party, which was very progressive and championed the welfare of poor Alabamians, both black and white. Wallace had the reputation as a "good-government" type of legislator who introduced many bills aimed at improving educational and working conditions for the working class. He asked Governor Folsom to appoint him a trustee of Tuskegee Institute, the premier black college in Alabama whose historic importance was unsurpassed in the nation. This is not to claim that Wallace did not share the prejudices of his social class about the inferior nature of blacks or about the need to maintain segregation of the races, but it is to insist that he was not identified as a "hater" or an ardent proponent of segregation. He recognized the importance of helping poor Alabamians of both races, and he made an effort to do so as a state representative.

When Wallace moved up the political ladder by winning election as a circuit judge in Alabama, he again had an opportunity to demonstrate fairness and decency in the way he treated black attorneys and defendants who appeared before him. In this situation, the testimony of J. L. Chestnut, a black attorney, is most compelling: "George Wallace was the first judge to call me Mister in a courtroom."[32] Chestnut continued to tell a story of defending poor black farmers who were suing a large corporation for money that had been unjustly denied them. When the corporation's attorneys appeared in court, they showed open contempt for his clients and for himself. Chestnut relates that Wallace, as the presiding judge, was upset by this behavior and ordered the opposing attorneys to refer to Chestnut's clients as "the plaintiffs" and to Chestnut as "Mr. Chestnut." J. L. Chestnut's testimony, which was freely given and with no obvious advantage to him, shows that Wallace was capable of treating black Alabamians fairly and with the respect that they deserved. This is not the behavior of a racist.

When in 1958, Wallace made his first run for governor, he espoused his moderate views. No one could run for governor in 1958 and not defend segregation, but Wallace did not make it the central issue in his campaign. When the Klan began to take an active role in the campaign of his opponent, Wallace denounced them. His campaign ran several newspaper advertisements deploring the Klan's activities in the campaign. In the end, he was endorsed by the Alabama NAACP; his opponent was endorsed by the Klan. In a televised address on the eve of the election, Wallace defended his record as a circuit judge, saying, "I want to tell the good people of this state, as a judge of the third judicial circuit, if I didn't have what it took to treat a man fair, regardless of his color, then I don't have what it takes be the Governor of your great state."[33]

Wallace lost. This was a staggering blow to a man who had worked to become governor of Alabama for most of his life. Wallace disappeared for a few days, and when he emerged, he uttered these famous words to Seymour Trammel, one of his campaign workers: "John Patterson out-nigguhed me. And boys, I'm not goin' to be out-nigguhed again."[34]

Wallace made good on his promise. He moved his family to Montgomery, opened a small law practice, and divided his time between his judicial duties and time on the road speaking to any audience he could find. He was so involved in politics that he neglected his growing family. Lurleen filed for divorce but was talked out of that extreme and politically disastrous action by George, who promised to spend more time with her and the family. Always looking for ways to keep himself in the public eye, Wallace took advantage of a staged encounter with Federal Judge Frank Johnson, an old college classmate, to pose as a defender of states rights against the federal judiciary. The United States Civil Rights Commission investigating voting rights in Alabama had requested voting records from six Alabama counties. When county officials refused to comply, the commission held hearing in Montgomery and issued subpoenas for the voting records. When Wallace as district judge for two of the counties announced that he would not comply with the subpoena, the commission went to federal court to get an order compelling Wallace to turn over the voting records. After several days of backtracking, and mindful that continued delay could mean time in jail for contempt of court, Wallace turned the records over to the grand jury, which promptly turned them over to the commission. Wallace promptly called a press conference to proclaim victory over the federal government and to give himself credit for "willing to risk my freedom to test . . . a grave constitutional question." He concluded, "This 1959 attempt to have a second Sherman's march to the sea has been stopped in the cradle of the Confederacy."[35] Wallace's actions and his televised news conference were the opening move in his run for the governorship. It is not necessary to recount the many ways in which Wallace's ruthless ambition led him to make common cause with the worst elements in the state in winning the governorship in 1962 and maintaining power and national attention until his presidential ambitions were ended by a deranged gunman in Maryland in 1972.

Wallace was a man of action. He was not given to thoughtful contemplation. He seemed to act by instinct, without considering the consequences of his action. The assassination attempt changed all that. Now Wallace spent long periods of time in hospital beds or rehabilitation facilities, where he had time to reflect on his actions and their consequences. It is during this time that he began to realize that he had caused suffering and pain to many people as he advanced his own political career. His subsequent effort to win their forgiveness therefore is not so much a dramatic conversion as it is a return to the ideals that motivated him as a young representative supporting the progressive policies of the Folsom administration.

RETIREMENT SPEECH

On April 2, 1986, over three hundred supporters gathered in the Alabama State House chamber to hear Wallace announce his decision about seeking another term. The Wallace who spoke on that day was but a dim shadow of his former self. Heavily medicated, seated in a wheelchair, hard of hearing, and his hands shaking from Parkinson's disease, Wallace had been under intense pressure from his son and close aides to announce his retirement from active politics. During his last term, he spent many days in bed and delegated significant power to his subordinates. Long gone was the fiery campaigner who aroused audiences and defied federal authority. But Wallace still enjoyed the attention of the media and the crowds of supporters who turned out for his public appearances. To add to the day's drama, he brought two speeches with him. One announced that he would run for re-election; the other announced his retirement from active politics. He stubbornly refused to tell even his son which speech he would read. The crowd cheered him when he was pushed to the dais and began to read his speech in a barely audible voice. When he reached the conclusion of the speech, his voice quavered, and tears filled his eyes.[36]

This speech as befits a ceremonial occasion focuses on values and follows a temporal pattern of discussing the past, the present, and the future. Wallace begins with an expression of appreciation to the voters of Alabama for their past support:

To be elected governor for even one term is the highest honor the people could bestow. But to be elected to serve four terms, and for the people to elect my wife Lurleen, also as governor is an honor without equal. And I can never begin to repay the people of this state for the confidence they have shown in me and my family for almost three decades.

Mentioning the long time that he has served as governor of Alabama provides Wallace with opportunity to reflect on the changes that he has seen during his tenure as governor.

But our state has come out of the depths of poverty in my lifetime. And today—thank God—our state is a vibrant part of this nation. Our future is bright and there are some exciting times ahead for our people.

He then states that he would like to be a part of the exciting times that are in the future.

I would like to be a part of those times. And I can say with confidence that I could continue in this role for a number of years. And while my health is good at the present time, I must do what is best in the long run for the people of the state and for me.

He confesses that arriving at his decision was not easy:

During the past few days, I have done much evaluation and much soul searching. And some who are younger may not fully realize that I was called upon to pay a high price for my involvement in political life.

He then recalls the attempt on his life while campaigning in Maryland and the consequent pain which he has endured ever since that day.

The five bullets that struck my body nearly 14 years ago inflicted me with a thorn in the flesh that has increasing taken its toll. And like the Apostle Paul, I have prayed for it to go away. But that is not to be.

He admits that "as I grow older the effect of my problem may become more noticeable and I may not be able to give you the fullest measure that you deserve from a governor throughout another term." The logical conclusion is that "I have climbed my last political mountain."

The image of climbing is extended and used for an emotional appeal: "But for now, I must pass the rope and the pick to another climber and say, 'Climb on.' 'Climb on to higher heights.' Climb on until you reach the very peak. Then look back and wave at me. For I, too, will still be climbing."

In a voice choking with emotion, Wallace admits that he has regrets about what has happened to him, but he vows to put the past behind him and to concentrate on the future:[37]

And while I may be tempted to dwell in the past and say, "Oh what might have been," I must realize, as did Peter the Great, that it is time to "Lay aside that which can never return" and think about the future.

He concludes the speech by vowing that "my heart will always belong to the people of Alabama. . . . But from the governmental and political arena, my fellow Alabamians, I must bid you a fond and affectionate farewell."

With its emphasis on traditional values of trust and confidence and responsibility in his leadership, Wallace celebrates the longevity of his tenure in office. By implication, he must have done something to merit such a renewed reward of office during those years. He also celebrates the progress that the state has made. Some members of the audience might have thought that this was a particularly ironic statement since Wallace made a career out of opposing the civil rights movement, which was the major factor responsible for that progress. But on the occasion of the old man's retirement from active politics, such comments would have been kept private. Perhaps all could agree that the state would face new challenges in the future and that the time had come to pass the pick and rope to a new person who could climb higher up the mountain and move the state forward into the twenty-first century. Although he resisted it up to the last minute, Wallace finally said goodbye to his first and only love: campaigning for political office.

George Wallace died in Montgomery, Alabama, on September 13, 1998, at the age of 79. Doctors tried to revive Wallace after he suffered respiratory and cardiac arrest. Wallace's son, George Wallace, Jr., and one of his daughters, Peggy Wallace Kennedy, were at his side when he died.[38] His passing was marked by an outpouring of commentary on the meaning of his career and remembrances of his past actions. Old adversaries such as John Lewis reflected on the change that had come over Wallace since the assassination attempt: "Mr. Wallace deserves recognition for seeking redemption for his mistakes, for his willingness to change and to set things right with those he harmed and with his God."[39] The *New York Times* noted, "The strength of will he showed in coming to terms with his paralysis and the way in which he continued afterwards with his political career impressed even his most implacable opponents."[40] Haynes Johnson, a political reporter who won a Pulitzer Prize for his coverage of the Selma campaign in an interview with Jim Lehrer on PBS called him a "tragic [figure] because he couldn't escape the prism of race."[41] The extent to which times had changed was inadvertently revealed by the coverage of his death by *Time* and *Newsweek*. Neither publication gave more than a half page to the story.[42]

NOTES

1. Stephan Lesher, *George Wallace: American Populist* (Reading, Mass.: Addison-Wesley, 1994), 492.

2. Lesher, *George Wallace*, 493.

3. Joseph P. Albright, "The Price of Purity," *New York Times Magazine*, September 1, 1974, 12.

4. B. Drummond Ayres Jr., "Southern Black Mayors Give Wallace Standing Ovation at a Conference," *New York Times*, November 19, 1973, 25.

5. Jody Carlson, *George C. Wallace and the Politics of Powerlessness: The Wallace Campaigns for the Presidency, 1964–1976* (New Brunswick, N.J.: Transaction Books, 1981), 188.

6. Ray Jenkins, "Black Vote for Wallace Is Put at 20–25% in Alabama Primary," *New York Times*, May 9, 1974, 50.

7. Tom Wicker, "Blacks for Wallace(!)," *New York Times*, May 12, 1974, E19.

8. "Fool's Errand," *New York Times*, November 12, 1975, 42.

9. B. Drummond Ayres Jr., "Wallace Opens 1976 White House Drive," *New York Times*, November 13, 1975, 1.

10. Jules Witcover, *Marathon: The Pursuit of the Presidency 1972–1976* (New York: Viking Press, 1977), 172.

11. Witcover, *Marathon*, 242.

12. Witcover, *Marathon*, 243.

13. Witcover, *Marathon*, 243.

14. Witcover, *Marathon*, 244.

15. The text of the speech is reprinted in part 2 of this volume, in "Trust the People: The 1976 Campaign Speech."

16. Witcover, *Marathon*, 256.

17. Carlson, *George C. Wallace*, 213.

18. Associated Press, "Final Totals in Florida Primary," *New York Times*, March 11, 1976, 33.

19. B. Drummond Ayres Jr., "Wallace Openly Despairs about His Political Future," *New York Times*, March 25, 1976, 30.

20. Robert Reinhold, "Surge by Carter on National Basis Indicated in Poll," *New York Times*, March 29, 1976, 1.

21. Carlson, *George C. Wallace*, 188.

22. Ray Jenkins, "U.S. Flag Back on Top in Alabama," *New York Times*, October 14, 1976, 1.

23. Thomas A. Johnson, "Last of Scottsboro 9 Is Pardoned. He Draws a Lesson for Everybody," *New York Times*, October 26, 1976, 1.

24. "Notes on People," *New York Times*, November 8, 1974, 45.

25. Lesher, *George Wallace*, 502.

26. Tom Gardner, "Lowery Rejects Wallace," *Montgomery Advertiser*, August 15, 1982, 1.

27. *Montgomery Advertiser*, August 15, 1982, 2.

28. *Montgomery Advertiser*, August 15, 1982, 2.

29. Quoted in B. L. Ware and Will Linkugel, "They Spoke in Defense of Themselves: On the Generic Criticism of Apologia," *Quarterly Journal of Speech* 59 (1973): 273–283. The text is reprinted in "Statement on the 30th Anniversary of the Selma March," in part 2 of this volume.

30. Joseph E. Lowery, "The Arc of Justice," *New York Times*, March 24, 1995, 31.

31. John Lewis, "Forgiving George Wallace," *New York Times*, September 16, 1998, 30.

32. *Wallace: Settin' the Woods on Fire*, produced and directed by Daniel McCabe and Paul Stekler (Washington, D.C.: PBS Video, 2000), videocassette.

33. The text is reprinted in "1958 Gubernatorial Campaign Election Eve Appeal," in part 2 of this volume.

34. Frady, *Wallace*, 131; Seymour Trammel recounts the incident on the video *Wallace: Settin' the Woods on Fire*.

35. Lesher, *George Wallace*, 139–140.

36. *Montgomery Advertiser*, April 3, 1986, 1. The text is reprinted in "Retirement Speech," in part 2 of this volume.

37. The conclusion of the speech is on the video *Wallace: Settin' the Woods on Fire*.

38. Associated Press, dispatch from Montgomery, Alabama, September 14, 1998.

39. Lewis, "Forgiving George Wallace," 30.

40. Editorial, *New York Times*, September 15, 1998, 35.

41. "Remembering George Wallace." *News Hour with Jim Lehrer*, PBS, September 14, 1998.

42. Lance Morrow, "Requiem for an Arsonist. George Corley Wallace, 1919–1998," *Time*, September 28, 1998, 54; "Legacy of a Healed Hater, George Wallace, 1919–1998," *Newsweek*, September 28, 1998, 51.

CHAPTER 9

Conclusion

For most of his time on the national political scene, George Wallace was seen through the prism of racism. His early record as a state legislator and circuit judge were unknown to the national audience. Thus he was defined by his actions in the racial crises that occurred in Alabama, from the stand in the schoolhouse door to the beating of the marchers in Selma. The reality is a little more complicated. Wallace began his career as a protégé of Jim Folsom, the progressive governor of Alabama who appointed Wallace a trustee of Tuskegee University. In the legislature, Wallace acquired a reputation as a progressive good-government type who introduced many bills to benefit the poor people of Alabama. As a circuit judge, he treated black attorneys and their clients with respect. When he ran for governor of Alabama in 1958, he attacked the Ku Klux Klan in speeches and newspaper advertisements. When he was criticized for helping a poor black defendant while serving as circuit judge, he defended that action in a statewide television address. These are not the actions of a racist— certainly not of a person who hates black people as a class.

The 1958 election is the key to understanding Wallace's subsequent behavior toward blacks. He lost the race and after long reflection decided that he lost because he was perceived as not being a strong defender of segregation. From then on, race became the byword in his subsequent campaigns. He decided to imitate the actions of the many southern demagogues that had dominated politics in that region for so long.

The English word *demagogue* comes from the Greek *demagogos,* which means "leader of the people." It has long been used as a disparaging term by supporters of the established order for their opponents, especially those who advocate change by appealing directly to the common people. It is commonly used to describe an unscrupulous politician who will use any means necessary to win and hold on to power. *The American Political Dictionary* defines a demagogue as "an unscrupulous politician who seeks to win and hold office through emotional appeals to mass prejudice and passions."[1] Waldo Braden contends that the essential defining characteristic of the demagogue is the use of a "rhetoric of exploitation . . . for one's own ends, to take advantage of another person's weakness, to gain rewards through manipulation and deception."[2] He further expands upon this definition: "The rhetoric of exploitation depends upon naiveté and concentrates upon sensitive issues, for example, poverty . . . and the race question. Feeding upon emotion, prejudice, and mythic concerns, it attracts listeners and readers who are in the throes of disappointment, frustration, and anxiety, and consequently are searching for easy solutions to their difficulties."[3] The social and political conditions of the southern states following the Civil War and Reconstruction made the region ripe for the rise of a succession of demagogues in a number of southern states. Braden in his study identifies 17 such men, ranging from Ben Tillman, Eugene Tallmadge, Theodore Bilbo, and Huey Long to George Wallace. He contends that they all employed a rhetoric of exploitation, using a strategy of aligning the have-nots against the entrenched elite to achieve their ends.[4] Unfortunately, the ends were often the achievement and the consolidation of personal power at the expense of genuine social reform. In what could be the epitaph of George Wallace, Braden concludes that "in the end, they were better showmen than they were reformers."[5]

The passage of the Voting Rights Act of 1965 changed the political landscape that had produced the southern demagogue. No longer was the South a one-party region whose politics were defined by the disenfranchisement of poor whites and almost all blacks. The all-white primary election in the Democratic Party, which was the only battleground for competing political interests, was replaced by genuine competition between the parties, and southern blacks, who had been excluded from the political process, now had their voting rights protected by the federal government. Wallace and the other southern governors who defied the federal government—including Orville Faubus of Arkansas, Ross Barnett of Mississippi, and Lester Maddox of Georgia—were the last of the southern demagogues. Of these men, only Wallace achieved a national following and became a player in presidential politics. One reason for his success and their failure in national politics is that he carefully avoided the use of racial epithets in his political speaking, relying instead on code words to convey his meaning. When Wallace promised to lock up street criminals or to put welfare loafers back to work, everyone knew that he was referring to black criminals and black men on welfare.

Wallace also found the pose of a populist champion of the working class to be an effective cover for his racially oriented politics. He got his biggest applause when he denounced "pointy-headed bureaucrats" and un-elected federal judges. Wallace understood long before other politicians did that the administrative state, with its regulations and enforcement mechanisms, had begun to chafe and grate on ordinary citizens. His larg-est constituency was in the South, and here people were particularly re-sentful at federal intervention in their communities to enforce the civil rights of black Americans. The genius of the American political system is its balancing of popular democracy with support of individual rights. When those two ideas conflict, as they did in the civil rights struggle in the South in the 1950s and 1960s, leadership is required to help the people understand and accept unpopular political decisions. The South did pro-duce such leaders in the person of Terry Sanford, the governor of North Carolina, who guided that state toward peaceful acceptance of the inte-gration of the public schools and other public facilities. But Wallace, who had enormous popularity and effective leadership skills, took a different path. Rather than risking any of his popularity on an attempt to help the people of Alabama understand the reasons for the court-ordered integra-tion of the public schools, he gambled that he could exploit racial fears and become a national political figure.

The limits of Wallace's concern for the working class are evident in his record as governor of Alabama. Wallace did accomplish some things that benefited his constituents. He got the legislature to make school textbooks free to all, and he established a system of two-year community colleges throughout the state. However, he did not make any effort to reform the tax system, which was one of the most regressive of all states. Families got free textbooks, but they paid for them with higher sales taxes. Students could go to community colleges, but they paid for them with higher taxes and fees.

Wallace's achievements as a public speaker were considerable. In an era when political messages were increasingly mass mediated and staged ei-ther as intimate programs or attack advertisements, George Wallace dem-onstrated that a political leader with a powerful message could through public speaking build a mass following. His speeches were neither ele-gantly written nor powerfully argued. None would be considered out-standing examples of effective organization. Yet all of them did what effective mimetic oratory does best. They reflected back to his followers their own feeling that they were victims of forces beyond their control. Wallace knew their frustrations; he shared their outrage that people who were better educated looked down on them and their beliefs with con-tempt. More important, he could express their rage and anger and focus it on those people and institutions they despised: pointy-headed intellec-tuals who provided the justification for the bureaucrats who issued rules and regulations that upset their traditional ways of doing things, and federal judges who enforced the rules and the hated laws without concern about the social dislocations their decisions caused.

Wallace spent a lifetime preparing for his role on the national political stage. From the early days growing up as a boy in Clio, Alabama, he had listened to people talk about politics. Never a serious student, Wallace got most of his information about the world from conversations with family and friends, not from reading and reflection. He learned the idioms of the people. He learned to talk to them using easily understood words and phrases based on their own experience to explain the sources of their difficulties and his ideas on how to deal with them. He had no difficulty identifying with them or their interests. He had nothing that passed for sophistication. He was a good old boy with his cheap, ill-fitting suits, his slicked-back hair, his habit of spitting, and his cocky demeanor. He was small-town country, and his supporters loved him for it. There is no disputing that Wallace was a powerful speaker who could easily bring a crowd to its feet to shout support for him. He was a demagogue who played on the fears and uncertainties of the people to gain power for himself. He stands as a warning of the challenges that democratic societies face during times of social unrest and confusion.

It is especially significant that Wallace was never interested in using power once he gained it. He was completely uninterested in the details of administration. Once he won an election, he was soon busy planning for the next campaign. He was desperate for public approval and hungered for the sound of public acclaim. He became what he was—the perfect mimetic orator who lived through the approval of his audience. That was both the reason for his success and the reason for his failure to accomplish anything that could properly be called a positive achievement for the people of his state and nation. He was all public gesture, and when the applause ended as the world changed and people found other leaders and other causes, he became a lonely old man full of regret and dreams of what might have been.

Wallace was eager to be taken seriously as a national figure, and he courted publicity assiduously. He staged confrontations with the federal government to show his willingness to defend the people of Alabama and their way of life against outsiders. He did get publicity, but inevitably, his intervention only hastened the actions he hoped to prevent. His stand in the schoolhouse door forced President Kennedy to commit the federal government to hasten the end of segregated schools in the South. His unwise intervention in the Selma march led to President Johnson proposing in a special address to Congress a broad law to protect voting rights. In both instances, Wallace also lost the battle to define the event. President Kennedy's address the night of the confrontation at the University of Alabama framed the situation in moral terms: "We are confronted primarily with a moral issue. It is as old as the Scriptures and is as clear as the American Constitution."[6] Wallace's attempt to breathe new life into the tired clichés about states rights could not compete with Kennedy's ringing defense of the freedom of all American citizens. Both President Johnson and Dr. Martin Luther King, Jr., defended the importance of the right to vote as the defining characteristic of a democratic society. Wallace, for all his bluster, could not compete with the eloquence of these speakers as they demonstrated that the policy he defended was outside the constitutional boundaries that defined American politics.

Wallace found an audience for his message in the 1968 presidential campaign. Civil rights legislation had not brought peace to urban ghettos, and President Johnson's escalation of the war in Vietnam had not brought peace to that nation either. Rebellious college students who mocked the patriotism of their elders and demonstrated against the war and the draft incensed many Americans. Wallace as a mimetic orator could easily express the outrage and anger of the white middle class at the many social disruptions that they could neither understand nor change. He preached law and order and promised to spank the unruly kids who heckled him. He carried five states—all in the South—and almost 14 percent of the total vote cast in the election.

Wallace's electoral success alarmed President Nixon, who adopted a strategy calculated to assure southerners that he would look out for their interests. The 1965 Voting Rights Act had destroyed the solidly Democratic South and radically changed its politics. Nixon wanted to ensure that the Republican Party would gain disaffected white Democrats who were Wallace voters. Nixon's public moves such as nominating a southerner for the U.S. Supreme Court and trying to limit school busing for integration were clearly aimed at attracting Wallace's supporters, but they did not dissuade Wallace himself from running against Nixon in 1972. Wallace and his staff were confident that their experience and their issues would enable Wallace to mount a serious run for the presidency. He was on his way when a deranged man fired a gun at him in a Maryland suburb and seriously wounded him. Unable to walk and in constant pain, Wallace could not campaign effectively. He attended the 1972 Democratic Convention and spoke briefly on a substitute plank for the party platform, but the powerful voice was subdued. Wallace would no longer be a serious force in American politics.

Wallace was still a force in Alabama politics, however, as he demonstrated by winning the governorship in 1974 and again in 1982. In the 1982 election, Wallace won with significant support from black voters who were willing to believe him when he told them that he was a changed man who regretted his past actions. In his last term, Wallace supported passage of a $310 million education bond issue, and reform of state's job injury laws. Also in his last term, Wallace returned to his good-government roots and worked closely with the state teachers' organization and organized labor in a failed attempt to reform the state tax system.

Wallace's life is an example of what can happen when ambition for power overcomes any moral scruples about gaining it or using it. Wallace knew as a young man that he would never be satisfied until he achieved his dream of becoming governor of the state of Alabama. From that moment, he devoted his considerable energy to accomplishing that one act. Although he was a mediocre student, he knew that the law was a likely avenue for political advancement, and so he became a lawyer. He ran for the state legislature to get his name before the people and later for circuit judge for the same reason. On weekends, he drove around the state meeting people and speaking to any group that would have him. In 1958 he ran for governor stressing his good-government background and his support for the working man. He was beaten by a man who accepted the support of the Klan. Wallace learned from his mistake. He would never be mistaken for a moderate on race relations again. Unfortunately, he did not learn that he could be outspoken in his support of segregation without encouraging violence and hatred of black citizens. He did win in 1962 and delivered his infamous declaration of "segregation today, segregation tomorrow, segregation forever." In the next four years, he was at the forefront of every attempt to deny the black citizens of Alabama their legal rights, including the basic right to vote.

In his old age, Wallace sought the forgiveness of those he wronged, and in his last term as governor, he appointed blacks to many positions on advisory boards in the state administration. He performed many symbolic acts such as appearing at the Dexter Avenue Baptist Church, where King had led the Montgomery bus boycott, and publicly greeting the marchers at the anniversary of the Selma march. Wallace was desperate for the approval of his former foes and worried about his place in history. Many of his old enemies accepted his pleas for forgiveness and publicly embraced him, but others held back, remembering the cost in human suffering that the Wallace years represented. He is remembered today for his defiant gestures and his blustery speeches. He was on the wrong side in a defining historical moment, and like many other losers, he is fading from memory.

NOTES

1. Jack C. Plano and Milton Greenburg, *The American Political Dictionary*, 4th ed. (Hinsdale, Ill.: Dryden Press, 1976), 118.

2. Waldo Braden, *The Oral Tradition in the South* (Baton Rouge: Louisiana State University Press, 1983), 85–86.

3. Braden, *Oral Tradition*, 86.

4. Braden, *Oral Tradition*, 89.

5. Braden, *Oral Tradition*, 105.

6. John F. Kennedy, "Radio and Television Report to the American People on Civil Rights, The White House, June 11, 1963," in *Papers of the Presidents of the United States, John F. Kennedy: Containing the Messages, Speeches, and Statements of the President, 1961–1963* (Washington, D.C.: United States Printing Office, 1962), 468–471.

PART II

Collected Speeches

1958 Gubernatorial Campaign Election Eve Appeal, May 27, 1958

My fellow Alabamians, it's a pleasure to speak to you in the closing days of this campaign and to ask for your support on June 3rd for Governor of Alabama. First, I would like to thank all of the people of this great state who cast their votes for me on May 6th and allowed me to get in the runoff in this governor's race. A lot of you good people in this television audience tonight cast your ballots for the fine candidates who were in the first primary but who lost out. You didn't make any mistake because speaking of the front-runners in that campaign, they were all high class individuals who would have made you a good governor had they been elected. So you made no mistake in casting your ballots for those who I consider front-runners.

I would like to ask you to join the Wallace campaign and to help elect George Wallace on June 3rd. One of the issues in this campaign, my friends, is who is the most experienced because during the next four years, I feel that the people of this state should have the most experienced man in the race for Governor as your Governor. There are many problems that will be confronting the people of this great state during the next four years. I would like to tell you that having served in the Legislature of your state for six years, I feel that this experience will be invaluable to me as your Governor. Any time that a man runs for governor, he advocates a program. The only way that this program can come into being is to be passed by the Alabama Legislature. Having served in that body for six years, I feel that I am more qualified to work with the Legislature of Alabama towards putting across a program that will help and benefit the people of this great state.

During the next four years, many problems will arise in the matter of segregation and civil rights as a result of judicial decisions. Having served as judge of the 3rd judicial circuit of Alabama, I feel, my friends, that this judicial experience will be invaluable to me as your Governor.

I also have had experience in representing the people of my district and of Alabama at national conventions. In 1948, I was a delegate to Philadelphia where I voted for Senator Richard Russell of Georgia for President, placed his name in nomination for Vice President, and voted against the so-called civil rights matters ten years ago. In 1956, it was my pleasure to again be a delegate to the Democratic Convention where I was chosen by the Alabama delegation to serve on the platform committee. And I led Alabama's civil rights fight in Chicago in 1956, in which, my friends, I, of course, helped other Southerners best the enemies of the South in many regards in that Convention. I have met the enemies of the South, such as Mennin Williams and Herbert Lehman and Roy Wilkins and the NAACP and the Americans for Democratic Action. And, therefore, fighting this group will be nothing new to George Wallace when I'm your Governor.

I have tried to take a positive approach to the problems that confront the people of this state during this campaign. And I want to tell you a little something about my positive approach. I also want to say before I do get into some of the positive matters in my campaign and in my platform, that I am one person that does not mind being questioned by anybody in this state about my record. I do not mind appearing on live television because I feel that the people of this Alabama—the people of Alabama have a right to know all about the record of George Wallace. And I feel that you have a right to know all about the record of my opponent and I am willing to tell you about George Wallace. I have heard those say when you talk about matters in a man's record, and when you mention matters in an opponent's record that you are talking about a smear campaign. They call it smear. But, my friends, I have said nothing in this campaign that was not the fact because I don't believe in smear and rumor, and I don't believe in a smut campaign. And, I have not, of course, I have, uh, I have not participated in any such type campaign during this Governor's race.

But I want to show the people of this campaign some of these smear sheets that have gone out all over Alabama against George Wallace. I have no underground movement to smear me in the alleyways and in byways. And, we in our campaign, have not participated in any sort of manner in such a campaign to the people of this state. I have in one, in my hand, one smear sheet that was circulated upon me that George Wallace was a draft dodger when I'm a disabled American veteran and saw combat service in the South Pacific. Here's another one that says I'm a former member of the Communist party which is, of course, the most silly and asinine statement ever made. Here's another one of half truths about a case in my court and not a thing in it is true, and, my friends, if it was true, I would not have received 4,800 votes in my county against 600 for the combined opposition. And my only opponent in this race, at the present time, received only 345 votes in my county. Here's another one, my friends, that says I used to be a professor at a school that is subversive. Here's another one that says I voted against segregation in 1951. Yes, I voted against the amendment here that they called a segregation amendment. And every man in the governor's race voted against it, including Mr. Todd, and Mr. Faulkner and Mr. Hawkins and Mr. Harrison and George Wallace. And, my friends, the two members of the Alabama Senate, who are today in the lieutenant governor's race, Mr. Skidmore and Mr. Boutwell, both voted against this silly amendment.

What did this amendment do? This amendment would have closed, in 1951, every school in Alabama, cut off every school teacher, closed every lunch room, cut off every bus and fired every mechanic, who works on the school busses if one school in Alabama were integrated. The Alabama Legislature thought so little of such an amendment that it voted it down overwhelmingly. And, my friends, I am one who believes that a positive approach ought to be made to the matter of segregation, and we ought not to allow the integrationists in this country to cause us to destroy that which we have built over the years. My friends, since my opponent, undoubtedly, and his henchman are circulating this smear sheet on me, saying that I voted against this amendment, it means, my friends, that they must be in favor of this amendment. Of closing down every school in Alabama, cutting off the pay to every schoolteacher, closing every lunchroom, and firing every bus driver and sending every school child home if one school is integrated. Yes, I'm against such an amendment as that, and I would not be for such an amendment as that as Governor of your state. My friends, I would close down the school that was integrated. I would transfer those peoples and teachers to other schools until it blows over. And then I would put them back in the court again and litigate with them some more. And then if they wanted to send any troops down into this section of the nation, they would be marching around an empty school house because there would not be any school children there if I were the Governor of this state.

My friends, on this same smear sheet that's circulated all over Alabama for the last ten months, they said George Wallace placed a negro boy on probation for reckless driving, and any reckless driving case in this state is usually a $25 fine. Yes, he was fined $25 and placed on probation because he deserved probation. What has that got to do with integration or segregation or mixed schools in Alabama? And I want to tell the good people of this state, as a judge of the third judicial circuit, if I didn't have what it took to treat a man fair, regardless of his color, then I don't have what it takes be the Governor of your great state. That's what I want to say about that type of smear sheet that has been circulated on me in this campaign.

My friends, I am interested in education. And I am going to see that we have the best education facilities possible in the next four years. We're going to raise school teachers salaries. We're going to build new school buildings. I am going to ask the Legislature to submit a bond issue to the people of this state for ratification to build school buildings all over Alabama. And we can submit a good sized bond issue that will not require any additional taxes. I'm going to see that every high school and college department in Alabama is accredited. My friends, we are going to move forward in the field of education. I'm going to help raise the pension program for the elderly people of this state to the maximum provided under the federal state matching program which is $60 per month. I have worked for six years in the Legislature of this state in behalf of the elderly people of Alabama. I have traveled and spoke at old age pension conventions from the Tennessee line to the Gulf of Mexico. I have not just started talking about the elderly people of Alabama when I became a candidate for Governor. I have been interested in them all the many years that I have been in government, and I have been endorsed by the largest old age pension association in Alabama, The Alabama Old Age Pension Institute.

My friends, I'm interested in the fine conservation program, the matter of seafood, the matter of forestry, the matter of attracting tourists into this great state to take advantage of our great scenic wonders and our great resort places. Tourist industry can become a great dollar industry for Alabama. I am interested in a strong National Guard. I am interested in using the power of the Governor's office to help the great textiles industry. I want to try and influence those in Washington to invoke those portions of the Reciprocal Trade Act that will protect the great textile industry from unfair foreign competition. And you good textile workers, let me say that I am the only candidate in the race for Governor that has mentioned your great industry and your great problem.

I am interested in re-apportionment of the legislative branch of the state government. My friends, the smaller counties of Alabama ought to be protected, but the larger counties of this state are entitled and justly so, to more representation in the legislative assembly. I shall work in good faith to see that the Alabama Legislature will submit to you, the people, an amendment to our Constitution that will give the larger counties of Alabama more voice in government.

I am interested in a continuation of a fine highway building program. And we should take part in the interstate road building program under which the federal government will put up 90% and the states 10%.

I am interested in agriculture. I was the son of a farmer. I was on the

WPA [Works Progress Administration] because my father was a farmer when I went to school. I am interested in placing a farmer in the Cabinet. I am interested in encouraging the poultry industry and the cattle industry and the dairy industry and the trucking industry. I helped take the tax off of feeds, seeds, and insecticides, and I'm going to help keep the tax off as the governor of your state.

I am interested in asking the Legislature and will ask the Legislature to pass a bill to give an immediate gas tax refund to the farmers of this state and make it unnecessary for them to keep books over a long period of time. And, in many instances, they lost their gas tax rebate because they were unable to keep the records required by the present law.

I am interested in the industry. And I am going to spend three months of my time in other parts of the nation from June until January of 1959 trying to find industry that's going to come South and talking them into coming into the cities and counties of Alabama. And all that the people of this great state find industrial employment and find it unnecessary to go to other parts of this nation to find such employment.

I am interested in segregation, and we shall keep segregation within the law. There will be no race mixing while I'm the Governor of your state. And there's plenty of intelligence and enough leadership in the peoples of Alabama and of the South to maintain peace among our people and keep segregation within the law. There will be no race mixing socially or educationally while I'm the Governor of your state.

And I want you to know that I mean that absolutely.

My friends, I'm interested in honest government. And I have today, a smear sheet in my hand signed by the friends of my opponent, in which he says that you should elect my opponent, who is a man who has not sold out to the big time politicians and the racketeers, who is not obligated to anyone in any way. I believe in honest government and nobody in this campaign has sold out to any racketeers and any such sheet as that is exactly what's called smear. I have engaged in no such tactics as that as a candidate for Governor.

My friends, I want to make you a good Governor. I hope you will consider my experience. I hope you will consider my positive, forward-looking program and elect me your governor on June 3rd. With divine guidance, I'll try and make you a good Governor.

Thank you very much.

The 1963 Inaugural Address

[This is the original text, with Wallace's own punctuation and spelling.]

Governor Patterson, Governor Barnett, from one of the greatest states in this nation, Mississippi, Judge Brown, representing Governor Hollings of South Carolina, Judge Perez, members of the Alabama Judiciary, members of the Alabama Congressional Delegation, members of the Alabama Legislature, distinguished guests, fellow Alabamians:

Before I begin my talk with you, I want to ask you for a few minutes patience while I say something that is on my heart: I want to thank those home folks of my county who first gave an anxious country boy his opportunity to serve in State politics. I shall always owe a lot to those who gave me that first opportunity to serve.

I will never forget the warm support and close loyalty at the folks of Suttons, Haigler's Mill, Eufaula, Beat 6 and Beat 14, Richards Cross Roads and Gammage Beat . . . at Baker Hill, Beat 8, and Comer, Spring Hill, Adams Chapel and Mount Andrew . . . White Oak, Baxter's Station, Clayton, Louisville and Cunnigham Place; Horns Crossroads, Texasville and Blue Springs, where the vote was 304 for Wallace and 1 for the opposition . . . and the dear little lady whom I heard had made that one vote against me . . . by mistake . . . because she couldn't see too well . . . and she had pulled the wrong lever. . . . Bless her heart. At Clio, my birthplace, and Elamville. I shall never forget them. May God bless them.

And I shall forever remember that election day morning as I waited . . . and suddenly at ten o'clock that morning the first return of a box was flashed over this state: it carried the message. . . . Wallace 15, opposition zero; and it came from the Hamrick Beat at Putman's Mountain where live the great hill people of our state. May God bless the mountain man . . . his loyalty is unshakeable, he'll do to walk down the road with.

I hope you'll forgive me these few moments of remembering . . . but I wanted them . . . and you . . . to know, that I shall never forget. And I wish I could shake hands and thank all of you in this state who voted for me . . . and those of you who did not . . . for I know you voted your honest convictions . . . and now, we must stand together and move the great State of Alabama forward.

I would be remiss, this day, if I did not thank my wonderful wife and fine family for their patience, support and loyalty . . . and there is no man living who does not owe more to his mother than he can ever repay, and I want my mother to know that I realize my debt to her.

This is the day of my Inauguration as Governor of the State of Alabama. And on this day I feel a deep obligation to renew my pledges, my covenants with you . . . the people of this great state.

General Robert E. Lee said that "duty" is the sublimest word on the English language and I have come, increasingly, to realize what he meant. I SHALL do my duty to you, God helping . . . to every man, to every woman, . . . yes, to every child in this state. I shall fulfill my duty toward honesty and economy in our State government so that no man shall have a part of his livelihood cheated and no child shall have a bit of his future stolen away.

I have said to you that I would eliminate the liquor agents in this state and that the money saved would be returned to our citizens. . . . I am happy to report to you that I am now filling orders for several hundred one-way tickets and stamped on them are these words . . . "for liquor agents . . . destination: . . . out of Alabama." I am happy to report to you that the big-wheeling cocktail-party boys have gotten the word that their free whiskey and boat rides are over . . . that the farmer in the field, the worker in the factory, the businessman in his office, the housewife in her home, have decided that the money can be better spent to help our children's education and our older citizens . . . and they have put a man in office to see that it is done. It shall be done. Let me say one more time . . . no more liquor drinking in your governor's mansion.

I shall fulfill my duty in working hard to bring industry into our state, not only by maintaining an honest, sober and free-enterprise climate of government in which industry can have confidence . . . but in going out and getting it . . . so that our people can have industrial jobs in Alabama and provide a better life for their children.

I shall not forget my duty to our senior citizens . . . so that their lives can be lived in dignity and enrichment of the golden years, nor to our sick, both mental and physical . . . and they will know we have not forsaken them. I want the farmer to feel confident that in this State government he has a partner who will work with him in raising his income and increasing his markets. And I want the laboring man to know he has a friend who is sincerely striving to better his field of endeavor.

I want to assure every child that this State government is not afraid to invest in their future through education, so that they will not be handicapped on every threshold of their lives.

Today I have stood, where once Jefferson Davis stood, and took an oath to my people. It is very appropriate then that from this Cradle of the Confederacy, this very Heart of the Great Anglo-Saxon Southland, that today we sound the drum for freedom as have our generations of forebears before us done, time and time again through history. Let us rise to the call of freedom-loving blood that is in us and send our answer to the tyranny that clanks its chains upon the South. In the name of the greatest people that have ever trod this earth, I draw the line in the dust and toss the gauntlet before the feet of tyranny . . . and I say . . . segregation today . . . segregation tomorrow . . . segregation forever.

The Washington, D.C. school riot report is disgusting and revealing. We will not sacrifice our children to any such type school system—and you can write that down. The federal troops in Mississippi could be better used guarding the safety of the citizens of Washington, D.C., where it is even unsafe to walk or go to a ballgame—and that is the nation's capitol. I was safer in a B-29 bomber over Japan during the war in an air raid, than the people of Washington are walking to the White House neighborhood. A closer example is Atlanta. The city officials fawn for political reasons over school integration and THEN build barricades to stop residential integration—what hypocrisy!

Let us send this message back to Washington by our representatives who are with us today . . . that from this day we are standing up, and the heel of tyranny does not fit the neck of an upright man . . . that we intend to take the offensive and carry our fight for freedom across the nation, wielding the balance of power we know we possess in the Southland . . . that WE, not the insipid bloc of voters of some sections . . . will determine in the next election who shall sit in the White House of these United States. . . . That from this day, from this hour . . . from this minute . . . we give the word of a race of honor that we will tolerate their boot in our face no longer . . . and let those certain judges put that in their opium pipes of power and smoke it for what it is worth.

Hear me, Southerners! You sons and daughters who have moved north and west throughout this nation . . . we call on you from your native soil to join with us in national support and vote . . . and we know . . . wherever you are . . . away from the hearths of the Southland . . . that you will respond, for though you may live in the fartherest reaches of this vast country . . . your heart has never left Dixieland.

And you native sons and daughters of old New England's rock-ribbed patriotism . . . and you sturdy natives of the great Mid-West . . . and you descendants of the far West flaming spirit of pioneer freedom . . . we invite you to come and be with us . . . for you are of the Southern spirit . . . and the Southern philosophy . . . you are Southerners too and brothers with us in our fight.

What I have said about segregation goes double this day . . . and what I have said to or about some federal judges goes TRIPLE this day.

Alabama has been blessed by God as few states in this Union have been blessed. Our state owns ten percent of all the natural resources of all the states in our country. Our inland waterway system is second to none . . . and has the potential of being the greatest waterway transport system in the entire world. We possess over thirty minerals in usable quantities and our soil is rich and varied, suited to a wide variety of plants. Our native pine and forestry system produces timber faster than we can cut it and yet we have only pricked the surface of the great lumber and pulp potential.

With ample rainfall and rich grasslands our live stock industry is in the infancy of a giant future that can make us a center of the big and growing meat packing and prepared foods marketing. We have the favorable climate, streams, woodlands, beaches, and natural beauty to make us a recreational mecca in the booming tourist and vacation industry. Nestled in the great Tennessee Valley, we possess the Rocket center of the world and the keys to the space frontier.

While the trade with a developing Europe built the great port cities of the east coast, our own fast developing port of Mobile faces as a magnetic gateway to the great continent of South America, well over twice as large and hundreds of times richer in resources, even now awakening to the growing probes of enterprising capital with a potential of growth and wealth beyond any present dream for our port development and corresponding results throughout the connecting waterways that thread our state.

And while the manufacturing industries of free enterprise have been coming to our state in increasing numbers, attracted by our bountiful natural resources, our growing numbers of skilled workers and our favorable conditions, their present rate of settlement here can be increased from the trickle they now represent to a stream of enterprise and endeavor, capital and expansion that can join us in our work of development and enrichment of the educational futures of our children, the opportunities of our citizens and the fulfillment of our talents as God has given them to us. To realize our ambitions and to bring to fruition our dreams, we as Alabamians must take cognizance of the world about us. We must redefine our heritage, re-school our thoughts in the lessons our forefathers knew so well, first hand, in order to function and to grow and to prosper. We can no longer hide our head in the sand and tell ourselves that the ideology of our free fathers is not being attacked and is not being threatened by another idea ... for it is. We are faced with an idea that if a centralized government assume enough authority, enough power over its people, that it can provide a utopian life ... that if given the power to dictate, to forbid, to require, to demand, to distribute, to edict and to judge what is best and enforce that will produce only "good" ... and it shall be our father ... and our God. It is an idea of government that encourages our fears and destroys our faith ... for where there is faith, there is no fear, and where there is fear, there is no faith. In encouraging our fears of economic insecurity it demands we place that economic management and control with government; in encouraging our fear of educational development it demands we place that education and the minds of our children under management and control of government, and even in feeding our fears of physical infirmities and declining years, it offers and demands to father us through it all and even into the grave. It is a government that claims to us that it is bountiful as it buys its power from us with the fruits of its rapaciousness of the wealth that free men before it have produced and builds on crumbling credit without responsibilities to the debtors ... our children. It is an ideology of government erected on the encouragement of fear and fails to recognize the basic law of our fathers that governments do not produce wealth ... people produce wealth ... free people; and those people become less free ... as they learn there is little reward for ambition ... that it requires faith to risk ... and they have none ... as the government must restrict and penalize and tax incentive and endeavor and must increase its expenditures of bounties ... then this government must assume more and more police powers and we find we are becoming government-fearing people ... not God-fearing people. We find we have replaced faith with fear ... and though we may give lip service to the Almighty ... in reality, government has become our god. It is, therefore, a basically ungodly government and its appeal to the psuedo-intellectual and the politician is to change their status from servant of the people to master of the people ... to play at being God ... without faith in God ... and without the wisdom of God. It is a system that is the very opposite of Christ for it feeds and encourages everything degenerate and base in our people as it assumes the responsibilities that we ourselves should assume. Its psuedo-liberal spokesmen and some Harvard advocates have never examined the logic of its substitution of what it calls "human rights" for individual rights, for its propaganda play on words has appeal for the unthinking. Its logic is totally material and irresponsible as it runs the full gamut of human desires ... including the theory that everyone has voting rights without the spiritual responsibility of preserving freedom. Our founding fathers recognized those rights ... but only within the framework of those spiritual responsibilities. But the strong, simple faith and sane reasoning of our founding fathers has long since been forgotten as the so-called "progressives" tell us that our Constitution was written for "horse and buggy" days . . . so were the Ten Commandments.

Not so long ago men stood in marvel and awe at the cities, the buildings, the schools, the autobahns that the government of Hitler's Germany had built . . . just as centuries before they stood in wonder of Rome's building . . . but it could not stand . . . for the system that built it had rotted the souls of the builders . . . and in turn . . . rotted the foundation of what God meant that men should be. Today that same system on an international scale is sweeping the world. It is the "changing world" of which we are told . . . it is called "new" and "liberal." It is as old as the oldest dictator. It is degenerate and decadent. As the *national* racism of Hitler's Germany persecuted a *national* minority to the whim of a *national* majority . . . so the *international* racism of the liberals seeks to persecute the *international* white minority to the whim of the *international* colored majority . . . so that we are footballed about according to the favor of the Afro-Asian bloc. But the Belgian survivors of the Congo cannot present their case to a war crimes commission . . . nor the Portuguese of Angola . . . nor the survivors of Castro . . . nor the citizens of Oxford, Mississippi.

It is this theory of international power politic that led a group of men on the Supreme Court for the first time in American history to issue an edict, based not on legal precedent, but upon a volume, the editor of which said our Constitution is outdated and must be changed and the writers of which, some had admittedly belonged to as many as half a hundred communist-front organizations. It is this theory that led this same group of men to briefly bare the ungodly core of that philosophy in forbidding little school children to say a prayer. And we find the evidence of that ungodliness even in the removal of the words "in God we trust" from some of our dollars, which was placed there as like evidence by our founding fathers as the faith upon which this system of government was built. It is the spirit of power thirst that caused a President in Washington to take up Caesar's pen and with one stroke of it make a law. A Law which the law-making body of Congress refused to pass . . . a law that tells us that we can or cannot buy or sell our very homes, except by his conditions . . . and except at HIS discretion. It is the spirit of power thirst that led the same President to launch a full offensive of twenty-five thousand troops against a university . . . of all places . . . in his own country . . . and against his own people, when this nation maintains only six thousand troops in the beleaguered city of Berlin. We have witnessed such acts of "might makes right" over the world as men yielded to the temptation to play God . . . but we have never before witnessed it in America. We reject such acts as free men. We do not defy, for there is nothing to defy . . . since as free men we do not recognize any government right to give freedom . . . or deny freedom. No government erected by man has that right. As Thomas Jefferson said, "The God who gave us life, gave us liberty at the same time; no King holds the right of liberty in his hands." Nor does any ruler in American government.

We intend, quite simply, to practice the free heritage as bequeathed to us as sons of free fathers. We intend to re-vitalize the truly new and progressive form of government that is less than two hundred years old . . . a government first founded in this nation simply and purely on faith . . . that there is a personal God who rewards good and punishes evil . . . that hard work will receive its just deserts . . . that ambition and ingenuity and incentiveness . . . and profit of such . . . are admirable traits and goals . . . that the individual is encouraged in his spiritual growth and from that growth arrives at a character that enhances his charity toward others and from that character and that charity so is influenced business, and labor and farmer and government. We intend to renew our faith as God-fearing men . . . not government-fearing men nor any other kind of fearing-men. We intend to roll up our sleeves and pitch in to develop this full bounty God has given us . . . to live full and useful lives and in absolute freedom from all fear. Then can we enjoy the full richness of the Great American Dream.

We have placed this sign, "In God We Trust," upon our State Capitol on this Inauguration Day as physical evidence of determination to renew the faith of our fathers and to practice the free heritage they bequeathed to us. We do this with the clear and solemn knowledge that such physical evidence is evidently a direct violation of the logic of that Supreme Court in Washington, D.C., and if they or their spokesmen in this state wish to term this defiance . . . I say . . . then let them make the most of it.

This nation was never meant to be a unit of one . . . but a united of the many . . . that is the exact reason our freedom loving forefathers established the states, so as to divide the rights and powers among the states, insuring that no central power could gain master government control.

In united effort we were meant to live under this government . . . whether Baptist, Methodist, Presbyterian, Church of Christ, or whatever one's denomination or religious belief . . . each respecting the others right to a separate denomination . . . each, by working to develop his own, enriching the total of all our lives through united effort. And so it was meant in our political lives . . . whether Republican, Democrat, Prohibition, or whatever political party . . . each striving from his separate political station . . . respecting the rights of others to be separate and work from within their political framework . . . and each separate political station making its contribution to our lives. . . .

And so it was meant in our racial lives . . . each race, within its own framework has the freedom to teach . . . to instruct . . . to develop . . . to ask for and receive deserved help from others of separate racial stations. This is the great freedom of our American founding fathers . . . but if we amalgamate into the one unit as advocated by the communist philosophers . . . then the enrichment of our lives . . . the freedom for our development . . . is gone forever. We become, therefore, a mongrel unit of one under a single all-powerful government . . . and we stand for everything . . . and for nothing.

The true brotherhood of America, of respecting the separateness of others . . . and uniting in effort . . . has been so twisted and distorted from its original concept that there is a small wonder that communism is winning the world.

We invite the Negro citizens of Alabama to work with us from his separate racial station . . . as we will work with him . . . to develop, to grow in individual freedom and enrichment. We want jobs and a good future for BOTH races . . . the tubercular and the infirm. This is the basic heritage of my religion, of which I make full practice . . . for we are all the handiwork of God.

But we warn those, of any group, who would follow the false doctrine of communistic amalgamation that we will not surrender our system of government . . . our freedom of race and religion . . . that freedom was won at a hard price and if it requires a hard price to retain it . . . we are able . . . and quite willing to pay it.

The liberals' theory that poverty, discrimination and lack of opportunity is the cause of communism is a false theory . . . if it were true the South would have been the biggest single communist bloc in the western hemisphere long ago . . . for after the great War Between the States, our people faced a desolate land of burned universities, destroyed crops and homes, with manpower depleted and crippled, and even the mule, which was required to work the land, was so scarce that whole communities shared one animal to make the spring plowing. There were no government handouts, no Marshall Plan aid, no coddling to make sure that our people would not suffer; instead the South was set upon by the vulturous carpetbagger and federal troops, all loyal Southerners were denied the vote at the point of bayonet, so that the infamous, illegal 14th Amendment might be passed. There was no money, no food and no hope of either. But our grandfathers bent their knee only in church and bowed their head only to God.

Not for a single instant did they ever consider the easy way of federal dictatorship and amalgamation in return for fat bellies. They fought. They dug sweet roots from the ground with their bare hands and boiled them in iron pots . . . they gathered poke salad from the woods and acorns from the ground. They fought. They followed no false doctrine . . . they knew what the wanted . . . and they fought for freedom! They came up from their knees in the greatest display of sheer nerve, grit and guts that has ever been set down in the pages of written history . . . and they won! The great writer, Rudyard Kipling wrote of them, that: "There in the Southland

of the United States of America, lives the greatest fighting breed of man
. . . in all the world!"

And that is why today, I stand ashamed of the fat, well-fed whimperers
who say that it is inevitable . . . that our cause is lost. I am ashamed of
them . . . and I am ashamed for them. They do not represent the people
of the Southland.

And may we take note of one other fact, with all trouble with communists that some sections of this country have . . . there are not enough
native communists in the South to fill up a telephone booth . . . and THAT
is a matter of public FBI record.

We remind all within hearing of this Southland that a Southerner, Peyton Randolph, presided over the Continental Congress in our nation's
beginning . . . that a Southerner, Thomas Jefferson, wrote the Declaration
of Independence, that a Southerner, George Washington, is the Father of
our country . . . that a Southerner, James Madison, authored our Constitution, that a Southerner, George Mason, authored the Bill of Rights and
it was a Southerner who said, "Give me liberty . . . or give me death,"
Patrick Henry.

Southerners played a most magnificent part in erecting this great divinely inspired system of freedom . . . and as God is our witness, Southerners will save it.

Let us, as Alabamians, grasp the hand of destiny and walk out of the
shadow of fear . . . and fill our divine destination. Let us not simply defend
. . . but let us assume the leadership of the fight and carry our leadership
across this nation. God has placed us here in this crisis . . . let us not fail
in this . . . our most historical moment.

You are here today, present in this audience, and to you over this great
state, wherever you are in sound of my voice, I want to humbly and with
all sincerity, thank you for your faith in me.

I promise you that I will try to make you a good governor. I promise
you that, as God gives me the wisdom and the strength, I will be sincere
with you. I will be honest with you.

I will apply the old sound rule of our fathers, that anything worthy of
our defense is worthy of one hundred percent of our defense. I have been
taught that freedom meant freedom from any threat or fear of government. I was born in that freedom, I was raised in that freedom. . . . I intend
to live in that freedom . . . and God willing, when I die, I shall leave that
freedom to my children . . . as my father left it to me.

My pledge to you . . . to "Stand up for Alabama," is a stronger pledge
today than it was the first day I made that pledge. I shall "Stand up for
Alabama," as Governor of our State . . . you stand with me . . . and we,
together, can give courageous leadership to millions of people throughout
this nation who look to the South for their hope in this fight to win and
preserve our freedoms and liberties.

So help me God.

And my prayer is that the Father who reigns above us will bless all the people of this great sovereign State and nation, both white and black.

I thank you.

Statement and Proclamation, University of Alabama, June 11, 1963

As Governor and Chief Magistrate of the State of Alabama I deem it to be my solemn obligation and duty to stand before you representing the rights and sovereignty of this State and its peoples.

The unwelcomed, unwanted, unwarranted and force-induced intrusion upon the campus of the University of Alabama today of the might of the Central Government offers frightful example of the oppression of the rights, privileges and sovereignty of this State by officers of the Federal Government. This intrusion results solely from force, or threat of force, undignified by any reasonable application of the principle of law, reason and justice. It is important that the people of this State and nation understand that this action is in violation of rights reserved to the State by the Constitution of the United States and the Constitution of the State of Alabama. While some few may applaud these acts, millions of Americans will gaze in sorrow upon this situation existing at the great institution of learning.

Only the Congress makes the law of the United States. To this date no statutory authority can be cited to the people of this Country which authorizes the Central Government to ignore the sovereignty of this State in an attempt to subordinate the rights of Alabama and millions of Americans. There has been no legislative action by Congress justifying this intrusion.

When the Constitution of the United States was enacted, a government was formed upon the premise that people, as individuals are endowed with the rights of life, liberty and property, and with the right of local self-government. The people and their local self-government formed a Central Government and conferred upon it certain stated and limited powers. All other powers were reserved to the states and to the people.

Strong local government is the foundation of our system and must be continually guarded and maintained. The Tenth Amendment to the Constitution of the United States reads as follows:

"The powers not delegated to the United States by the Constitution nor prohibited by it to the states, are reserved to the states respectively, or to the people."

This amendment sustains the rights of self-determination and grants the State of Alabama the right to enforce its laws and regulate its internal affairs.

This nation was never meant to be a unit of one . . . but a united of the many . . . that is the exact reason our freedom-loving forefathers established the states, so as to divide the rights and powers among the many states, insuring that no central power could gain master government control.

There can be no submission to the theory that the Central Government is anything but a servant of the people. We are God-fearing people—not government-fearing people. We practice today the free heritage bequeathed to us by the Founding Fathers.

I stand here today, as Governor of this sovereign State, and refuse to willingly submit to illegal usurpation of power by the Central Government. I claim today for all the people of this State of Alabama those rights reserved to them under the Constitution of the United States. Among those powers so reserved and claimed is the right of state authority in the operation of the public schools, colleges and Universities. My action does not constitute disobedience to legislative and constitutional provisions. It is not defiance—for defiance sake, but for the purpose of raising basic and fundamental Constitutional questions. My action is a call for strict adherence to the Constitution of the United States as it was written—for a cessation of usurpation and abuses. My action seeks to avoid having state sovereignty sacrificed on the altar of political expediency.

Further, as the Governor of the State of Alabama, I hold the supreme executive power of this State, and it is my duty to see that the laws are faithfully executed. The illegal and unwarranted actions of the Central Government on this day, contrary to the laws, customs and traditions of this State is calculated to disturb the peace.

I stand before you today in place of thousands of other Alabamians whose presence would have confronted you had I been derelict and neglected to fulfill the responsibilities of my office. It is the right of every citizen, however humble he may be, through his chosen officials of representative government to stand courageously against whatever he believes to be the exercise of power beyond the Constitutional rights conferred upon our Federal Government. It is this right which I assert for the people of Alabama by my presence here today.

Again I state—this is the exercise of the heritage of freedom and liberty under the law—coupled with responsible government.

Now, therefore, in consideration of the premises, and in my official capacity as Governor of the State of Alabama, I do hereby make the following solemn proclamation:

WHEREAS, the Constitution of Alabama vests the supreme executive powers of the State in the Governor as the Chief Magistrate, and said Constitution requires of the Governor that he take care that the laws be faithfully executed; and,

WHEREAS, the operation of the public school system is a power reserved to the State of Alabama under the Constitution of the United States and Amendment 10 thereof; and,

WHEREAS, it is the duty of the Governor of the State of Alabama to preserve the peace under the circumstances now existing, which power is one reserved to the State of Alabama and the people thereof under the Constitution of the United States and Amendment 10 thereof.

NOW THEREFORE, I, George C. Wallace, as Governor of the State of Alabama, have by my action raised issues between the Central government and the Sovereign State of Alabama, which said issues should be adjudicated in the manner prescribed by the Constitution of the United States; and now being mindful of my duties and responsibilities under the Constitution of the United States, the Constitution of the State of Alabama, and seeking to preserve and maintain the peace and dignity of this State, and the individual freedoms of the citizens thereof, do hereby denounce and forbid this illegal and unwarranted action by the Central government.

Wallace for President: The 1964 Campaign Speech

Patriotic Americans have a great duty before them. It is a duty that will require patience, persistence and courage.

We must have patience to continually point to the truth. We must exercise that patience even in the most violent storm of recriminations against us by those who seek through centralized authority to vanquish freedom in the name of freedom, to destroy human rights and dignity in the name of civil rights, to inspire hatred and chaos in the name of love and peace.

Our efforts will require character, individualism and vitality. It will require that we exercise the heritage bequeathed to us by those who stood firm against adversity, fought their way across this country, and established a strong virile United States.

We must re-evaluate the political philosophy of our governmental structure. We must take stock of our values and fully investigate the questions which have been raised as to our political direction as a nation.

We have witnessed a scheme to create national chaos in recent months. Much has been written and said about the "hate" that is purportedly prevalent in our society. Much has been written and said regarding the "haters." Invariably those who are identified as the purveyors of "hate" are:

Those who believe in the rights of the individual states.

Those who believe in fiscal responsibility.

Those who object to amendment of the Constitution of the United States without regard to the basic precepts of the Founding Fathers.

Those who stand firm for the retention of the checks and balances system of government.

Those who object to a socialist ideology under which a few men in the executive and judicial branches of our government make decisions and laws without regard to our elected representatives who reflect the decisions of the people.

These people—I, among them—have been denounced as haters, hate-mongers and demagogues.

Yes, I have made speeches. I have criticized. I have denounced policies that I believe to be detrimental to our country and our people. I have, in good conscience, forcefully fought every device that I felt reduced our freedoms, our rights as a people to make our own decisions, all as guaranteed by the Constitution. I have, when the issue was forced, legally defied the physical actions which seek to break the laws of our nation and tear away the fabric of this republic.

I intend to continue to represent convictions which will tend to help preserve constitutional government and states' sovereignty.

For those of the leftist ideology to term those convictions as "hate" is to attempt to perpetrate one of the biggest lies ever placed on the market in this age of the propagandist and the sellers of the Big Lie.

In selling the Big Lie, the left-wing endeavors to destroy all opposition to their program of venomous destruction of our American Republic and to cloak their hatred for its system in an hysterical denunciation of "hate" at any and all who dare raise their voices in protest.

It has been written that:

"Nothing is so shameful as those who hide their own shamefulness behind attempts to shame others. Nothing could be so hateful—if anyone wishes to be hateful—as those who hide their own hatreds by charging someone else with hate."

I am campaigning today because the world is at war between two ideals of government. I am here to campaign today because I believe we can no longer comfortably contemplate that war from afar.

There is an ideal that believes government can manage the people and—by management and manipulations—bring about a utopian life.

This ideal has come to be a predominant aim in Washington, D.C. Basically, the practice of this ideal requires a shift from a government based upon and acting through the will of the people and guided by the consummate wisdom of the people, to an authoritarian government based upon and acting by the wisdom of a select group of men.

We see practitioners of that ideal on the United States Supreme Court, afraid to submit to the wisdom of the people in amending the Constitution as prescribed by law. Such legal amendment procedure requires two-thirds of the States' approval and is subject to open debate and honest truth—and deliberate action. We find these men reaching outside the realm of legal precedent, ignoring the basic precepts as established by the Founding Fathers. This rule of men rather than law gains momentum in absurdity as a single federal judge, not elected by the people, begins to govern an entire state of people, confident that he has the wisdom he is sure that the people do not have, and answerable only to those select few to whom he owes his seat of power.

This gathering of absolute power by men, into a central body of government, was greatly feared by the Founding Fathers of this country. With rights and powers divided among separate State governments, close to and answerable to the citizens of each State, no single group could hope to gain control over the people. But with the right and powers of the States destroyed, with power centralized into one seat of control, tyranny—benevolent or other wise—is assured over the people.

Through this central management of people, we find the nation's Capitol becomes a jungle where citizens fear to walk the streets at night. We find high school football games played in secret because of the anarchy engendered under the label of "brotherhood" in Philadelphia. We are witness to little school children in New York being taken, against their parents will, out of their neighborhood schools and bussed across town into neighborhoods where grown men are afraid to walk, and taxi drives refuse to ply their trade. This management is carried out under the banner of "morality," "democracy" and "humanity." Those who feel anything for the children and their parents and object to people being manage about like checkers are labeled as "bigots and demagogues."

We are subjected to roving bands of irresponsible street rioters who are encouraged to break the laws by the irresponsible power gatherers in Washington, who themselves have violated the Constitution, broken the law, and now depend upon engendering irresponsibility in others for their support.

We are faced with the astounding spectacle for the first time in a civilized nation of high officials calling for the passage of a so-called civil rights bill for fear of threat of mob violence. A mob movement which includes at least several communist indoctrinated leaders.

I have spoken against this bill across the length of this country. I began speaking when most people did not know the contents of the bill—a sad commentary on this nation's public information facilities which unfortunately have, in the majority, claimed freedom FOR the press, but have forgotten what freedom OF the press really means—a dedication to supply—not distortions of America, nor a zeal to manage the people's thinking—but rather a duty to supply the facts to the people, in the faith that the American people have the decency and the consummate wisdom to reach decisions in the best interest of their country when given those ungarnished facts. Somewhere along the way news management TO the people has become synonymous with political management OF the people.

Time does not permit my discussing that bill tonight. But it is an ungarnished fact of truth that the official Communist Party of the United States is an enthusiastic supporter of it. Well they might be, for this bill takes a long step toward transferring private property to public domain under a central government. It is this way in Russia. It places in the hands of a few men in central government the power to create a regulatory police arm unequaled in Western civilization—power to investigate, to arrest, to charge, and to try a citizen without a jury of his peers—power to control the voting booth—power to invade private property without compensation or due process of law—power to enter every community, every business and level the American citizen to a common denominator called "equality," that is necessary for central planning and management of an entire people by governmental authority.

And with this power, this bill hands over to a few men indiscriminate control of billions of dollars, to use as they will—to intimidate, to withhold livelihood from those who would oppose their power, and to reward those who would aid in perpetuating that power. Under any name, it will create a dictatorship the like of which we or our fathers have not witnessed. It will bring about the ultimate in tyranny. It will make government master and God over man.

In all my speeches and utterances, I have never spoken one word of evil or demagoguery against any race, or any religion, or any culture. I believe that people have the wisdom, the sense of justice and the decency to govern their own local affairs.

I believe that people of each state must live with their specific conditions, must raise their families and develop their children under particular conditions peculiar to that State—as must the people of Alabama. And I have faith in the wisdom of the people of each State to make decisions in the best interest of all. I have faith in the decency and the Christianity of the people that their sense of justice is right. This is called freedom. I do not have faith that a central government operating at the caprice of a few powerful men is capable of those decisions—nor do I consider them as keepers of the wisdom of the people.

I want to offer you the choice of supporting the American philosophy of government close to the governed and by the governed in preference to control by a federal judge and accompanying federal police executing decisions made in Washington, D.C. If your local school board does something with your children that you do not like, I want that school board answerable to you, so that you can change that decision by majority vote. I do not want that school board answerable only to a federal judge over whom you exercise no control, and before whose decision you are helpless.

The United States is made up of separate races, separate religions, separate cultures, languages and separate States. We have always been a united of many divergences, for this has been our freedom, this has been our secret of dynamics, our will to creativeness. From these fountain heads of differences have come the diversities of free men before the open forum of honest controversy and rich contribution from which decisions are arrived at that speak the will and the wisdom of free and diverse people.

But now there are those who would amalgamate us into a unit of the one, subservient to a powerful central government, with laws designed to equalize us into the common denominator necessary for a slave people. If we follow this course of making government our master, we shall soon discover, and too late, that everything that is not forbidden by law, is required by law—by law that can change in a moment at the whim of a few powerful men in central government.

I am sure you have been to a county fair or carnival and looked in one of those crooked mirrors that distorts your image into grotesque figures. That is the way I feel when I read the majority of the nation's press. A grotesque distortion—so that when a vast mob is organized by leaders, and that mob is set upon a town, throwing bricks, invading private property, causing chaos and violence—the news media distort this picture to inveigle the reader into believing that the police are attacking the mob—that men sworn to uphold the law, are in reality, vicious attackers upon poor innocent bystanders. We have seen it happen over and over again, in nation after nation—the riots, the demonstrations, the violence, the bombings, the demands.

We have read the newspapers when they called Chaing-Kai-Shek, "Black Jack" Chiang, because he would not allow the so-called "agrarian reformers," their rights—these "agrarian reforms" were led by Mao Tse Tung and now as the world know—they are not "agrarian reformers," but communists.

We can all recall how Batista of Cuba suddenly became a "butcher." Castro was played up in the press as a crusading democratic leader who only wanted to gain "rights" for his people—until he got in power. Then it was too late.

This is the same press that talks of "responsibility" and labels defenders against this trained conspiracy as "irresponsible racists," and "bigots," and "demagogues." Surely a pattern of action and propaganda that has circled the globe in slavery—surely, when that pattern and that propaganda reaches our very doorstep we shall have the power of sight to recognize it.

We know by way of actual declaration that the leaders of world communism intend to attempt to destroy our political system. We know that our system under the Constitution, guaranteeing the dissemination of power among the 50 states, preventing a concentration of central authority, is a frustrating road block to communism and its liberal forerunners. Hence, we have witnessed a venomous attack on all who believe in states sovereignty. We have witnessed a propaganda barrage of emotionalism that creates a climate of hysteria in promoting and justifying deliberate violations of those rights by judicial edict and by physical force.

We have been subjected to oceans of emotional propaganda that justifies the breaking of the law and a flagrant violation of the Constitution, with the law breakers and the violators gathering the central authority that they usurp from the states.

We know that to succeed Communism must destroy the basis upon which our system of jurisprudence was founded. With decisions of the present based upon precedent of the past as guidelines for the future, our legal system leaves little opportunity for communism to invoke revolutionary perversion and prostitution of purpose.

We have seen our legal system breached. We have seen it abandoned by a federal judiciary, basing its decision upon the twilight zone of psychology, psychiatry and sociology. The communist rules supreme in these fields of double talk.

We have witnessed this abandonment of our legal principles amidst a campaign against the Constitution of the United States—a campaign that calls our principles "out-dated" and "behind the times."

We have witnessed this departure from the basic precepts of our legal system—this flaunting of the law—along with an emotional wave of propaganda for the "democratic way of life" and the "human rights" that have just suddenly begun to damage our "image" with the rest of the world.

We know that communism hates our system of division of duty and authority within the federal government. Communism cannot destroy a system whereby representatives of the people make the law—where the Executive Branch executes those laws—and only those laws—and where the Judiciary referees the contentions arising from the administration of those laws—and only those laws. A communist hates this system. He hates the Congress for the Congress is representative of the people. It is unwieldy. It is large. It has differing opinions—differing prejudices. It is rampant with debate and deliberation—and most important, with truths. Communism cannot survive where there is truth.

A communist applauds government by executive or judicial edict. A president can be forcibly removed and his authority easily assumed. A judiciary of only nine men may be deceived, or brainwashed or corrupted. But a Congress represents the people and is directly responsible to the people—it represents the authority OF the people.

We have seen our Constitution violated. We know that the Executive branch has made law without constitutional sanction. We have witnessed numerous judicial edicts that range from actual amendment of the Constitution, to centralizing power over education, to outlawing the reading of the Bible in our public schools.

The venom of this attack upon our system which was designed for the greatest liberty to the greatest number is an appalling and alarming revolution.

The person whether he be a public official or an individual citizen, who attempts to stand in some manner of opposition to this express train of liberal revolution can be virtually destroyed by a flailing thresher of propaganda that smears him with a wide range of deprecating adjectives which can deceive and mislead the American public. This emotional wave of propaganda serves a purpose of silencing opposition and of creating such an atmosphere of charged emotionalism that factual knowledge goes by the board.

I am alarmed and I believe the responsible citizens of America are alarmed.

We negotiated away a third of Europe, half of Germany and all of the Balkans after the blood-bath of World War II. These people are now in slavery. The proud and gallant Poles who fought so bravely now live without freedom—as is the case with the Czechs and Hungarians and millions more—all subject to the butchery of Communism.

Have you looked at your map lately? A map that has colored in red the part of the world that is now under the domination of Communism? If you have not, you will be amazed and astounded.

World analysts are now quite coolly predicting that the whole of South America will be next unless there is forceful, forthright action on the part of the United States.

What has been the official line of policy of our State Department through all these years? I quote: "We search for areas that might provide an overlapping interest between Communism and ourselves and seek to work out a cooperative atmosphere." Unquote.

In other words, Communist Russia selects a country—it is always a free country—makes menacing moves, stages riots and street demonstrations, bombing and violence—which our press dutifully reports as "the people, wanting their rights." Then the Communists say let's sit down and negotiate on how much central power you are going to put through in order to "satisfy these people"—let us determine how much communism you are going to allow in the government of this country. Our State Department marches to the negotiating table and decides, while the frightened people of the country look on. If the leaders of the country refuse to accept a coalition communist govern, they are labeled "fascist" and "bigots" by our press and they have their guns and ammunition cut off—such as Chiang Kai Shek or Diem. If they do accept the coalition Communist government, our press hails this as a "great victory"—such as Laos was proclaimed a few months ago. But today it is agreed that the people of Laos have been taken over completely by Communism—the Communism we helped establish.

If we concede that this world give-away has been the result of just fuzzy bumbling while looking for areas of "overlapping" interests, then why must it always be a free nation which is subject to negotiation? Why cannot we sit down and look for some overlapping interest in Poland—and say to the Communists: "Let us negotiate. We want some Polish patriots put in positions of power in the Polish government, and we want your troops withdrawn. Let us have some 'overlapping' interest in the cause of freedom."

After all, the American taxpayer is now financing food for the Russians in order to save the internal pressure on Mr. Khrushchev. We might propose to cut off that wheat. We might arm the underground patriots of Cuba, furnishing the necessary air cover. We might then offer troops to any South American government requesting them, to mop up the Saboteurs, the fifth-columnists, the rioters and the communist-trained street fighters. We might then cut off aid to the Communist Sukarno and force acceptance of decent men into his government. We might call together the Western nations of the world with this rededication to principle instead of betrayal and bring economic and political pressures to bear to negotiate freedom for our valiant allies Poland, Hungary, Czechoslovakia, East Germany and other nations.

We are feeding and supporting half the Communist nations of the world at this moment. What is our return? Let us re-evaluate our position.

The socio-liberal will snort that this is impossible. He will raise the old spectre of fear—for he trades on fear. If victory for freedom is impossible, then surrender to communism is inevitable and we can begin fitting the yokes of slavery to the necks of our children even now as the riots and mobs lap at the streets of these United States.

We are involved in a war for the minds of people—our people. We are living in a new kind of warfare—a warfare of propaganda that is waged unceasingly and ruthlessly. It is a warfare of which we know little—and sadly in which we hold small skills.

We must make the decision now to Stand Up for America in our foreign affairs and for Americanism in our internal affairs.

We must not allow ourselves to be emotionalized into giving up the last bastion of freedom.

The Civil Rights Movement: Fraud, Sham, and Hoax, July 4, 1964

We come here today in deference to the memory of those stalwart patriots who on July 4, 1776, pledged their lives, their fortunes, and their sacred honor to establish and defend the proposition that governments are created by the people, empowered by the people, derive their just powers from the consent of the people, and must forever remain subservient to the will of the people.

Today, 188 years later, we celebrate that occasion and find inspiration and determination and courage to preserve and protect the great principles of freedom enunciated in the Declaration of Independence.

It is therefore a cruel irony that the President of the United States has only yesterday signed into law the most monstrous piece of legislation ever enacted by the United States Congress.

It is a fraud, a sham, and a hoax.

This bill will live in infamy. To sign it into law at any time is tragic. To do so upon the eve of the celebration of our independence insults the intelligence of the American people. It dishonors the memory of countless thousands of our dead who offered up their very lives in defense of principles which this bill destroys.

Never before in the history of this nation have so many human and property rights been destroyed by a single enactment of the Congress. It is an act of tyranny. It is the assassin's knife stuck in the back of liberty.

With this assassin's knife and a blackjack in the hand of the Federal force-cult, the left-wing liberals will try to force us back into bondage. Bondage to a tyranny more brutal than that imposed by the British monarchy which claimed power to rule over the lives of our forefathers under sanction of the Divine Right of kings.

Today, this tyranny is imposed by the central government which claims the right to rule over our lives under sanction of the omnipotent black-robed despots who sit on the bench of the United States Supreme Court.

This bill is fraudulent in intent, in design, and in execution.

It is misnamed. Each and every provision is mistitled. It was rammed through the Congress on the wave of ballyhoo, promotions, and publicity stunts reminiscent of P. T. Barnum.

It was enacted in an atmosphere of pressure, intimidation, and even cowardice, as demonstrated by the refusal of the United States Senate to adopt an amendment to submit the bill to a vote of the people.

To illustrate the fraud—it is not a Civil Rights Bill. It is a Federal Penal Code. It creates Federal crimes which would take volumes to list and years to tabulate because it affects the lives of 192 million American citizens. Every person in every walk and station of life and every aspect of our daily lives becomes subject to the criminal provisions of this bill.

It threatens our freedom of speech, of assembly, or association, and makes the exercise of these Freedoms a federal crime under certain conditions.

It affects our political rights, our right to trial by jury, our right to the full use and enjoyment of our private property, the freedom from search and seizure of our private property and possessions, the freedom from harassment by Federal police and, in short, all the rights of individuals inherent in a society of free men.

Ministers, lawyers, teachers, newspapers, and every private citizen must guard his speech and watch his actions to avoid the deliberately imposed booby traps put into this bill. It is designed to make Federal crimes of our customs, beliefs, and traditions. Therefore, under the fantastic powers of the Federal judiciary to punish for contempt of court and under their fantastic powers to regulate our most intimate aspects of our lives by injunction, every American citizen is in jeopardy and must stand guard against these despots.

Yet there are those who call this a good bill.

It is people like Senator Hubert Humphrey and other members of Americans for Democratic Action. It is people like Ralph McGill and other left-wing radical apologists.

They called it a good bill before it was amended to restore the right to trial by jury in certain cases.

Yet a Federal judge may still try one without a jury under the provisions of this bill. It was the same persons who said it was a good bill before the amendment pretending to forbid busing of pupils from neighborhood schools. Yet a Federal judge may still order busing from one neighborhood school to another. They have done it, they will continue to do it. As a matter of fact, it is but another evidence of the deceitful intent of the sponsors of this bill for them to claim that it accomplished any such thing.

It was left-wing radicals who led the fight in the Senate for the so-called civil rights bill now about to enslave our nation.

We find Senator Hubert Humphrey telling the people of the United States that "non-violent" demonstrations would continue to serve a good purpose through a "long, busy and constructive summer."

Yet this same Senator told the people of this country that passage of this monstrous bill would ease tensions and stop demonstrations.

This is the same Senator who has suggested, now that the Civil Rights Bill is passed, that the President call the fifty state Governors together to work out ways and means to enforce this rotten measure.

There is no need for him to call on me. I am not about to be a party to anything having to do with the law that is going to destroy individual freedom and liberty in this country.

I am having nothing to do with enforcing a law that will destroy our free enterprise system.

I am having nothing to do with enforcing a law that will destroy neighborhood schools.

I am having nothing to do with enforcing a law that will destroy the rights of private property.

I am having nothing to do with enforcing a law that destroys your right—and my right—to choose my neighbors—or to sell my house to whomever I choose.

I am having nothing to do with enforcing a law that destroys the labor seniority system.

I am having nothing to do with this so-called civil rights bill.

The liberal left-wingers have passed it. Now let them employ some pinknik social engineers in Washington, D.C., to figure out what to do with it.

The situation reminds me of the little boy looking at the blacksmith as he hammered a red-hot horseshoe into the proper shape. After minutes of hammering, the blacksmith took the horseshoe, splashed it into a tub of water and threw it steaming onto a sawdust pile. The little fellow picked up the horseshoe, dropped it quickly. "What's the matter, son," the blacksmith said, "is that shoe too hot to handle?" "No sir," the little boy said, "it just don't take me long to look at a horseshoe."

It's not going to take the people of this country long to look at the Civil Rights Bill, either. And they are going to discard it just as quickly as the little boy tossed away the still hot horseshoe.

But I am not here to talk about the separate provisions of the Federal Penal Code. I am here to talk about principles which have been overthrown by the enactment of this bill. The principles that you and I hold dear. The principles for which our forefathers fought and died to establish and to defend. The principles for which we came here to rededicate ourselves.

But before I get into that, let me point out one important fact. It would have been impossible for the American people to have been deceived by the sponsors of this bill had there been a responsible American press to tell the people exactly what the bill contained. If they had had the integrity and the guts to tell the truth, this bill would never have been enacted. Whoever heard of truth put to the worst in free and open encounter? We couldn't get the truth to the American people. You and I know that that's extremely difficult to do where our newspapers are owned by out-of-state interests. Newspapers which are run and operated by left-wing liberals, Communist sympathizers, and members of the Americans for Democratic Action and other Communist front organizations with high-sounding names.

However, we will not be intimidated by the vultures of the liberal left-wing press. We will not be deceived by their lies and distortions of truth. We will not be swayed by their brutal attacks upon the character and reputation of any honest citizen who dares stand up and fight for liberty.

And, we are not going to be influenced by intellectually bankrupt editors of the Atlanta Journal and Constitution, one of whom has presided over the dissolution of the once great Atlanta Constitution. We can understand his bitterness in his bleak failure, but we need not tolerate his vituperative and venomous attacks upon the integrity and character of our people. These editors, like many other left-wingers in the liberal press, are not influenced by tradition. Theirs is a tradition of scalawags. Their mealy-mouthed platitudes disgrace the honored memory of their predecessors—such men of character as Henry Grady, Joel Chandler Harris, and Clarke Howell, men who made the name of the Atlanta Constitution familiar in every household throughout the South. They are not worthy to shine the shoes of those great men.

In this connection I want to pay my highest respects and compliments to the dedicated men of Atlanta and of Georgia who gave to the people of their state what is destined to become the true voice of the south. I have reference to the great newspaper the *Atlanta Times*. It is a sad commentary on the period in which we live that it is necessary for the people of a great city to start their own newspaper in order to get the truth. I hope you have some success in this venture and I assure you that there will be many subscribers in the State of Alabama including myself.

As I have said before, that Federal Penal Code could never have been enacted into law if we had had a responsible press who was willing to tell the American people the truth about what it actually provides. Nor would we have had a bill had it not been for the United States Supreme Court.

Now on the subject of the court let me make it clear that I am not attacking any member of the United States Supreme Court as an individual. However, I do attack their decisions, I question their intelligence, their common sense and their judgment, I consider the Federal Judiciary system to be the greatest single threat to individual freedom and liberty in the United States today, and I'm going to take off the gloves in talking about these people.

There is only one word to describe the Federal judiciary today. That word is "lousy."

They assert more power than claimed by King George III, more power than Hitler, Mussolini, or Khrushchev ever had. They assert the power to declare unconstitutional our very thoughts. To create for us a system of moral and ethical values. To outlaw and declare unconstitutional, illegal, and immoral the customs, traditions, and beliefs of the people, and furthermore they assert the authority to enforce their decrees in all these subjects upon the American people without their consent.

This is a matter that has been of great concern to many legal authorities. The Council of State Governments composed of representatives of the fifty States sponsored the proposal just last year seeking to curb the powers of this body of judicial tyrants. The Conference of Chief Justices of all of the state Supreme Courts of this nation has also issued an historic statement urging judicial restraint upon the Court. This latter group said, "the value of a firm statement by us lies in the fact that we speak as members of all the state appellate courts with a background of many years experience in the determination of thousands of cases of all kinds. Surely there are those who will respect the declaration of what we believe."

"It has long been an American boast that we have a government of laws and not of men. We believe that any study of recent decisions of the supreme court will raise at least considerable doubt as to the validity of that boast."

In addition, the state legislatures have for years flooded the Congress with resolutions condemning usurpations of power by the Federal judiciary.

The court today, just as in 1776, is deaf to the voices of the people and their repeated entreaties: they have become arrogant, contemptuous, high-handed, and literal despots.

It has been said that power corrupts and absolute power corrupts absolutely. There was never greater evidence as to the proof of this statement than in the example of the present Federal Judiciary.

I want to touch upon just a few of the acts of tyranny which have been sanctioned by the United States Supreme Court and compare these acts with the acts of tyranny enumerated in the Declaration of Independence.

The colonists objected most strenuously to the imposition of taxes upon the people without their consent.

Today, the Federal judiciary asserts the same tyrannical power to levy taxes in Prince Edward County, Virginia, and without the consent of the people. Not only that, but they insist upon the power to tell the people for what purposes their money must be spent.

The colonists stated, "he has refused to pass other laws for the accommodation of large districts of people, unless those people would relinquish the right of representation in the legislature, a right inestimable to them and formidable to tyrants only." Today, the Federal judiciary, in one of its most recent decisions, has deprived the American people of the right to use the unit system of representation in their own state governments for the accommodation of large districts of people, and has itself prescribed the manner in which the people shall structure the legislative branch of their own government, and have prescribed how the people shall allocate the legislative powers of state government.

More than that they have even told the American people that we may not, with a majority of the people voting for the measure, or with two-thirds of those voting, or even if by unanimous consent, adopt a provision in our state constitutions to allocate the legislative power of state government in any manner other than as prescribed by the court.

One justice of the United States Supreme Court said in this connection, and I quote, "to put the matter plainly, there is nothing in all the history of this Court's decisions which supports this Constitutional rule. The Court's draconian pronouncement which makes unconstitutional the legislatures of most of the fifty states finds no support in the words of the constitution in any prior decision of this court or in the 175-year political history of our Federal union. These decisions mark a long step backward into the unhappy era where a majority of the members of this court were thought by many to have convinced themselves and each other that the demands of the constitution were to be measured not by what it says by their own notions of wise political theory." Two other Justices of the Court said, "such a massive repudiation of the experience of our whole past in asserting destructively novel Judicial power demands analysis of the role of this Court and our Constitutional scheme. . . . It may well impair the Court's position as the ultimate organ of the Supreme Law of the Land. . . ."

The only reason it is the Supreme Law of the Land today is because we have a President who cares so little for freedom that he would send the armed forces into the states to enforce the dictatorial decree.

Our colonial forefathers had something to say about that too. The Declaration of Independence cited as an act of tyranny the fact that, ". . . Kept among us in times of peace standing armies without the consent of the legislature." Today, 188 years later, we have actually witnessed the invasion of the State of Arkansas, Mississippi, and Alabama by the armed forces of the United States and maintained in the state against the will of the people and without consent of state legislatures. It is a form of tyranny worse than that of King George III who had sent mercenaries against the colonies because today the Federal Judicial tyrants have sanctioned the use of brother against brother and father against son by federalizing the National Guard.

In 1776 the colonists also complained that the monarch ". . . Has incited domestic insurrections among us." Today, we have absolute proof that the Federal Department of Justice has planned, supervised, financed and protected acts of insurrection in the southern states, resulting in vandalism, property damage, personal injury, and staggering expense to the states.

In 1776 it was charged that the monarchy had asserted power to ". . . Dissolve representative houses and to punish . . . For opposing with manly firmness his invasions of the rights of the people. . . ." Today, the Federal judiciary asserts the power not only to dissolve state legislatures but to create them and to dissolve all state laws and state judicial decrees, and to punish a state governor by trial without jury ". . . For opposing with manly firmness his invasions of the rights of the people. . . ."

The colonists also listed as acts of tyranny: ". . . The erection of a multitude of new offices and sent hither swarms of officers to harass our people and to eat out their substance . . . ;"

". . . Suspending our own legislatures and declaring themselves invested with the power to legislate for us in all cases whatsoever;"

". . . Abolishing the free system of the English laws . . .";

—it had "abdicated government here";

—refusing to assent to the laws enacted by the people, ". . . Laws considered most wholesome and necessary for the public good";

—and ". . . For depriving us in many cases, of the benefits of trial by jury . . . ; For taking away our charters, abolishing our most valuable laws, and altering fundamentally form of our government; for suspending our own legislatures and declaring themselves invested with power to legislate for us in all cases whatsoever."

The United States Supreme Court is guilty of each and every one of these acts of tyranny.

Therefore, I echo the sentiments of our forefathers who declared: "a prince, whose character is thus marked by every act which may define a tyrant, is unfit to be the ruler of a free people." Ladies and gentlemen, I have listed only a few of the many acts of tyranny which have been committed or specifically sanctioned by the United States Supreme Court. I feel it important that you should know and understand what it is that these people are trying to do. The written opinions of the court are filled with double talk, semantics, jargon, and meaningless phrases. The words they use are not important. The ideas that they represent are the things which count.

It is perfectly obvious from the left-wing liberal press and from the left-wing law journals that what the court is saying behind all the jargon is that they don't like our form of government. They think they can establish a better one. In order to do so it is necessary that they overthrow our existing form, destroy the democratic institutions created by the people, change the outlook, religion, and philosophy, and bring the whole area of human thought, aspiration, action and organization, under the absolute control of the court. Their decisions reveal this to be the goal of the liberal element on the court which is in a majority at present.

It has reached the point where one may no longer look to judicial decisions to determine what the court may do. However, it is possible to predict with accuracy the nature of the opinions to be rendered. One may find the answer in the Communist Manifesto. The Communists are dedicated to the overthrow of our form of government. They are dedicated to the destruction of the concept of private property. They are dedicated to the object of destroying religion as the basis of moral and ethical values. The Communists are determined that all natural resources shall be controlled by the central government, that all productive capacity of the nation shall be under the control of the central government, that the political sovereignty of the people shall be destroyed as an incident to control of local schools. It is their objective to capture the minds of our youth in order to indoctrinate them in what to think and not how to think.

I do not call the members of the United States Supreme Court Communists. But I do say, and I submit for your judgment the fact that every single decision of the court in the past ten years which related in any way to each of these objectives has been decided against freedom and in favor of tyranny.

A politician must stand on his record. Let the Court stand on its record. The record reveals, for the past number of years, that the chief, if not the only beneficiaries of the present Court's rulings, have been duly and lawfully convicted criminals, Communists, atheists, and clients of vociferous left-wing minority groups. You can't convict a Communist in our Federal court system. Neither can you convict one of being a Communist in Russia, China, or Cuba. The point is that the United States Supreme Court refuses to recognize the Communist conspiracy and their intent to "bury us."

Let us look at the record further with respect to the court's contribution to the destruction of the concept of God and the abolition of religion. The Federal court rules that your children shall not be permitted to read the Bible in our public school systems. Let me tell you this, though. We still read the Bible in Alabama schools and as long as I am governor we will continue to read the Bible no matter what the Supreme Court says. Federal courts will not convict a "demonstrator" invading and destroying private property. But the Federal courts rule you cannot say a simple "God is great, God is good, we thank Thee for our food," in kindergartens supported by public funds.

Now, let us examine the manner in which the Court has continuously chipped away at the concept of private property. It is contended by the left-wing liberals that private property is merely a legal fiction. That one has no inherent right to own and possess property. The courts have restricted and limited the right of acquisition of property in life and have decreed its disposition in death and have ruthlessly set aside the wills of the dead in order to attain social ends decreed by the court. The court has substituted its judgment for that of the testator based on social theory.

The courts assert authority even in decree the use of private cemeteries. They assert the right to convert a private place of business into a public place of business without the consent of the owner and without compensation to him. One justice asserts that the mere licensing of a business by the state is sufficient to convert it into control by the Federal judiciary as to its use and disposition. Another asserts that the guarantees of equal protection and due process of law cannot be extended to a corporation. In one instance, following the edicts of the United States Supreme Court, a state Supreme Court has ordered and directed a private citizen to sell his home to an individual contrary to the wishes of the owner.

In California we witnessed a state Supreme Court taking under advisement the question as to whether or not it will compel a bank to make a loan to an applicant on the basis of his race.

We have witnessed the sanction by the courts of confiscatory taxation.

Let us take a look at the attitude of the court with respect to the control of the private resources of the nation and the allocation of the productive capacity of the nation. The Supreme Court decisions have sanctioned enactment of the civil rights bill. What this bill actually does is to empower the United States government to reallocate the entire productive capacity of the agricultural economy covered by quotas and acreage allotments of various types on the basis of race, creed, color and national origin. It, in effect, places in the hands of the Federal government the right of a farmer to earn a living, making that right dependent upon the consent of the Federal government precisely as is the case in Russia. The power is there. I am not in the least impressed by the protestations that the government will use this power with benevolent discretion. We know that this bill authorizes the President of the United States to allocate all defense productive capacity of this country on the basis of race, creed, or color.

It does not matter in the least that he will make such allocations with restraint. The fact is that it is possible with a politically dominated agency to punish and to bankrupt and destroy any business that deals with the Federal government if it does not bow to the wishes and demands of the president of the United States.

All of us know what the court has done to capture the minds of our children. The Federal judiciary has asserted the authority to prescribe regulations with respect to the management, operation, and control of our local schools. The second Brown decision in the infamous school segregation case authorized Federal district courts to supervise such matters as teacher hiring, firing, promotion, the expenditure of local funds, both administratively and for capital improvements, additions, and renovations, the location of new schools, the drawing of school boundaries, busing and transportation of school children, and, believe it or not, it has asserted the right in the Federal judiciary to pass judgment upon the curricula adopted in local public schools. A comparatively recent Federal court decision in a Florida case actually entered an order embracing each and every one of these assertions of Federal supervision.

In ruling after ruling, the Supreme Court has overstepped its constitutional authority. While appearing to protect the people's interest, it has in reality become a judicial tyrant. It's the old pattern. The people always have some champion whom they set over them . . . And nurse into greatness. This, and no other, is the foot from which a tyrant springs, after first appearing as a protector.

This is another way of saying that the people never give up their liberties . . . And their freedom . . . But under some delusion.

But yet there is hope.

There is yet a spirit of resistance in this country which will not be oppressed. And it is awakening. And I am sure there is an abundance of good sense in this country which cannot be deceived. I have personal knowledge of this. Thirty-four percent of the Wisconsin Democrats supported the beliefs you and I uphold and expound.

Thirty percent of the Democrats in Indiana join us in fighting this grab for executive power by those now in control in Washington. And, listen to this, forty-three percent of the Democrats in Maryland, practically in view of the nation's capitol, believe as you and I believe.

So, let me say to you today. Take heart. Millions of Americans believe just as we in this great region of the United States believe.

I shall never forget last spring as I stood in the midst of a great throng of South Milwaukee supporters at one of the greatest political rallies I have ever witnessed. A fine-looking man grabbed my hand and said: "Governor, I've never been south of South Milwaukee, but I am a Southerner!" Of course, he was saying he believed in the principles and philosophy of the southern people . . . Of you here today and the people of my state of Alabama.

He was right. Being a southerner is no longer geographic. It's a philosophy and an attitude.

One destined to be a national philosophy—embraced by millions of Americans—which shall assume the mantle of leadership and steady a governmental structure in these days of crises.

Certainly I am a candidate for President of the United States.

If the left-wingers do not think I am serious—let them consider this. I am going to take our fight to the people—the court of public opinion—where truth and common sense will eventually prevail. At this time, I have definite, concrete plans to get presidential electors pledged to me on the ballots in the following states: Florida, Georgia, South Carolina, North Carolina, Virginia, New York, Indiana, Illinois, Wisconsin, Missouri, Kentucky, Arkansas, Tennessee, and of course Alabama, Mississippi and Louisiana. Other states are under serious consideration. A candidate for President must receive 270 electoral votes to win. The states I am definitely going to enter represent 218 electoral votes.

Conservatives of this nation constitute the balance of power in presidential elections. I am a conservative.

I intend to give the American people a clear choice. I welcome a fight between our philosophy and the liberal left-wing dogma which now threatens to engulf every man, woman, and child in the United States. I am in this race because I believe the American people have been pushed around long enough and that they, like you and I, are fed up with the continuing trend toward a socialist state which now subjects the individual to the dictates of an all-powerful central government.

I am running for President because I was born free. I want to remain free. I want your children and mine and our prosperity to be unencumbered by the manipulations of a soulless state. I intend to fight for a positive, affirmative program to restore constitutional government and to stop the senseless bloodletting now being performed on the body of liberty by those who lead us willingly and dangerously close to a totalitarian central government.

In our nation, man has always been sovereign and the state has been his servant. This philosophy has made the United States the greatest free nation in history. This freedom was not a gift. It was won by work, by sweat, by tears, by war, by whatever it took to be—and to remain free. Are we today less resolute, less determined and courageous than our fathers and our grandfathers? Are we to abandon this priceless heritage that has carried us to our present position of achievement and leadership? I say if we are to abandon our heritage, let it be done in the open and full knowledge of what we do.

We are not unmindful and careless of our future. We will not stand aside while our conscientious convictions tell us that a dictatorial Supreme Court has taken away our rights and our liberties. We will not stand idly by while the Supreme Court continues to invade the prerogatives left rightfully to the states by the constitution.

We must not be misled by left-wing incompetent news media that day after day feed us a diet of fantasy telling us we are bigots, racists and hate-mongers to oppose the destruction of the constitution and our nation.

A left-wing monster has risen up in this nation. It has invaded the government. It has invaded the news media. It has invaded the leadership of many of our churches. It has invaded every phase and aspect of the life of freedom-loving people. It consists of many and various and powerful interests, but it has combined into one massive drive and is held together by the cohesive power of the emotion, setting forth civil rights as supreme to all. But, in reality, it is a drive to destroy the rights of private property, to destroy the freedom and liberty of you and me. And, my friends, where there are no property rights, there are no human rights. Red China and Soviet Russia are prime examples.

Politically evil men have combined and arranged themselves against us. The good people of this nation must now associate themselves together, else we will fall one by one, an unpitied sacrifice in a struggle which threatens to engulf the entire nation.

We can win. We can control the election of the president in November.

Our object must be our country, our whole country and nothing but our country.

If we will stand together—the people of this state—the people of my state—the people throughout this great region—yes, throughout the United States—then we can be the balance of power. We can determine who will be the next president.

Georgia is a great state. Atlanta is a great city. I know you will demonstrate that greatness in November by joining Alabama and other states throughout the South in electing the next president of the United States. We are not going to change anything by sitting on our hands hoping that things will change for the better. Those who cherish individual freedom have a job to do.

First, let us let it be known that we intend to take the offensive and carry our fight for freedom across this nation. We will wield the power that is ours—the power of the people.

Let it be known that we will no longer tolerate the boot of tyranny. We will no longer hide our heads in the sand. We will reschool our thoughts in the lessons our forefathers knew so well.

We must destroy the power to dictate, to forbid, to require, to demand, to distribute, to edict, and to judge what is best and enforce that will of judgment upon free citizens.

We must revitalize a government founded in this nation on faith in God.

I ask that you join with me and that together, we give an active and courageous leadership to the millions of people throughout this nation who look with hope and faith to our fight to preserve our constitutional system of government with its guarantees of liberty and justice for all within the framework of our priceless freedoms.

Speech to the Joint Session of the Alabama Legislature, March 18, 1965

Governor Allen, Mr. Speaker, Senator Mathews and members of the Joint Session of the Legislature of Alabama assembled:

We see a most unprecedented order—unprecedented in the annals of American history having been rendered by a Federal Court here in Montgomery, Alabama.

We stopped the so-called march from Selma to Montgomery, Alabama, because we understood ourselves that at that time what a colossal undertaking it would be to provide safety and security, not only to the marchers but the vehicular traffic of the other citizens of this State and Nation who customarily used that highway.

To show you that we understood when others did not, and evidently the Federal Courts did not, I have a telegram in my hand from one of the leaders of the march that says we expect you to meet health and safety needs of 5,000 marchers.

This telegram addressed to me, the Governor of Alabama.

To meet health and safety needs of 5,000 marchers Sunday 21 of March, over 12 miles of U.S. Highway 380, of 300 marchers Monday 22, Tuesday, 23, Wednesday 24, and Thursday March 25 on the same highway to Montgomery; of 5,000–10,000 demonstrators who need some facilities within Montgomery, Thursday 25 on the final 4 miles to the State Capitol.

State responsibility can be met adequately by providing the following minimum needs: six equipped ambulances; two mobile aid stations; nine 300 gallon water trailers; portable toilet facilities; two rubbish disposal trucks and containers;

mobile radio communications for coordination; adequate medical personnel—physicians, nurses and aidmen; State control, protection and coordination of all above medical and public health activities. The original sent to Governor Wallace, copies to Hosea Williams, SCLC, Auburn Avenue, Atlanta; Col. Albert Lingo, Executive Offices of Alabama, State Troopers, State Capitol, Montgomery, Alabama; Dr. Fred Solomon, College of Medicine, Howard University, Washington, D.C.

Signed Aaron O. Wells, M.D., Medical Committee for Human Rights, Hosea Williams, Coordinator of March on Montgomery, Southern Christian Leadership Conference.

Great and dedicated men of the past worked diligently and honestly to establish the integrity and the justice of our court system.

From their work has come a faith by the people in the Courts and a dignity and respect accorded the courts that has been the rock upon which our house of freedom has rested—but of course that integrity and faith has been shaken in the last number of years.

Now they say our Courts are too slow. We must therefore submit to the speedier expedience of mob rule. That a Federal judge concurs and prostitutes our law in favor of that mob rule while hypocritically wearing the robes and clothed in the respect built by great and honest men is a tragedy and a sorrow beyond any words.

Here are a few examples of what Judge Johnson embraces as "peaceful demonstrations":

These demonstrators, wielding knives, have slashed the clothing of law enforcement officers. They have thrown bricks and bottles at law enforcement officers and at passing automobile, including a car driven by a member of the Alabama Legislature.

They have smashed windows, have invaded courtrooms in Perry and Dallas Counties. They have laid down in the streets, refusing to let even ambulances pass through. They have invaded the front yards and front porches of private homes and refused to move.

They have been granted the right to deny the use of public streets and sidewalks to other citizens to the exclusive use of the demonstrators.

They are mobs employing the street warfare tactics of the Communists and it is upon these people and upon their anarchy that a Federal judge, presiding over a mock court, places a stamp of approval as their "rights."

And now that Federal Judge compounds the anarchy by ordering the State of Alabama to protect this street army on its march from Selma.

Perhaps it would be well to see what plans were necessary for a one-day demonstration in Washington. Official sources tell us what the Federal Government did to keep the march on Washington peaceful.

Under military planning directed by Lt. Colonel John Downey, 4,000 combat troops including one Marine Battalion were stationed in Washington and maintained on an alert status.

In addition to these troops, the Army provided an additional 2,500 combat battalion troops which were held available at Army Posts on the outskirts of Washington.

Twenty-six teams of two to four men a team were assigned to selected areas of Washington for the purpose of observing and reporting any disorder.

All leave for members of the Police Department was canceled for the week of August 25 in order that the Force would be at its full strength of 2,900 men.

In addition 500 civilian reserves were on duty in outlying precincts to preserve the peace around the perimeter of the district.

In fact, without going into any more details it took nearly 30,000 people to provide a peaceful march of one day in Washington and it cost $805,000 for the one day in Washington.

We have reliable information that over 200 nationally known entertainers are coming into this state for this demonstration. The call has gone out from the demonstration leaders for every left-wing, pro-Communist, Fellow Traveler and Communist in the country to be here and we know that we can expect them along with the usual number of dupes and poor misguided individuals.

Any reasonable person can see that this well planned, well financed assault is going to be much more difficult to control than was the one-day march on Washington. May I remind you again that we have practically all of the same groups behind the Alabama demonstrations who planned and instigated the Washington march.

If this financial burden were imposed upon the State, the money would be taken from moneys which otherwise would be used for the care of our sick and infirm, both white and Negro—which would provide for the care of tuberculosis patients, both white and Negro—which provide for our program for aid to dependent children, the majority of whom are Negroes, and many other people of our State whose care and comfort and health depend on such funds.

It would cost an estimated $350,000 to $400,000 of state funds to handle this march completely by ourselves in this city.

We have 600 state troopers today who have been taken away from protecting the other people of our state in order to protect demonstrators and to police the areas in which they happen to be located.

I am sure that if the facts were known there are a number of Alabamians who have met their deaths on the highways because of the lack of protection in the last number of weeks—either from drunken drivers or careless drivers who would have been taken off the highways had the law enforcement officials been carrying on their normal duties.

We see today a foreign philosophy that says to the people, "You need not bother to work and meet qualifications of a free man. All you must do is demonstrate and cause chaos and create a situation whereby our propagandists, masquerading as newsmen, may destroy faith in local law enforcement so that we may take all police powers unto the central government."

That is the ominous price that the irresponsible demonstrators pay—many of them communist-trained to bring about such a development.

Such a development is taking place. And sadly, the Negroes used as tools in this traditional type of communist street warfare have no conception of the misery and slavery they are bringing to their children.

Before the Civil Rights Act was passed by Congress, Mr. Robert Kennedy said, "If we can just pass this Act, it will take the issues out of the streets and put them in the court." I said then it would do no such thing for the issue is but a single, clearly-defined issue—preservation or destruction of the United States of America.

There shall be no end to the street chaos—only temporary respites while the collectivist press builds up another phony issue by which the trained demonstrators may again take to the streets in riotous disorder.

I say to you tonight that the street warfare and demonstrations that once plagued Czechoslovakia, that ripped Cuba apart, that destroyed Diem in Vietnam, that raped China—that has torn civilization and established institutions of this world into bloody shreds, now courses through the streets of America, rips asunder the town of Selma and laps at the doorstep of every American, black and white.

I am the Governor of this State elected by you the people. I have fought for you and I have spoken across this land for you. I have kept faith with you.

Tonight I would like to offer words that are something more than words of alarm. Not that I have anything against proper alarm—for were it not for the alarm sounded by Patrick Henry, we might not tonight be products of a free people.

Tonight, I should like to ask you—the people of Alabama—for restraint. I am asking you to stay away from the points of tension if at all possible.

I do not ask you for cowardice but I ask you for restraint in the same tradition that our outnumbered forefathers followed. I ask you not to play into the hands of the enemies of our Nation and our freedom.

I ask you to hold firm and I ask you to exercise that superior discipline that is yours. I ask you to do if you will the same as you did when I stood at Tuscaloosa, Alabama. Please stay home. Let's have peace.

Outside the door of my office there stands a monument and on it these words are written:

> Fame's temple boasts no higher name,
> No king is grander on his throne;
> No glory shines with brighter gleam;
> The name of "Patriot" stands alone.

I ask you tonight for patriotism in its finest hour and its highest duty and I ask you too to restrain yourselves and I ask if at the time this march takes place if you will stay at your work bench, that you will stay at your home, and that you will let this matter be handled by those in authority.

Our security forces have today told us after thorough studies what it will take to police this march. For maximum security on a fifty-mile walk, when there was only 10 miles to be secured in Washington, it will take 2,057 personnel on a 24-hour shift, 163 cars and 15 buses.

It will take 4,114 men on a 12-hour shift and a like increase in the number of vehicles and on an 8-hour shift it will take 6,171 law enforcement personnel for maximum security.

For limited security on a 24-hour shift it will take 772 personnel—on a 12-hour shift, 1,544 and on an 8-hour shift, 2,314.

The other day the leader of the demonstrations said in an open Federal Court that "I will not obey an unjust order"—he said "the order issued to me by the Federal Court was unjust and I do not have to obey an unjust order."

I say this order is unjust—I say that many orders of the Federal Courts that have been issued are unjust. But whether they are unjust or not, if anarchy is not to prevail, we must obey even though it be galling.

Even though it provokes our heritage, we still must obey an order of a court when it becomes a final order.

So we will obey—we will do our duty. We will not abdicate our responsibilities to provide protection in as best as we can because that is the duty of your Governor and the State. I said on national television that we would obey court orders even though those who lead demonstrations say that they will decide whether the order is just or unjust. In view of the circumstances outlined and with awareness of the serious nature of this insensible burden placed on the State of Alabama, I intend to call on the President of the United States to provide sufficient federal civil authorities or officers to provide for the safety and welfare of the citizens in and along the route of the proposed march and to provide for the safety and welfare of the so-called demonstrators. I hope the Legislature of the State will approve.

The Federal courts have created this matter. They can help us out of the same. Let's you and I—the people of Alabama—see that this march is peaceful.

Let's show the people of this Nation our superior discipline in times of distress and then when this march has been concluded peacefully I shall ask, along with you, that those in authority who had influence upon these to ask for a cessation of these continuous demonstrations and let the Courts of this land decide the issues involved.

And I say to you in conclusion tonight that my prayers are that God will bless all the people of this great and sovereign state, both white and black, and say that our administration will continue to try to provide a better life for all the citizens of this state, regardless of their race, color, creed, religion or national origin.

I sincerely hope that the Legislature of this state and the people of Alabama will stand with me in this crisis that we face here in Alabama.

Stand Up for America: The 1968 Campaign Speech

Thank you very much ladies and gentlemen. And I am sure tonight that you have shaken the eyeteeth of the liberals of both national parties here in Memphis, Tennessee. I am sure from your attendance here tonight that those throughout the country know that the overwhelming majority of the American people are sick and tire of tweedle-dee and tweedle-dum. I'm very grateful to you folks for the fact that you have made it possible to be on the Tennessee ballot, by signing the petitions, so that you might have the opportunity and give opportunities to other Tennesseans to vote for this movement in November. So I want to thank you on the first public political appearance that I have made in the last several weeks, to tell you that I am appreciative of the fact that so many of you have thought of us in Alabama durin' the last several weeks and several months, and of course we are on a fund-raising drive and we appreciate the fact that you have contributed in that regard—because we don't have two national party treasure chests like the two national parties at the moment and so when they ask me at press conferences and on television and radio "where are you going to get the money to run for the Presidency?" and I think they've gotten that answer here in Tennessee from the average man on the street.

And there are millions of people in this country who think exactly as you do. If this were not true, and I have the experience, the reception necessary to make up my mind to run—all the way from Concord, California—I wouldn't be here on a political mission tonight. Because there's no need to butt your head against a brick wall. But I know the people in this region of the country are offerin' leadership to this movement which has millions of supporters from one end of the country to the other.

And I been from one end of the country to the other, and to California last year to comply with the California ballot law that said we must get 66,000 people to register in the American Independent Party to get on the ballot. And all the press—most of the press—and news media said "it can't be done," because the law was written to keep this movement off the ballot in California. We not only got 66,000 people who went and re-registered, we got 107,000 people who went and re-registered. An on May 4, in Texas, durin' their primary day and I believe ten candidates runnin' for Governor and other offices, the Texas law was changed to make it impossible to get on the ballot, in my judgment. 15,000 people had to go to the precinct conventions on the day of the primary, May 4, and no one knew where our precinct conventions were going to be held, because the other two parties held theirs at the courthouse and other public accommodation places, and so on May 4, election day in Texas, 2,000 more people attended the precinct conventions of the American Party in 30 counties than the combined total of the Republican and Democratic parties in 254 counties.

And some of the politicians in the state capitol of Austin, Texas, said a week before that, "We hadn't heard anything about this movement in Texas. But the other day the same politicians said, "We were surprised and shocked at the support this movement has." Well if they'll go out and ask the average man on the street in Texas or Memphis or any other city in the country, they'll find that there are millions, as I said a while ago, who think as we do.

The only thing I'm gonna say about race tonight is this: that I am grateful for the fact that the people in our state—of all races—and in this state have thought so much of me and my family during the last several weeks and several months. And in 1966 my wife was the candidate for Governor and had two opponents in the general election. And contrary to what I resent as portrayal of people like you and me as being racists and against people because of color, my wife received more Negro votes than did either one of her two opponents in the general election and over at Selma, Alabama, where they made a mountain out of a molehill because we maintained law and order, on election day half of those who voted were members of the Negro race—6,500 voters—my wife received 11,400 votes in round numbers to a combined total of 3,800 for her two opponents, and in the all-Negro precincts and ward in that city my wife received 87½% of the Negro vote. So we are not fighting to defend the system that has made it possible for people of all races, colors, creeds and religions and national origins to live in peace and freedom. When they say you and me are racist and a hate-monger and a fascist, it's because they cain't logically argue against the position we take. And so they write us off. And when

I was in California and made the announcement that we had made ballot position one newsman said, "Haven't you changed yo position? Don't you talk differently now than you used to?" I said, No, I talk basically the same as I did from the first day I got into politics, but you drew a conclusion in your mind about Tennesseeans and Alabam'ans and wrote it without listenin' to us and you didn't pay any attention to what we said in the past, but you've got to pay attention to what we say now." I invite the people in Memphis and Tennessee and the country of all races and colors to support us in November because we want to say the system that makes it possible for good people whoever they might be to live in peace and freedom and to restore back constitutional movement in this country.

Now what are we talkin' about and what are some of the issues in this country that confront people in Memphis? They have taken away the right of people to determine the policies of democratic domestic institutions. The National Democratic party and National Republican party both have drawn together to take away the right of people in Memphis to control the policies of their schools, the education of their children, to run their own hospitals, the seniority and apprenticeship list of their own labor unions, or their business and now recently, Democrats and Republicans in Congress, including some from your own state, have joined to pass a law, that will put you in jail without a trial by jury, because you don't want to sell or lease yo' property to somebody that they think you ought to sell or lease it to, and one of the first. . . . And you know, these national Republican leaders in Tennessee and throughout the country, they say, "You may take some votes away from the National Republican party and the National Democratic party might win." Well, if Mr. Nixon and Mr. Rockefeller stand for the same things that Mr. McCarthy and Mr. Humphrey stand for, what difference does it make who. . . . Now if you want to beat the National Democratic party for the sake of beating them, that's one thing. But if you want to beat them for the sake of changing trends in the country, that's another. And if you elect the National Republican party in November, one week after they are inaugurated you'll want to put them out and you'll have to wait four years to do it. Let's put 'em both out in November.

They not gonna get by with that. And they've looked down their noses at the average man on the street too long. They've looked at the bus driver, the truck driver, the beautician, the fireman, the policeman, and the steelworker, the plumber, and the communication worker and the oil worker and the little businessman and they say, "We've gotta write a guideline. We've gotta tell you when to get up in the mornin'. We've gotta tell you when to go to bed at night. And we gonna tell both national parties the average man on the street in Tennessee and Alabama and California don't need anybody to write him a guideline to tell him when to get up.

And you know, what do you hear from the liberals in Tennessee and the country? "We believe in free choice," they say. "Let every man choose." Well, we had a school system in Alabama that allowed people to choose to go to any school they want a go to regardless of their race or color. You had that in Tennessee. The Courts recently have stricken it down because they filed a court suit in which they said not enough people have chosen to go to school from this side of Los Angeles to this side of Los Angeles, and not enough people from this side of Memphis have chosen to go to school on this side of Memphis! And we said, "Well, they could choose if they so desired. What are we gonna do about that?" An' the Justice Department says "That's your problem." And the Federal court wrote a decision that's now been affirmed by the Fifth Circuit Court of Appeals and also the Supreme Court of our country that says that you can choose, if you choose properly, but if you don't choose right, we gonna choose fo you. They want you to choose if you choose correctly, but they look down they nose at Alabamians and Tennesseeans and the work'n man in California. And I want to say that one of the first things we going to do when we get into the White House, and we going to do it within the law, we going to turn back to you these domestic institutions.

In California, they voted on the matter of housin' not too long ago, in 1966, and the people of that state voted 4½ million to 2 million that they wanted to dispose of their property in the manner they saw fit. And the Supreme Court of your country said, "You cain't vote that way." And they struck it down. And the people of Oklahoma voted on the matter of apportionment of their legislature. And the Supreme Court said, "The people of Oklahoma cain't vote that way." Well, why cain't the people of California and Oklahoma and Tennessee vote to dispose of their property in the manner they see fit or apportion their legislature in the manner they see fit? It never has been unconstitutional for them to do that and it is not unconstitutional now, just because the Supreme Court of our country said so but they too can violate the law. And they have the power but they don't have the right. And recently they wrote a decision, the other day, in which they gave the police some authority [stop and frisk]. And you know why they wrote that decision? It's because of you who are assembled here. They are hearing from the people of this country and when they can change the law at their own whim, I say they go beyond the law and I'm gonna appoint some different sorts of judges when attrition takes its toll.

They say you cain't pray in a public school anymore—oh, that's violatin' the law, they say. And you know, the other day the Supreme Court of this country ruled that a communist can work in a defense plant without a security clearance and I wouldn't believe a communist with a security clearance, and when I get to be President—if you elect me President, I tell you what I'm gonna do. And I'm gonna do it within the law. I'm gonna take every communist out of every defense plant in Tennessee. Yes, we fight the communists in Southeast Asia and let 'em run wild in this country and if you don't think people aren't tired of it you oughta been with me in California. And you know when we were out in California we have a professor—I'm not talkin' about all professors, but here's an issue in the campaign—we got these pseudo-theoriticians, and these pseudo-social engineers that we find on some college campuses and we find in some pulpits and we find on some judges' benches and we find in some newspaper editors' offices—they guide line writers. They wanna tell you how to do. And those that write guidelines, some of 'em have pointed heads and cain't even park a bicycle straight. I'm not talkin' about the true intellectuals, we need true intellectuals in this country. I'm talkin' about the kind that assaults the Pentagon. I'm talking about those who lay on railroad tracks and stop defense shipments. I'm talkin' about those kind. And the folks in our country's sick and tired of those kind of folks, and when I was in California one UCLA professor, who made a speech derogatory of Alabamians in which they referred to us as rednecks—and I said, "Yes, our necks are red from workin' in the sun. I've seen some folks whose necks won't ever get red cause they've got too much hair on their necks."—You know he made a speech and he draws about $40,000 a year on the tax money in California, and I said "you hard-workin' taxpayers are payin' him $40,000 a year and he makes a speech in which he calls for the burnin' down of the city." He said he oughta burn this town down. And they say that's academic freedom and free speech. And I said, "I wanna tell you, the first public college professor in my state who makes a statement drawing tax money that he wants to burn the town down, my little wife's gonna fire him so fast he won't know what's struck him."

Another great issue that faces the American people is the breakdown of law and order. And you know those in high places in this country have helped to bring about the breakdown of law and order because they said we must remove the causes, we must remove the reasons, and the leadership of both national parties are sayin' we gotta remove the causes for the destruction of the internal security of our country, and I tell you that no small group of people in this country, regardless of who they happen to be, have the right to destroy the security of 200-odd millions of people in this country and do you know who's responsible for the breakdown of law and order in this country? It's those who want to lose the war in Viet Nam. It's militants, activists, revolutionaries, anarchists and communists, that's who. And I'm not talkin' about race. The overwhelmin' majority of the people in our country—of all races—are just as sick and tired of this breakdown of law and order as those of us who assemble here tonight. And yet I'm asked the question when you talk about law and order, and local government, the property ownership system, "Aren't you bein' a racist?" Well, it is a sad day in the country when you cain't talk about law and order unless they wanna call you a racist. I tell you that's not true and I resent it and they gonna have to pay attention 'cause all people in this country, in the great majority, the Supreme Court of our country has made it impossible to convict a criminal and if you walk out of this buildin' tonight, and someone knocks you in the haid, the person who knocked you in the haid will be out of jail before you get in the hospital, and on Monday they'll try the policeman if you don't watch out. I want to say that you in Memphis and wherever you might live, better be proud of the police and firemen in this country because I . . . One of the first things I'm gonna do if you elect me president is to give my moral support to the police of this country and tell them that I'm gonna give you the moral support of the President of the United States. We don't need any national police force. Just let the police in Memphis and Little Rock and Los Angeles and New York enforce the law like they know how to enforce it without fear or favor and we'll have peace in the land and you know it's a sad day in our country when people in high places cannot even run for public office without being slain. And yet we have heard people in high places speak that you've got a right to obey the laws you wanna obey and to disobey those you don't wanna obey. And if that prevails we'll have anarchy. I don't like some of the laws that they passed on us, and I don't like some of the court orders, but we got to obey them whether we like them or not. And one reason I'm runnin' for the Presidency is we gonna change some court orders and some laws in the proper constitutional manner.

You know, the president of our country—and even though I don't support President Johnson—he's the president of our country and he travels the length and breadth of this country, he did sometime ago, and whether we agree with him or not, and I've always been opposed to him politically, but he is the president and he is entitled to the respect that office is due. Not only personal respect, but he is entitled to respect as the president of our country. And yet he went to California not so long ago, and while he was there his personal safety was impaired, his life was impaired and threatened, and when he went to the cardinal's funeral in New York some time ago, he had to go in the side door because a group of anarchists threatening the personal safety of the President of the United States. And when he was in California a group of anarchists lay down in front of his automobile. I want to tell you as I said on television the other night, you elect me the president, and I go to California, or I come to Tennessee, and a group of anarchists lay down in front of my automobile, it's gonna be the last one they ever gonna wanna lay down in front of. And yet we find today some of these politicians on the national scene that all of a sudden are talking about law and order themselves and you know down in Selma, Alabama, the *Washington Post* they wrote about what a great holy crusade it was—to come down a group of anarchists of all races, to impair the safety of people in Selma. To block trade, commerce and traffic. Yet the other day when I announced for the presidency in Washington, D.C., the *Washington Post* had an editorial in which they said we shouldn't let them come to this town and block out trade and commerce, we ought to put a stop to it. Well, they advocated the breakdown of law and order in Selma, they created themselves a Frankenstein and now they callin' on help and you and me gonna help Washington and Selma in November.

Hypocrites? You got more hypocrites there than any place I know. And in Berkeley, they talked about open housin' there, y'know everybody had a runnin' academic fit about open housin'. They voted on it twice in Berkeley and voted against it, so you see hypocrisy, bad faith, and lack of candor hasn't helped race relations in our country but it has hurt them. And I say we ought to be honest with people, and that's the reason I believe that people of all races are eventually gonna support this movement, because they'd rather have somebody honest talking; to them than some hypocritical liberal who lives in Washington.

You know, I can remember not long ago in Detroit, Michigan, when you talk about the breakdown of law and order, Governor Romney said, "President Johnson didn't send troops on time." President Johnson said, "You didn't ask for 'em on time." Governor Romney says, "They too many papers to fill out." President Johnson says, "You didn't fill out enough papers." And then my wife gets a telegram from Mr. Ramsey Clark, who's another advocate of the breakdown of law and order, unwittingly maybe, wrote my wife a letter, two pages, explaining to her how you have to go about gettin' federal troops in case of the breakdown of domestic tranquility. You got to hold up your right hand and swear before so many notary publics; you got to hold your left hand and swear to satisfy the left-wingers in the country; and you got to fill out duplicate copies to one bureau, triplicate copies to another, quintipulet copies to another, and octopulet copies to another. And my wife says, "you know, this is amusin' and confusin', George, how difficult it is to get troops! I remember we got 'em in Alabama, Arkansas and Mississippi and didn't even ask for 'em." They thought it was politically expedient to violate the Constitution insofar as Alabama was concerned, but they're finding now that it's not expedient to violate it even insofar as a deep southern state is concerned.

And another issue, and there are many issues in the campaign, that we'll develop as we go along, is our involvement in Southeast Asia. And I don't impugn anybody's motives in the top echelons of our government. I have been to classified and confidential briefin's when I was Governor of Alabama with other governors, the cabinet of the President, the President, the Vice President, and the Joint Chiefs of Staff. It is a frustrating and exasperating experience, the matter of Vietnam. And there is no simple, utopian solution to our involvement there. There are several things we should have learned about this involvement. Is that we should never have become involved by ourselves, because it is just as much to the interests of Western Europe and the non-communist nations of Asia to defend against communist aggression as it is for the United States and we should have looked them in the face.

And whether you agree with our involvement or not, we've got 500,000 American servicemen and other allied servicemen who are totally committed between life and death at this very minute, and some of them are bein' killed in Southeast Asia and so we should look our European allies in the face and say, "We need you and you need us. But our nuclear shield is your deterrent to communist aggression. We know that Eastern European nations were lost and sold out evidently at Yalta, but Western Europe, we stabilized you after the war, we loaned you money, we built back your industries and glad we stabilized you because you have been in a stabilized position, a deterrent to further communist aggression." And we should tell our neighbors in Asia the same thing. "But you gonna help us, and you gonna go with us, and if you don't help us and you don't go with us and don't quit tradin' with the North Vietnamese and the communist enemies of ours, we not only gonna cut off foreign aid, but we gonna make you pay back every dime that you borrowed from us."

And advise Mr. DeGaulle who's been flirtin' with the communists and they are now about to stab him in the back, you cain't deal with the communists except from a position of strength and I'm not talkin' about rattlin' sabers and rockets, I'm talkin' about bein' strong fiscally, economically, industrially, agriculturally, militarily because that in itself is a deterrent to a possible third world war. But Mr. DeGaulle evidently has seen the British pound devalued because of socialistic overspending, spending which has brought no return to the British people. I'm not against spending money. I believe in spending money. The government oughta build schools and roads and harbors—that is an investment. When I was governor of our state, and durin' my late wife's administration, we had the largest highway program in Alabama's history, the largest hospital program, we had the largest school program with more colleges and trade schools built to serve the average citizen of our state of all races than at any time in our history. And we borrowed some money to do some of these things with. But we didn't borrow any money to build bridges in Cuba; we didn't borrow any money to build any bridges in Yugoslavia; we built them in Alabama and there's a real difference. And Mr. DeGaulle evidently wants to see the American dollar devalued, which has been devalued enough through inflationary processes in our country. When he has some dollars he wants to drain our gold out. And so, we find that he gets hundred-million here and a hundred-million there. We ought to tell Mr. DeGaulle, "If you gonna keep on takin' gold fo' yo' dollahs when you don't have to, we gonna do some old cab-drivin' logic in our business relations with you which would be just as good or better than some of the pseudo-theoreticians logic"—I used to be a cab driver in college, is the reason I say cab-drivin' logic. Their fierce contact with life teaches them some things that some of our pseudo-social-engineers never learn, in college, and so, what I would do, I would just say, "You owe us 7 billion dollahs from World War I and write it up on the wall—7 billion dollahs— and when you wanted 100 million in gold we'd just put 100 million under it and subtract it and say you owe us six billion, nine hundred million." They say it's so complicated and it really isn't all that complicated, we just need some common sense in some of the decisions of our government.

I sincerely hope that the negotiations bein' carried on in France are fruitful and that we have an honorable peace. I hope that, and I pray for that, and you do too. But one way that I think we can help conclude this war, if it has to commence on a large scale because they break down, is that we should stop the morale buildup by the communists in our own country. When we say, today, academic freedom, and free speech and the right of dissent, give people the right to advocate treason, it's not dissent. Land you know you have a right to dissent about the war, and you have a right to say that I don't think we ought to be in the war, if that's the way you feel. Because that is free speech, and that is a freedom we possess. But every man on the street understands the difference between honest dissent and that which is not honest. And when a professor at Berkeley, the University of California, rises and makes a speech and says let us organize a freedom brigade and go fight the American imperialist soldiers in Southeast Asia and they print that in Hanoi, Peking and Moscow, and boost the morale of the communists who then kill some more American troops and then up at Rutgers University one—and many have said this— "I long for a communist victory" he says, and when they said, "Do you want to fire this man?" They said "Academic freedom!" We going to de- stroy academic freedom in this country if we continue to abuse it and if you'll elect me the president, the first thing I'm gonna do, is have my attorney general to call for an indictment against any one callin' for com- munist victory and we see if we can't put 'em under a good jail. There is a great difference in honest dissent and an overt act of treason and when I've said that in some places they've said, "Wallace would jail the Senate." I never said any such thing. I said that I would jail traitors, and dissenters are . . . entirely . . . two different definitions as far as I'm personally con- cerned. Yes, and you find also on some college campuses in our country organizations raisin' money, blood and clothes for the Viet Cong com- munists and flyin' the V.C. flag and they say, "Well, that's dissent. That's academic freedom." And I say that a few of them ought to be dragged by the hair on their heads and stuck under a good jail and that would stop that and that's what we are gonna do when I get to be president.

When I was out in California they was gonna raise everything under the sun against this movement cause they are disturbed now about it, about this movement, and after this crowd here in Memphis they gonna be doubly disturbed. When I was out in Los Angeles they had to write that Wallace flies the Confederate flag on the capital—like we didn't fly the American flag. Well, no flag flies higher in the hearts of Alabamians and Tennesseeans than the American flag. But one reason we love the American flag is because it embraces the flags of all our states and the flags of our heritage, which includes the flag of the Confederacy. We flew the Confederate flag to commemorate the centennial of the War between the States. And the American flag flies on the same spot on the capital grounds in Alabama since the year 1917—before I was born. And a contingency of Ohio troops put the flag up. And they put it in the wrong place—it was Ohio folks that did it—and what I said in California—we might fly the Confederate flag, but there's one thing for sure. Where you see the Confederate flag flyin' you won't see any Viet Cong flags flyin'. And you won't see anybody raisin' money and blood and clothes for the communists. Land I am proud of the condition of support for our country in Tennessee and our great section of the country and in the Volunteer State.

Now, you know while I was out there they talked about napalm, and I want to tell you this. I don't want to hold you here too long because [Some in crowd yell back "NO! NO!"] you been here a long time but let me tell you this, while I was in California a group of folks was marchin' on all the college campuses sayin' we ought not to have napalm and we against killin' civilians. Well, I'm against killin' civilians, too, and I'm sorry that any civilian is killed in any war. But the communists cause the killing of civilians, not the people of our country. Were it not for the communists no civilians would be bein' killed any place—not in Southeast Asia or any place else. But during World War II, my young friends who might attend college who are here tonight, when you hear somebody stand up and beat his chest and say we got to stop killin' civilians in Hanoi, and his organization has opposed the dropping of napalm, you ask him what his organization said durin' World War II when were on the same side as the communists and you know the communist *Daily Worker* and every front organization in Tennessee and California said we ought not to be in this war. That's when Germany and Russia were at peace with each other. But the day after the night that Germany invaded Russia, the communist *Daily Worker* and every front organization came out and said we must join this war and defend and fight this war, and we did fight, and I was against Nazism because it's just as mean and terrible as communism, and we fought Nazism but we were on the same side and we saved the communist system at Leningrad, at Stalingrad, with 10 billion dollars of materials manufactured in Tennessee and Alabama. And every time we dropped a thousand tons of bombs on Tokyo, Berlin, and Rome, these same groups who today decry the bombing of cities said "Bomb 'em some mo. Kill all the civilians in these countries." So when they tell you, my young friends, they don't want any civilians killed, they talking about civilians in the communists' capitols. They didn't mind killin' all the civilians in the non-communist capitols of the world in fightin' Russia. So when they tell you they for peace and for civilians, they lyin' to you. And if you pay any attention to them and you an objective person, you gonna wake up short one day because they not one ounce of truth in any organization in the country that advocates the breakdown of law and order on the one hand and their leaders then wind up in Hanoi, Peking and Moscow. And have you seen the likes in this country of people in high places winin' and dinin' folks who advocate the breakdown of law and order and then themselves wind up some place callin' for communist victory. I don't understand it, and people in Tennessee don't understand it and so they going to get the ax in November.

So you know they say if you run for the presidency, can you win? Well, let me tell you this. It doesn't take but a plurality to win when three or more are runnin'. In our electoral college system that Senator Dirksen said the other day, "We going to have to change this thing on account of this Wallace fellow." We at least got 'em talkin' about changing the Constitution which is something that no movement in the country like this has ever done before. But you know if I get 34% of the vote in Tennessee and the other two parties get 33% apiece, then we win the electoral vote of the state. You can win without a majority. Not that we don't have a majority viewpoint, but it is a political fact that you can win on less than a majority.

And you know I went to Wisconsin four years ago with all these things they said about me, with no time and no money and no organization, and we got 35% of the vote in the Democratic primary in Wisconsin four years ago; and we got 30% in Indiana and got 44% in Maryland and they counted the votes. I don't know how many I'd have gotten if I'd counted them myself.

You know this was on a television show, from one of our speeches but I's like to tell it again. You know we were leading in Maryland with no organization, just the grass roots people, but we were leading in that state about 8 or 9 o'clock that night with about several hundred thousand votes already reported and they called the mayor of Baltimore on the television and he as a big-time politician, naturally. They said, "What do you think about it?" And of course he said, "It's a sad day in the free State of Maryland!" He said, "We won't ever live this down if we exist another thousand years! What has come over the people of the free state of Maryland?" Well, if he'd gone out and asked a good cab driver he could of told him but they don't ask cab drivers anymore, they ask some fella like I said a moment ago, who cain't park his bicycle straight. About that time there was a request for a recapitulation of the vote. Well, bein' from Alabama, I wasn't sure what recapitulation was. But I knew I was goin' to find out. And about 10 o'clock the head recapitulator of Maryland came on the television and he said "We have had a request for recapitulation. And we have thoroughly recapitulated and upon this recapitulation Governor Wallace is now behind." I'm not quite sure what it is yet, but if anybody in Memphis ever tells you they gonna recapitulate on you, you better watch 'em, they gonna do somethin' to you.

We've learned how to recapitulate ourselves and we've learned many things since 1964 and they've learned a lot of things about us. And to those Republicans who say "you might cause us to lose," let me say that I withdrew in 1964 from those states I was qualified in because I didn't want to split the vote up and I withdrew, and they ran a poor campaign as you know. So since the Gallup poll the other day showed that there are more independent voters than there are Republican voters, maybe somebody ought to withdraw for us.

And remember this also, they've talked about the people of our nation, they've talked about throwin' it into the House. Well, we're not runnin' to throw it into the House. We're running to win. But that question comes up and the only time I answer it is that it's asked. But if it were thrown into the House and no one got a majority in the electoral college, since both parties stand for the same identical philosophy, we have nothing to lose and everything to gain. And so, don't let 'em talk that to you in the newspapers. And remember this, they keep talkin' about our people are sick in the country. They say our people are sick. The people of our nation are as good and fine a people as ever populated the Unites States and I'm tired—I tell you who's sick. It's some of the leadership in this country that's sick. When the newspapers, the *Washington Post,* and the *New York Times,* and the *Milwaukee Journal* and the other large newspapers when they write an editorial about you and me you remember that the editorial writer's one man and you are one man and you one woman and your attitude and mine is just as good about these matters or better as theirs. So, don't let that worry you when they tell you that some newspaper said—well, you said so and you represent just as many votes as the editor of any newspaper in the country good or bad. And let me tell you this— they are not always right. I remember when Mao Tse Tung was comin' to power in China. What did the *New York Times* and the *Newsweek* and the *Time* magazine that makes fun of people even in death—yeah that's what they do and I resent that too, if you want to know the truth about it. They said, they said Mao Tse Tung is an agrarian reformer, he wants to help the poor people of China and Chiang Kai-Shek oughta be thrown out. It turned out they were mistaken. Mao Tse Tung was a communist who wanted to destroy the United States and so they were not right then, were they? And many people in the armed services while they was in the South Pacific they knew from private to general that Mao Tse Tung was a communist but not the smart folk who sometimes try to mold public opinion in this country, they didn't see that from their ivory towers; and when Ben Bella was down there in Algeria they said the same things—"He's a good man"—he turned out to be a communist. And when Castro was in the hills of Cuba they brought him up to Washington and New York and they introduced him on national television as the George Washington of Cuba and he was said by the *New York Times* to be the Robin Hood of the Caribbean. And every cab driver in Alabama said he was a communist. By instinct, they knew. And they always right.

And so my friends, as one writer has said, the people of this nation look to the soul of the South to help place this nation back on the road to sanity. And there are millions of people who are as good as we in other parts of the country but their leadership has let them down. And they lookin' to us. And if you don't believe it you go with me to Milwaukee or to Escanaha, Michigan, to Macomb, Ohio, to Tacoma, Washington, to Fontana, California, you can see that they dependin' on you. And I again say that my prayer is, as I said in the opening of the end of my Inaugural address when I was inaugurated Governor of Alabama, that God would bless all of the people of this state and of this country, regardless of their race or color. And I'll tell you what you do, if you'll go out and work for us from now on till this campaign's over, I'll come back to Tennessee prior to the election and you and me together will continue to shake the eyeteeth of the liberals in both national parties. Thank you all very much.

Send Them a Message: The 1972 Campaign Speech

The people of Florida, many who come from all over the United States and thus represent a cross section of American public opinion, have a unique opportunity. They can start the grass roots movement to take back the National Democratic Party unto themselves. Too long this party has been controlled by the so-called intellectual snobs who feel that big government should control the lives of American citizens from the cradle to the grave. The people want to be left alone from the unnecessary control of big government. As a candidate for the Democratic Party nomination, I ask for the support of Floridians whether white or black, rich or poor, whether they belong to management, labor or business, or whether they are in active pursuits or retired, whether they are native born citizens or citizens by choice. Yes, our offering is a new beginning of hope for the American people.

The essential stands I take among others will be: peace through strength; superior offensive and defensive capabilities of our military forces second to none; then we will always be in a position to negotiate with our enemies.

A continuation of a viable space program which is tied directly to national defense.

A fair tax system that levies taxes on the multi-billion and multi-million dollar foundations which are now virtually tax exempt, whose purposes are other than strictly charitable. The levying of taxes upon the estimated 150 billion dollars' worth of church commercial property now in competition with businesses and industries in our free enterprise system.

A reduction in taxes for the individual and businesses and industry to be replaced with revenues from those now evading taxes through special laws passed in their special interests. This will put people back to work because the demand for consumer goods by individuals will stimulate production activity. This should be of the highest priority. Get people back to work.

Protection of the social security trust fund from other uses so that pensions can be raised and social security taxes reduced on individuals and those whose incomes are low.

The discontinuance of foreign aid programs except where determined to be in our national interest, and no foreign aid to Communist countries or those countries who aid the Communists.

Continued withdrawal from Vietnam and never again commit American troops to fight a no win war. No recognition of Castro Cuba.

Curtailment of Federal spending to bring about a balanced budget.

A farm program that will not have the farmer at the bottom of the economic ladder as he is now.

Reasonable restriction, but not prohibiting the investment of American capital to build plants in foreign countries when the loss of jobs to American workers in those plants not built are relocated abroad was not offset by gains to the overall economy of the Nation and to the Nation's work force.

The restoration of our maritime fleet to the position of No. 1 in the world.

A return to law and order. Action by the Federal Government in its proper role in cooperation with the States and political subdivisions to make it safe to walk on the streets of the cities of our nation and for the curtailment of other criminal activities and 100% support for the law enforcement personnel and firemen of the Nation.

The appointment of Judges to the Supreme Court who will not decree their own political, social and economic philosophy into court-made law.

A reasonable welfare program for those who are disabled and blind and handicapped and for the elderly, but a curtailment of welfare programs that are designed to pay able-bodied individuals not to work.

The return to local control of public education on a nondiscriminatory basis. A return to freedom of choice and the neighborhood school concept. A complete halt to involuntary busing to achieve a sort of balance, and the reopening of schools now closed under Federal Court orders, HEW [Health, Education and Welfare] departmental regulations and/or by action of the Justice Department where such openings are desired by the citizens and officials of the States and/or local school districts.

Those in this campaign who have served in the Congress of the United States have had their opportunity to keep our military strength superior but have either failed in their efforts or have supported a weakened military posture.

They have made no significant effort to tax those ultra-rich who escape taxation and give relief to lower income groups proportionately.

They have failed to keep social security taxes reasonable and to give meaningful social security benefits to those entitled, especially to our senior citizens.

They have voted to give away our money by the billions to those who not only did not appreciate it, but who in many cases worked against the interests of the United States. They voted to give aid to our Communist enemies and those who were aiding the Communists.

We are the leaders of the free world, but we cannot act as the world's policemen. We should require our allies in the NATO Alliances and other parts of the world to shoulder a larger burden of the manpower requirements and cost involved in these alliances. We do not have sufficient manpower to shoulder over and above our share of thee burden, and the cost over the years has aided in bringing on our balance of payment problem which threatens our economic well being and the economic stability of the free world.

Those who were in the Congress at the time did not support a win-the-war policy in Vietnam or their influence in such direction was nil.

They all support the recognition of Red China, which means they would, in my opinion, recognize Castro Cuba.

They have supported every liberal give-away program that brought no return to the American people but has debauched our money and resulted in economic controls on management and labor and resulted in the highest deficit spending in our history which is the prime cause of inflation.

They took no effective action to curtail the loss of American worker jobs to cheap foreign labor.

They were serving in the Congress and at the same time presiding over the relegation of our maritime fleet to a position below that of other great powers.

They served in the Congress while crime grew to run rampant in the Country and saw it rise every year in the Nation's Capitol to the point where it is unsafe for even them to walk much less ride in the streets of Washington, D.C. Those in the Senate who are candidates voted against the nominee to the Supreme Court from Florida because, in my opinion, he thought and expressed himself as an average Floridian, and that is unthinkable, so they think. If a Floridian is not good enough for the Supreme Court, then maybe their thinking is not good enough for Floridians.

Those candidates in this race from the Senate either voted or supported, and it is a matter of record, to bus little children in Florida to achieve racial balance. They voted or supported to a man the destruction of neighborhood schools—they voted or supported to a man destruction of freedom of choice in the public schools and voted against an amendment to treat States outside of the South the same as Southern States are treated relative to public schools.

Therefore, these candidates who serve in the Congress and who did serve there have voted in a great majority of cases opposite to the way most Floridians in the Congress voted and opposite to the way the overwhelming majority of Floridians would have voted had they been members of the Congress. They have helped to bring about the ills we now suffer. But now they tell us that they want to save us from their own deeds.

This senseless business of trifling with the health and safety of your child, regardless of his color, by busing him across state lines, and city lines and into kingdom come has got to go. I said many years ago, if we don't stop the Federal takeover of the schools, there'd be chaos. Well, what've we got? Chaos.

This thing they've come up with of busing little children to schools is the most atrocious, callous, cruel, asinine thing you can do for little children. These pluperfect hypocrites who live in Maryland or Virginia and they've got their children in a private school. Well on election day the chickens are coming home to roost. They gonna be sorry they bused your little children and had something to do with it. So, my friends on election day you give 'em a good jolt. You give 'em the St. Vitus Dance.

Trust the People: The 1976 Campaign Speech

By the thousands, Americans write to me each week. They are concerned. And rightly so.

They are justly proud of our American heritage. They know to lose our heritage would be to surrender all that is sacred. They know now more than ever we must be wise and strong.

They know our nation is surrounded on all sides by great mountains of accumulated troubles. They don't like the looks of what's happening to us.

They know America has ended up on a road that seems to lead us only to dead ends and blind passageways.

They want to get America on the right road to achieve new greatness in meeting the challenges of our times.

They believe—as I believe—that the challenges of our times can be met by a determined America whose policy is fairness and firmness and who will get about the business of putting our house in order before it is too late.

They want strong, honest and unblinking leaders with salt in their blood to guide our dreams into reality and to clear the skies of the darkness of international fumbling and internal deterioration.

They want leaders to fill the gap between promises and performances with action for America. Men who when faced in a pinch with political consequences will not yield. Men who can recognize a diplomatic double cross before it hits us. Men with backbone who do not go kowtowing off to our enemies in a show of spineless weakness.

They want a return of local government without the octopus confusion and complexities of a federal government to frustrate them with bureaucratic strings attached to money that belongs to the taxpayers.

They want to be rid of the frustrated feeling that they are a statistic devoid of personality or freedoms in a federal government computer to be checked on by bureaucrats at their whim and will.

They want to determine their lives and the lives of their families without the frustration of federally-appointed judges to determine their future and their children's future for them.

They want to find a way for local government and state government to continue to exist without bankruptcy and without breaking the back of the taxpayer in ever increasing sales tax and property taxes.

They want to have their share in America and in what America is doing without the frustration of the political ransom of their votes for attention.

They want America to quit wasting millions of dollars in a UN experiment that has never produced peace and where the show goes on to embarrass and downgrade our country's prestige.

They want realistic hope to clutch to their hearts in these critical times and a sense of security that our national leaders are guiding our nation in the right direction and not falling for trickery.

They want to be rid of the feeling that they don't count and that what they think won't change anything in a society where they do count and their thoughts should guide our nation.

When all about rages a never-ending storm of permissiveness, inflation, crime, social disturbances, economic problems and despair, they want to think there's a new day ahead for America.

They are not so naive as to think things will ever be like a "they lived happily after" fairy tale. What they seek is reasonable and within our grasp. They want security and a job without fear they will lose it. They want to be able to count on something.

I say these Americans and all Americans are entitled to all of this.

A new day when our government and our national leaders will trust the people and they can be trusted by the people.

A new day when men and women are free in the true sense that they may plan their lives without direction and ruling by a bureaucratic government far removed from their lives.

A new day of law and order and an atmosphere of decency for us to raise our children into decent men and women.

A new day when we can end the epidemic of inflationary frustration and doubt and apathy and hopelessness that clutches America at the throat.

We have watched as a whole new cast of names and faces have come on the stage in the leadership of our government. They were to be different but nothing has really changed. The script is unchanged with the same old lines. Only the actors are different. It is the old politics at work with new faces.

We have watched national leaders play trial and error political games with our lives while they offer up hollow hopes of brighter things that never seem to come.

We have watched the hypocrisy of our national leaders who speak one way and act another in search of votes while our lives are jolted and jarred by their own appointees and by federal judges with politically-motivated edicts that choke hope and destroy happiness in the name of justice and undermine the foundation of our rights.

We have seen our national leaders drag out old political policies and parade them before the American people as new dreams when, in fact, they are the same old nightmares.

We have heard them talk of change. But let's not fool ourselves. The change of which they speak is forced upon the majority and is always at the expense of the majority and in the name of so-called progress.

It's the average citizens who pay the bill. The truth is the politicians often think there is a silent majority because they are too involved in listening to the pressure groups to hear the loud roar of the majority crying out across this land for an answer to what ails America.

When they ignore the majority, they destroy the people's hopes for the best government and add to the frustration that big government and big bureaucracy have overwhelmed them with. I believe as the majority of Americans believe, that government closest to the people is the best government. The best government cannot exist if the majority is silent. Government of the people, by the people and for the people becomes a hollow nothing if the majority is, indeed, silent.

We have watched our national leaders attempt to lull our people into a false sense of security while they play politics with the nation's safety and prestige as they go kowtowing to Peking and Moscow backed up by the biggest public relations buildup since Barnum.

We have watched as they try to convince the people we can do business with Communists and come out with something for the free world. All the while history tells a different story. Yalta and Berlin and Hungary and Korea and Vietnam and Cuba and the Paris Peace Talks proved that it is the impossible dream that we can do business with Communists bent on world domination and come out with something for the free world. Yet they offer up the impossible dream as hope to a people reaching out for any light out of the darkness into which these leaders plunged America.

We've got to have the wisdom to junk the Old Politics of the last two decades that have blindly led on to dead-end roads of doubt, disaster, drift, despair and defeat at home and abroad.

We've got to have the wisdom and strength to win us respect among all nations and all peopled of the world without buying friends that double cross us. We've got to make prosperity and opportunity real in America without bureaucratic interference in our lives. We've got to let the American worker know he is not neglected and let the American family be safe and secure in the happiness of the home and raise up realistic hope for all our people, rich and poor, young and old, black and white. We've got to provide a decent standard of living for every American and job security in America's capacity for greatness.

We've got to cancel out the Old Politics that believes we can support the whole world and police the whole world and still be strong ourselves for if our strength is sapped again and again we will end up weak and enslaved.

We've got to have a clean start where the people are trusted and the government is trusted for we have paid the full price for half truths and deceptions that have led us to the brink of disaster.

We've got to cure our land of the crippling paralysis of apathy and once again bring our people back into a government that is personal and close to their needs and wishes.

We've got to have a strong faith in God in whom we will trust to meet all challenges to our liberty and freedoms.

We've got to have a total and irreversible commitment to America.

That is not too much to ask. It is the real hope and the real dream for which the majority yearn in the light of what is happening to us.

America must be saved. America will not be saved by those who cry wolf in the street or by those who offer hope with hands tainted with political shame or by those who offer false dreams that become nightmares or by those who simply do not love America.

America will be saved by decent men and women who dare to dream the decent dream of a decent America.

America will be saved by the courage and wisdom of men and women who believe in a government of the people, by the people and for the people and not in a government of the government by the government and for the government.

I believe we can cure what ails America. But to cure America, we've got to bring the majority of Americans back into the mainstream of American government.

We can bridge the gap from darkness to a new dawn of greater things for America when all of us lock hands together to stand up for America and get involved in America.

There is no other way. United in a common cause, in a clean start with real hope, I believe all things are possible for America against all odds and all enemies.

I believe together with God on our side, we can cure what ails America.

Then we must make certain we will never let our country get in this shape again.

This is the course I believe America must follow and this is what I will work for in 1976 as a spokesman for average citizens who support our cause to restore America.

Retirement Speech,
April 12, 1986

I come before you this afternoon with great humility and with deep appreciation to the people of Alabama. They have honored me and my family like no man or no family has ever been honored in the history of this state.

To be elected governor for even one term is the highest honor the people could bestow. But to be elected to serve four terms, and for the people to elect my wife Lurleen, also as governor is an honor without equal. And I can never begin to repay the people of this state for the confidence they have shown in me and my family for almost three decades.

Together, we have shared good times and prosperous times. We have seen progress, and we have been partners in the development of our great state.

But during the hard times, when we looked into the painful faces of the hungry and the unemployed, and we saw the tears of the desperate parents who could not properly feed or clothe their children, I called on you to join together and to help each other and you have responded.

As a child of the Depression, I have lived in both the "Old South" and the "New South." I have seen the results of the Depression which has held us back. But together, we have come through those dark times.

The "Old South" resisted federal encroachment into our everyday affairs, just as the "New South" does today. But our state has come out of the depths of poverty in my lifetime. And today—thank God—our state is a vibrant part of this nation. Our future is bright and there are some exciting times ahead for our people.

I would like to be a part of those times. And I can say with confidence that I could continue in this role for a number of years. And while my health is good at the present time, I must do what is best in the long run for the people of the state and for me.

During the past few days, I have done much evaluation and much soul searching. And some who are younger may not fully realized that I was called upon to pay a high price for my involvement in political life. In 1972, I was the leading candidate for the Democratic nomination for President when I was shot by a would-be assassin in Laurel, Maryland. I was doing what I had promised the people of Alabama I would do when they elected me governor. And that is to take our viewpoint to the people of the nation. And while my first love has always been the governorship of this state, I wanted to show that someone from Alabama could be elected president.

The five bullets that struck my body nearly 14 years ago inflicted me with a thorn in the flesh that has increasing taken its toll. And like the Apostle Paul, I have prayed for it to go away. But that is not to be.

I realize, in my own mind, that although I am doing fine at the present time, as I grow older the effect of my problem may become more noticeable and I may not be able to give you the fullest measure that you deserve from a governor throughout another term.

In light of this, and after much prayerful consideration, I feel that I must say that I have climbed my last political mountain. But there are still some personal hills that I must climb.

But for now, I must pass the rope and the pick to another climber and say, "Climb on." "Climb on to higher heights." Climb on until you reach the very peak. Then look back and wave at me. For I, too, will still be climbing. And in my melancholy moments, when I am tempted to think of the past . . . My service as governor . . . and my campaign in 1972 when I was shot, I may be inclined to do, as did Peter the Great upon reflecting of the death of his mother, when he remembered what the Apostle Paul said about not grieving for such things, and the Voice of Edras, "Call me again the day that is past."

And while I may be tempted to dwell in the past and say, "Oh what might have been," I must realize, as did Peter the Great, that it is time to "Lay aside that which can never return" and think about the future.

But for now, I conclude by telling you that my heart will always belong to the people of Alabama.

And I expect to be around for quite a few years to do whatever I can. But from the governmental and political arena, my fellow Alabamians, I must bid you a fond and affectionate farewell.

Statement on the 30th Anniversary of the Selma March, March 10, 1995

My friends, I have been watching your progress this week as you retrace your footsteps of 30 years ago and cannot help but reflect on those days that remain so vivid in my memory. Those were different days and we all in our own ways were different people. We have learned hard and important lessons in the 30 years that have passed between us since the days surrounding your first walk along Highway 80.

Those days were filled with passionate convictions and a magnified sense of purpose that imposed a feeling on us all that events of the day were bigger than any one individual. Much has transpired since those days. A great deal has been lost and a great deal has been gained, and here we are.

My message to you today is, Welcome to Montgomery.

May your message be heard.

May your lessons never be forgotten.

May our history be always remembered.

Chronology of Major Speeches

April 10, 1958   Joint appearance with other candidates at American Legion Post in Geneva, Alabama

April 11, 1958   Speech at Tuscaloosa Law Day Program

April 12, 1958   Speeches at Guntersville and Athens, Alabama

April 15, 1958   Speeches at Auburn, Opelika, and Fairfax, Alabama

April 16, 1958   Speeches at Camp Hill, Dadeville, Newsite, and Alexander City, Alabama

April 17, 1958   Speeches at Mobile and Baldwin, Alabama

May 1, 1958   Campaign Rally at Union Springs, Alabama

May 1, 1958   Speech at Birmingham, Alabama

May 2, 1958   Campaign rally at Mobile, Alabama

May 3, 1958   Speeches at Huntsville and Jasper City, Alabama

May 5, 1958   Final campaign rally at Montgomery City Auditorium

May 9, 1958   Statewide television address

May 11, 1958   Interview with Birmingham television station

May 12, 1958   Address to the Annual Convention of Alabama Association of Insurance Agents, Birmingham, Alabama

May 16, 1958   Speech at Russelville, Alabama

May 16, 1958   Statewide Television address on the Ku Klux Klan

May 17, 1958   Speeches at Moulton, Russelville, and Red Bay, Alabama

May 19, 1958   Speeches at Tuscumbia, Florence, and Athens, Alabama

May 20, 1958   Speeches at Huntsville, New Hope, Scottsboro, Bryant, Fort Payne, and Rainsville, Alabama

May 21, 1958   Speeches at Centre, Piedmont, Jacksonville, Anniston, and Tallidega, Alabama

May 22, 1958   Speeches at Ashland, Roanoke, LaFayette, Pepperell Mill, and Lanett, Alabama

May 23, 1958   Speeches at Opelika, Dadeville, Alexander City, Childersburg, and Birmingham, Alabama

May 24, 1958   Speeches at Guntersville, Albertville, Boaz, Altalia, and Gadsden, Alabama

May 25, 1958   Rally at Birmingham, Alabama

May 26, 1958   Statewide television address, Birmingham, Alabama

May 27, 1958	Speeches at Greenville, Andalusia, Evergreen, Brewton, and Robertsdale, Alabama
May 29, 1958	Speeches at Lamar, Fayetteville, Tuscaloosa, Sulligent, Fayette, and Northport, Alabama
May 30, 1958	Speeches at Hamilton, Guin, Winfield, Caron Hill, and Columbiana, Alabama
May 31, 1958	Speeches at Jasper, Cullman, Oneonta, and Pell City and television address from Birmingham, Alabama
June 1, 1958	Final campaign rally, Scottsboro, Alabama
November 21, 1961	Speech before the Alabama Freemasons
April 2, 1962	Rally speeches in Russelville, Pull, Campbell, Hackleberg, Hamilton, Guin, Winfield, and Fayette, Alabama
April 3, 1962	Appearance at Moundville, Alabama; speech given by Minnie Pearl, due to Wallace's laryngitis
April 4, 1962	Speeches at Brent, Centreville, Mapiersville, Jemison, Thursly, and Clayton, Alabama
April 5, 1962	Rally at Wetumpka, Alabama
April 7, 1962	Joint appearance with other candidates at Scottsboro's Monday Trade Day
April 8, 1962	Speeches in Madison County, Alabama
April 9, 1962	Rally at opening of campaign headquarters in Fairfield, Alabama
April 10, 1962	Speech at joint appearance with other candidates, American Legion Post, Geneva, Alabama
April 11, 1962	Speech at Tuscaloosa Law Day Program
April 12, 1962	Speeches at Guntersville, Hartselle, and Athens, Alabama
April 15, 1962	Speeches at Auburn, Opelika, and Fairfax, Alabama
April 16, 1962	Rallies at Camp Hill, Dadeville, Newsite, Alexander City, and Sylacauga, Alabama
April 17, 1962	Rally at Mobile, speech at Baldwin, Alabama
October 5, 1962	Speech delivered at Alabama Democratic Dinner
November 15, 1962	Speech to Alabama State Chamber of Commerce, Birmingham, Alabama
January 14, 1963	Inaugural Address, Montgomery, Alabama

February 3, 1963	Greek Orthodox Church 15th anniversary, Montgomery, Alabama
February 11, 1963	DAR Good Citizenship Girls, Montgomery, Alabama
March 8, 1963	Address to joint session of Alabama Legislature, first special session
March 19, 1963	Address to joint session of Alabama Legislature, second special session
April 17, 1963	Speech at groundbreaking, site of Millers Ferry Dam
April 21, 1963	Testimony before the House Judiciary Committee on a proposed constitutional amendment guaranteeing freedom of worship, Washington, D.C.
April 26, 1963	Message to the State Senate, second special session
May 7, 1963	Message to the State Legislature, regular session
	Remarks at groundbreaking, Lockheed Missiles and Space Company's Research and Engineering Center, Huntsville, Alabama
June 2, 1963	Appearance on *Meet the Press*
June 11, 1963	"School House Door" speech, University of Alabama
June 28, 1963	Veterans of Foreign Wars convention, Mobile, Alabama
	Testimony before the U.S. Senate Committee on Commerce in opposition to Senate Bill 1732
July 15, 1963	Speech before South Carolina Broadcaster Association, Myrtle Beach, South Carolina
July 24, 1963	Speech before the Miami-area Kiwanis Club, Miami, Florida
August 10, 1963	Address to the Citizens' Council of Louisiana, Inc., Shreveport, Louisiana
September 6, 1963	Message to the House of Representatives, Alabama Legislature
September 8, 1963	Broadcast to the citizens of Alabama on the situation in the public schools
October 14, 1963	Report to the citizens of Birmingham, Jefferson County
November 3, 1963	Appearance on panel discussing civil rights, WNAC-TV, Boston
November 4, 1963	"Practice of Segregation of the Races," Harvard College, Boston, Massachusetts

November 5, 1963	"A Major Fraud," Dartmouth College, Hanover, New Hampshire
November 6, 1963	"Brown v. School Board and the Law of the Land," Smith College, Northhampton, Massachusetts
November 7, 1963	"The Southern Legal Philosophy," Brown University, Providence, Rhode Island
January 7, 1964	Speech at Colorado State University, Fort Collins, Colorado
January 8, 1964	Speech at the University of Denver
January 9, 1964	Speech at the University of Arizona, Tucson, Arizona
January 10, 1964	Speech at UCLA, Los Angeles, California
January 13, 1964	Speech at the University of Oregon, Eugene, Oregon
January 14, 1964	Speech at the University of Washington, Seattle
January 16, 1964	Speech at the University of Victoria, British Columbia, Canada
February 12, 1964	Speech at the University of Cincinnati
	Speech sponsored by the American Opinion Library, Cincinnati
February 13, 1964	Speech at the Ohio State University
February 13, 1964	Speech for central Ohio chapter of Sigma Delta Chi
February 17, 1964	Speech at the University of Minnesota
February 19, 1964	Speech at the University of Wisconsin, Madison
February 20, 1964	Speech to the Rotary Club, Madison, Wisconsin
March 5, 1964	Address before the State Safety Coordinating Committee, Montgomery, Alabama
March 19, 1964	Speech formally opening campaign for Democratic presidential nomination, Appleton, Wisconsin
March 20, 1964	Speech at Civic Auditorium, Oshkosh, Wisconsin
March 23, 1964	Speech at Whitewater State College, Wisconsin
March 24, 1964	Speech at St. Norbert College, De Pere, Wisconsin

March 25, 1964   Speech at Green Bay, Wisconsin

March 27, 1964   Speech at Chippewa Falls, Wisconsin

March 30, 1964   Speech at La Crosse, Wisconsin

April 1, 1964   Speeches in Sheboygan and Manitowoc, Wisconsin

April 3, 1964   Speeches in Milwaukee and Madison, Wisconsin

April 4, 1964   Speeches in Janesville and Marquette University, Milwaukee, Wisconsin

April 20, 1964   Speech at Earlham College, Richmond, Indiana

April 21, 1964   Speech at Vincennes University, Indiana

April 23, 1964   Speech at Indiana University

April 29, 1964   Speech at Notre Dame University, South Bend, Indiana

April 30, 1964   Statement before the House Committee on the Judiciary in support of a proposed constitutional amendment guaranteeing the freedom of religious worship

May 15, 1964   Interview on the *Today Show*

                      Speech in Marlow Heights, Maryland

June 4, 1964   Speech before the National Press Club, Washington, D.C.

June 11, 1964   Address to the Organization Against Communism, Cleveland, Ohio

June 16, 1964   Speech to the Conservative Party of Texas, Dallas, Texas

June 17, 1964   Speech at Baton Rouge, Louisiana

June 23, 1964   Speech to U.S. Junior Chamber of Commerce, Dallas, Texas

June 25, 1964   Campaign rally at Mississippi State Coliseum, Jackson, Mississippi

June 26, 1964   Rally at Columbia Township Auditorium, Columbia, South Carolina

June 27, 1964   Rally at State Fairgrounds, Richmond, Virginia

July 4, 1964   Rally at Southeastern Fairgrounds, Atlanta, Georgia

July 9, 1964   Speech to the Lions International Convention, Toronto, Canada

July 10, 1964   Speech to the Alabama American Legion Convention, Mobile, Alabama

July 14, 1964   Speech at Little Rock, Arkansas

July 19, 1964   Televised appearance on *Face the Nation*

                      Speech before joint session of Alabama Legislature on congressional redistricting

August 6, 1964   Address to the joint session of the Alabama Legislature

August 21, 1964   Testimony before the Platform Committee, National Democratic Convention, Atlantic City, New Jersey

September 4, 1964 Speech before the State Safety Coordinating Committee, Montgomery, Alabama

September 11, 1964 Speech at Inland Docks plant, Phenix City, Alabama

September 16, 1964 Speech in Hammond, Indiana

Speech before the Southern Tuberculosis Conference, Atlanta, Georgia

September 21, 1964 Address before the joint session of the Alabama Legislature, second special session

October 25, 1964 Interview on *Meet the Press*

January 7, 1965   Address before the Tennessee School Boards Association, Nashville, Tennessee

February 16, 1965 Address before the joint session of the Alabama Legislature, first special session

March 11, 1965   Statement before the U.S. Subcommittee on Constitutional Amendments

March 14, 1965   Interview on *Face the Nation*

March 18, 1965   Speech before the Alabama Education Association, Birmingham, Alabama

Address to the joint session of the Alabama Legislature on the proposed Selma to Montgomery Civil Rights March

March 30, 1965   Reply to petition presented to the governor after the Selma to Montgomery Civil Rights March

April 11, 1965   Appearance on *Meet the Press*

April 14, 1965   Speech before the Governor's Traffic Safety Conference

April 15, 1965   Remarks at groundbreaking, Clairborne Lock and Dam, Monroeville, Alabama

Speech before the Alabama Farm Bureau Federation, Montgomery, Alabama

May 21, 1965   Address to the Alabama Legislature, regular session

June 6, 1965   Speech to the Louisiana Grand Masons, Baton Rouge, Louisiana

July 16, 1965   Speech to the American Legion Convention, Alabama District, Huntsville, Alabama

August 6, 1965   Message to the House of Representatives, Alabama Legislature

September 9,   Address to joint session of the Alabama Legislature
1965

September 23,   Speech before the Chamber of Commerce, New Orleans,
1965   Louisiana

September 30,   Address before the joint session of the Alabama Legislature
1965

November 11,   Speech at the Veterans Day program, Birmingham, Alabama
1965

January 28,   Speech delivered at Jones Law School, Montgomery, Alabama
1966

February 24,   Statement regarding Lurleen Wallace's candidacy for governor
1966

March 17, 1966   Speech before the Alabama Education Association, Birming-
                        ham, Alabama

April 1, 1966   Statement before the Special Subcommittee on State Taxation of
                        Interstate Commerce, Committee on the Judiciary, U.S. House
                        of Representatives

June 22, 1966   Address before the Louisiana State Legislature, Baton Rouge,
                        Louisiana

June 23, 1966   Speech to the Governor's Conference on Emergency Planning,
                        Montgomery, Alabama

July 26, 1966   Address to the joint session of the Alabama Legislature

August 18, 1966   Address to the joint session of the Alabama Legislature

January 25,   Statement before the Senate Finance Committee on Termination
1967   of Welfare Funds, Washington, D.C.

February 8,   Statement announcing candidacy for president of the United
1967   States, Montgomery, Alabama

February 17,   Speech before the Citizens Councils of America Leadership
1967   Conference, New Orleans, Louisiana

April 23, 1967   Interview on *Meet the Press*

April 27, 1967   Speech in Pittsburgh, Pennsylvania

September 2,   Speech in Baton Rouge, Louisiana
1967

October 6, 1967   Speech delivered at the University of Missouri-Kansas City

October 31,   Speech to the Comstock Club, Sacramento, California
1967

November 26, 1967   Speech delivered at campaign rally in Long Beach, California

February 19, 1968   Speech in Pittsburgh, Pennsylvania

September 22, 1968   Television interview on *Face the Nation*

October 1, 1968   Television interview aired on KDKA, Pittsburgh, Pennsylvania

October 2, 1968   Speech in Canton, Ohio

October 3, 1968   Speech in Toledo, Ohio

October 24, 1968   Speech at Madison Square Garden rally

October 27, 1968   Paid political broadcast on NBC

January 18, 1971   Inaugural Address, Montgomery, Alabama

January 19, 1971   Speech to the joint session of the Alabama Legislature, Montgomery, Alabama

March 18, 1971   Speech to the Alabama Education Association, Birmingham, Alabama

March 21, 1971   Address to the joint session of the Alabama Legislature, Montgomery, Alabama

April 28, 1971   Address before the Eighth Annual Safety Conference, Montgomery, Alabama

May 4, 1971   Speech to the joint session of the Alabama Legislature, Montgomery, Alabama

July 22, 1971   Speech to the joint session of the Alabama Legislature, Montgomery, Alabama

October 25, 1971   Speech before the World Peace Luncheon, Birmingham, Alabama

November 15, 1971   Address to the joint session of the Alabama Legislature, Montgomery, Alabama

December 18, 1971   Speech to the Birmingham Chamber of Commerce, Birmingham, Alabama

January 13, 1972   Statement of candidacy for president of the United States, Tallahassee, Florida

February 19, 1972   Speech in Melbourne, Florida

March 6, 1972   Speech to the joint session of the West Virginia Legislature, Wheeling, West Virginia

March 8, 1972   Speech to the Young Men's Hebrew Association, Miami Beach, Florida

March 11, 1972   Speech in Orlando, Florida

March 12, 1972   Documentary film supporting Wallace candidacy, broadcast statewide

Appearance on ABC Television "News Broadcast of Issues and Answers," Miami Beach, Florida

April 16, 1972   Speech in Detroit, Michigan

May 9, 1972   Speech in Dearborn, Michigan

May 15, 1972   Speeches in Wheaton and Laurel, Maryland

July 11, 1972   Address to the Democratic National Convention, Miami Beach, Florida

January 3, 1973 Remarks at Governor's Special Luncheon, Montgomery, Alabama

March 15, 1973   Address before the Alabama Education Association, Birmingham, Alabama

April 5, 1973   Statement before the Subcommittee on Domestic Finance of the Committee on Banking and Currency of the U.S. House of Representatives, Washington, D.C.

April 26, 1973   Speech before the Tenth Annual Traffic Safety Conference, Montgomery, Alabama

May 1, 1973   Address to the joint session of the Alabama Legislature, Montgomery, Alabama

June 15, 1973   Speech to the Alabama Association of Life Underwriters, Montgomery, Alabama

July 4, 1973   Speech at the Spirit of America Festival, Decatur, Alabama

July 10, 1973   Speech to the Multi-State Transportation Advisory Board, Montgomery, Alabama

July 15, 1973   Speech to the Democratic Party Advisory Commission on Delegate Selection, Atlanta, Georgia

July 20, 1973   Testimony to the Delegate Selection Commission Meeting, Democratic Party, Atlanta, Georgia

October 17, 1973 Address to the Future Farmers of America Convention, Kansas City, Missouri

October 26, 1973	Speech to the ABC Drug Enforcement Administration School, Montgomery, Alabama
October 31, 1973	Speech to the Special Education Teachers' Institute, Montgomery, Alabama
November 14, 1973	Speech to the Alabama Baptist Convention, Greensboro, Alabama
November 18, 1973	Speech to the Black Mayors Conference, Montgomery, Alabama
November 29, 1973	Speech to the Conference on Technology Assessment and Environmental Quality, Montgomery, Alabama
December 7, 1973	Speech to the Governor's Conference on Physical Fitness, Montgomery, Alabama
January 14, 1974	Speech to the Sheriff's Association, Prattville, Alabama
January 27, 1974	Speech to the United Mine Workers of America, Birmingham, Alabama
February 19, 1974	Speech welcoming President Nixon to Honor America Day, Huntsville, Alabama
February 22, 1974	Opening speech for the Democratic primary, Montgomery, Alabama
April 23, 1974	Address to the Annual Convention of the PTA, Tuscaloosa, Alabama
May 7, 1974	Speech on winning the primary, Montgomery, Alabama
May 15, 1974	Speech on the 100th anniversary of Alabama State University, Montgomery, Alabama
June 7, 1974	Speech to the Troy University School of Nursing, Montgomery, Alabama
July 26, 1974	Speech to the Leadership Conference for Educators, Montgomery, Alabama
August 15, 1974	Address to the Greater New Orleans Chamber of Commerce, New Orleans, Louisiana
August 16, 1974	Speech to the National Legislative Conference, Albuquerque, New Mexico
August 21, 1974	Speech to the Marion Institute Alumni Association Dinner, Marion, Alabama
November 7, 1974	Speech at the Alabama Progressive Baptist State Convention, Dexter Avenue Baptist Church, Montgomery, Alabama

January 20,   Inaugural Address, Montgomery, Alabama
1975

January 21,   Address to the joint session of the Alabama Legislature, Mont-
1975   gomery, Alabama

February 23,   Speech to the National Governor's Conference
1975

May 5, 1976   Address to the joint session of the Alabama Legislature, Mont-
                      gomery, Alabama

February 1,   Address to the joint session of the Alabama Legislature, Mont-
1977   gomery, Alabama

January 3, 1978   Address to the joint session of the Alabama Legislature, Mont-
                      gomery, Alabama

April 2, 1986   Retirement speech, Montgomery, Alabama

March 10, 1995   Statement on the 30th Anniversary of the Selma March, Mont-
                      gomery, Alabama

Selected Bibliography

MANUSCRIPTS AND ARCHIVAL MATERIAL

The Wallace papers are not as easily available to scholars as are the papers of most political figures of the twentieth century. The Alabama Department of Archives and History in Montgomery, Alabama, has the papers from Wallace's years as governor of the state. The papers for his first term are catalogued and are available to scholars. The papers for his later terms have not been organized and catalogued, and this poses problems for their use. When Wallace left office in 1987, he donated his personal papers and the papers from his presidential campaigns to the Wallace Foundation with the intention that eventually they would be part of a Center for the Study of Southern Politics. Unfortunately, the funds necessary to establish and administer such an institution did not materialize. The Wallace Foundation closed its office. The uncatalogued papers were boxed and stored in a warehouse in Montgomery, where they are unavailable for use by scholars.

BOOKS ABOUT WALLACE AND SOUTHERN POLITICS

Bass, Jack, and Walter DeVries. *The Transformation of Southern Politics: Social Change and Political Consequences since 1945*. New York: Basic Books, 1976.

Black, Earl. *Southern Governors and Civil Rights: Racial Segregation as a Campaign Issue in the Second Reconstruction*. Cambridge, Mass.: Harvard University Press, 1976.

Botsch, Robert Emil. *We Shall Not Overcome: Populism and Southern Blue-Collar Workers*. Chapel Hill: University of North Carolina Press, 1980.

Brauer, Carl. *John F. Kennedy and the Second Reconstruction.* New York: Columbia University Press, 1977.

Canfield, James Lewis. *A Case of Third Party Activism: The George Wallace Campaign Workers and the American Independent Party.* Washington, D.C.: University Press of America.

Carson, Clayborne, David Garrow, Gerald Gill, Vincent Harding, and Darlene Clark Hine, eds. *The Eyes on the Prize Civil Rights Reader.* New York: Penguin Books, 1991.

Carlson, Jody. *George C. Wallace and the Politics of Powerlessness: The Wallace Campaigns for the Presidency, 1964–1976.* New Brunswick, N.J.: Transaction Books, 1981.

Carter, Dan T. *The Politics of Rage: George Wallace, the Origins of the New Conservatism, and the Transformation of American Politics.* New York: Simon & Schuster, 1995.

Cash, W. J. *The Mind of the South.* New York: Alfred A. Knopf, 1941.

Chester, Lewis, Godfrey Hodgson, and Bruce Page. *An American Melodrama: The Presidential Campaign of 1968.* New York: Viking Press, 1969.

Clark, E. Culpepper. *The Schoolhouse Door: Segregation's Last Stand at the University of Alabama.* New York: Oxford University Press, 1993.

Crass, Phillip. *The Wallace Factor.* New York: Mason/Charter, 1976.

Crawford, Alan. *Thunder on the Right: The "New Right" and the Politics of Resentment.* New York: Pantheon Books, 1980.

Dorman, Michael. *The George Wallace Myth.* New York: Bantam, 1976.

Faber, Harold. *The Road to the White House. The Story of the 1964 Election by the Staff of the New York Times.* New York: New York Times, 1965.

Fager, Charles E. *Selma, 1965: The March That Changed the South.* 2nd ed. Boston: Beacon Press, 1985.

Frady, Marshall. *Wallace.* New York: Random House, 1996.

Garrow, David J. *Protest at Selma: Martin Luther King, Jr., and the Voting Rights Act of 1965.* New Haven, Conn.: Yale University Press, 1978.

Greenhaw, Wayne. *Watch Out for George Wallace.* Englewood Cliffs, N.J.: Prentice-Hall, 1976.

Hofstadter, Richard. *The Paranoid Style in American Politics and Other Essays.* New York: Alfred A. Knopf, 1965.

House, Jack. *George Wallace Tells It Like It Is.* Selma, Ala.: Dallas, 1969.

———. *Lady of Courage: The Story of Lurleen Burns Wallace.* Montgomery, Ala.: League Press, 1969.

Jones, Bill. *The Wallace Story.* Northport, Ala.: American Southern, 1966.

Kennedy, Robert Francis, Jr. *Judge Frank M. Johnson.* New York: G. P. Putnam's Sons, 1978.

LeMay, Curtis E. *America Is in Danger.* New York: Funk & Wagnalls, 1968.

Lesher, Stephan. *George Wallace: American Populist.* Reading, Mass.: Addison-Wesley, 1994.

Lienesh, Michael. *Redeeming American: Piety and Politics in the New American Right.* Chapel Hill: University of North Carolina Press, 1993.

The Life of George Wallace: "Our Kind of Man." Clayton, Ala.: Friends of George C. Wallace, 1970.

Lipset, Seymour, and Earl Raab. *The Politics of Unreason: Right Wing Extremism in America, 1790–1970.* New York: Basic Books, 1970.

Logue, Cal M., and Howard Dorgan. *The Oratory of Southern Demagogues.* Baton Rouge: Louisiana University Press, 1981.

Lubell, Samuel. *The Hidden Crisis in American Politics.* New York: Norton, 1970.

Novak, Michael. *Choosing Our King: Powerful Symbols in Presidential Politics.* New York: Macmillan, 1974.

Permaloff, Anne, and Carl Grafton. *Political Power in Alabama: The More Things Change.* Athens: University of Georgia Press, 1995.

Sachs, Patricia, ed. *George Wallace: A Rebel and His Cause.* New York: Universal, 1968.

Sherrill, Robert. *Gothic Politics in the Deep South.* New York: Grossman, 1968.

Sims, George E. *The Little Man's Big Friend: James E. Folsom in Alabama Politics, 1946–1958.* Tuscaloosa: University of Alabama Press, 1985.

Smith, Stephen. A. *Myth, Media, and the Southern Mind.* Fayetteville: University of Arkansas Press, 1985.

Synon, John J. *George Wallace. Profile of a Presidential Candidate.* Kilmarnook, Va.: Manuscripts, 1968.

Thompson, Hunter S. *Fear and Loathing on the Campaign Trail '72.* San Francisco: Straight Arrow Books, 1973.

Wallace, Cornelia. *C'Nelia.* Philadelphia: Holman, 1976.

Wallace, George C. *Hear Me Out.* Anderson, South Carolina: Droke House, 1968.

———. *Stand Up for America.* Garden City, N.Y.: Doubleday, 1976.

Wallace, George, Jr. *The Wallaces of Alabama: My Family.* Chicago: Follett, 1975.

White, Theodore. *The Making of the President, 1964.* New York: Atheneum, 1965.

———. *The Making of the President, 1968.* New York: Atheneum, 1969.

———. *The Making of the President, 1972.* New York: Atheneum, 1973.

Wills, Garry. *Nixon Agonistes.* Boston: Houghton Mifflin, 1970.

Witcover, Jules. *Marathon: The Pursuit of the Presidency 1972–1976.* New York: Viking Press, 1977.

ARTICLES

Ace, Goodman. "Southern Discomfort." *Saturday Review,* October 1, 1966, 11.

Alsop, Stewart. "The Little Man in the Catbird Seat." *Saturday Evening Post,* March 25, 1968, 20.

"Answer to Wallace." *New Republic,* March 9, 1968, 8.

"Bomber on the Stump." *Time,* October 16, 1968, 20.

Brill, Steven. "George Wallace Is Even Worse Than You Think He Is." *New York,* March 17, 1975, 37.

Buckley, William F., Jr. "The Power of George Wallace." *National Review,* November 19, 1968, 1152–1153.

Conway, M. Margaret. "The White Backlash Re-Examined: Wallace and the 1964 Primaries." *Social Science Quarterly* 49 (1968): 710–719.

Crawford, Kenneth. "What George Is Doing." *Newsweek,* May 27, 1967, 45.

"Enigma in the South." *Time,* May 12, 1967, 20–21.

Evans, Rowland, and Robert Novak. "Wallace Tactics Lure G.O.P. Right Wing." Syndicated column, February 23, 1968.

Frady, Marshall. "Governor and Mister Wallace." *Atlantic Monthly* 220 (August 1967): 35–40.
———. "The Return of George Wallace." *New York Review of Books*, October 30, 1975, 16–26.
"George's Asphalt Jungle." *Time*, May 10, 1968, 30–31.
"George Wallace Tells His Plans." *U.S. News & World Report*, September 30, 1968, 34–36.
Gilbert, Christopher P., Timothy R. Johnson, and David A. M. Peterson. "The Religious Roots of Third Candidate Voting: A Comparison of Anderson, Perot, and Wallace Voters." *Journal for the Scientific Study of Religion* 34 (1995): 470–481.
Goldwater, Barry. "Don't Waste a Vote on Wallace." *National Review*, October 22, 1968, 1060–1061.
Goldzwig, Steven R., and George N. Dionisopoulos. "John F. Kennedy's Civil Rights Discourse: The Evolution from 'Principled Bystander' to Public Advocate." *Communication Monographs* 56 (1989): 179–198.
Hardwick, Elizabeth. "Mr. America." *New York Review of Books*, November 7, 1968.
Harte, Thomas B. "The Rhetoric of Pox: Invention in George Wallace's Speech at Cape Girardeu, Missouri." *Central States Speech Journal* 23(1972): 202–205.
Hogan, J. Michael. "Wallace and the Wallacites: A Reexamination." *Southern Speech Communication Journal* 50 (Fall, 1984): 24–48.
"How Wallace Fared on His Trip North." *U.S. News & World Report*, May 8, 1967, 12.
"How Wallace Sees the Issues." *U.S. News & World Report*, March 20, 1967, 57–60.
Jenkins, Ray. "Wallace." *New York Times Magazine*, April 7, 1968, 27–90.
Kimball, Penn. "The Politics of Style." *Saturday Review*, June 8, 1968, 26.
Knap, Thaddeus L. "George Wallace Maps His Way to the White House." *New Republic*, April 29, 1967, 7–9.
Lardner, George, Jr. "Politics of Protest Aids Wallace Cause." *Washington Post*, September 14, 1968, A3.
———. "Wallace Unveils Platform." *Washington Post*, October 14, 1968, 1.
Leamer, Lawrence. "Out West with Candidate Wallace." *New Republic*, December 16, 1967, 11–13.
"Legacy of a Healed Hater: George Wallace, 1918–1998." *Newsweek*, September 28, 1998, 51.
Lipset, Seymour Martin. "George Wallace and the New U.S. New Right." *New Society*, October 3, 1968, 477–483.
Lipset, Seymour Martin, and Earl Raab. "The Wallace Whitelash." *Transaction* 7 (December 1969): 23–35.
"Long Says Wallace Leads in the South." *New York Times*, May 31, 1968, 30C.
Makay, John J. "George C. Wallace: Southern Spokesman with a Northern Audience." *Central States Speech Journal* 19 (Fall 1968), 202–207.
———. "The Rhetoric of George C. Wallace and the 1964 Civil Rights Law." *Communication Quarterly* 18 (1970): 26–33.
———. " The Rhetorical Strategies of Governor George Wallace in the 1964 Maryland Primary." *Southern Speech Journal* 36 (Winter 1970): 164–175.
Martin, Harold H. "George Wallace, the Angry Man's Candidate." *Saturday Evening Post*, June 15, 1968, 23–25.

Meyer, Frank. S. "Principles and Heresies: The Populism of George Wallace." *National Review,* May 16, 1967, 527.

"A New Look at Wallace: What He May Do to the Election." *U.S. News & World Report,* January 29, 1968, 56–57.

"On the Campaign Trail with Wallace." *U.S. News & World Report,* May 15, 1967, 20.

Pettigrew, Thomas F., Robert T. Riley, and Reve D Vannerman. "George Wallace's Constituents." *Psychology Today* 5 (February 1972), 47–49.

"The Racist Candidate." *New York Times,* February 9, 1968, 26.

"Requiem for an Arsonist: George Corley Wallace 1919–1998." *Time,* September 28, 1998, 54.

Reston, James. "Wallace's Electoral College Blackmail." *New York Times,* February 18, 1968, 28.

Roberts, Steven V. "Civil Servants: Wallace Voices Their Frustration." *New York Times,* October 27, 1968, 6E.

Rogin, Michael. "Wallace and the Middle Class: The White Backlash in Wisconsin." *Public Opinion Quarterly* 30 (1966): 98–108.

Rohler, Lloyd. "Conservative Appeals to the People: George Wallace's Populist Rhetoric." *Southern Communication Journal* 64 (1999): 316–322.

Rosenfield, Lawrence W. "George Wallace Plays Rosemary's Baby." *Quarterly Journal of Speech* 55 (1969): 36–44.

Rugaber, Walter. "Wallace: He Also Runs." *New York Times,* June 23, 1968, sec. 4, 2E.

———. "Wallace's Drive in South Decried." *New York Times,* June 18, 1968, 35C.

"The Spoiler." *Newsweek,* April 3, 1967, 34.

"The Spoiler." *Newsweek,* May 8, 1967, 39–40.

"Southern Black Mayors Give Wallace Standing Ovation at a Conference." *New York Times,* November 19, 1973, 25.

"Stand Up for George." *Newsweek,* December 4, 1967, 31–32.

Swanson, David L. "The Rhetoric of Political Revolt: George C. Wallace." *Speaker and Gavel* 6 (1969): 45–54.

"The Third Man Theme." *Newsweek,* August 26, 1968, 28.

"A Third Party in '68? The George Wallace Story." *U.S. News & World Report,* March 20, 1967, 54–57.

"Up to the Bourgeoisie." *Newsweek,* September 30, 1968, 24–25.

"Wallace and His Folks." *Newsweek,* September 16, 1968, 25–28.

"Wallace Campaign: Getting Ready for Another Run." *Congressional Quarterly Weekly Report,* 179 (October 30, 1971), 2220–2225.

"Wallace Describes Slaying as 'Tragic.'" *New York Times,* April 6, 1968, 24C.

"Wallace Drops Presidential Bid; Denies Any Deals." *New York Times,* July 20, 1964, 1.

"Wallace in the West." *Time,* December 9, 1967, 27.

"Wallace Invites Others into Race." *New York Times,* March 24, 1968, 27.

"Wallace Likely to Win Primary Today; Seeks Black Support for National Bid." *New York Times,* May 7, 1974, 30.

"Wallace Opens 1976 White House Drive." *New York Times,* November 13, 1975, 1.

"Wallace Race in '68—As Governors See It." *U.S. News & World Report,* September 25, 1967, 77.

"Wallace Sets Fire to the '68 Campaign." *U.S. News & World Report,* September 30, 1968, 32–33.

"Wallace Watching." *New Republic*, March 2, 1968, 5.

"Wallace's Army: The Coalition of Frustration." *Time*, October 18, 1968, 16–20.

"The Wallaces: More Clues to '68 Plans." *U.S. News & World Report*, January 30, 1967, 14.

"Wallace's New Math," *Newsweek*, January 15, 1968, 18.

"What's Happening to the Democrats," *U.S. News & World Report*, December 18, 1967, 31–33.

Wicker, Tom. "George Wallace: A Gross and Simple Heart." *Harper's*, April, 1967, 41–49.

Widick, B. J. "Rebellion in the Shops: Why They Like Wallace." *Nation*, October 14, 1968, 358–359.

DISSERTATIONS AND THESES

Armstrong, Forrest Harrell. "George C. Wallace: Insurgent on the Right." Ph.D. dissertation, University of Michigan, 1970.

Cooper, James Pershing. "The Rise of George C. Wallace: Alabama Politics and Policy, 1958–1966." Ph.D. dissertation, Vanderbilt University, 1987.

Fadely, Lawrence Dean. "George Wallace, Agitator Rhetorician: A Rhetorical Criticism of George Corley Wallace's 1968 Presidential Campaign." Ph.D. dissertation, University of Pittsburgh, 1974.

Grasmick, Harold George. "Social Change and the Wallace Movement in the South." Ph.D. dissertation, University of North Carolina, 1973.

Hogan, J. Michael. "George Wallace's Political Revivalism: A Case Study in the Political Application of Religious Rhetorical Strategies." M.A. Thesis, University of Wisconsin, 1977.

Husbands, C. T. "The Campaign Organizations and Patterns of Popular Support of George C. Wallace in Wisconsin and Indiana in 1964 and 1968." Ph.D. dissertation, University of Chicago, 1972.

Hynson, Lawrence McKee, Jr. "Status Inconsistency, Classification and the George Wallace Support in the 1968 Presidential Elections." Ph.D. dissertation, University of Tennessee, 1972.

Makay, John Joseph. "The Speaking of Governor George C. Wallace in the 1964 Presidential Primary." Ph.D. dissertation, Purdue University, 1969.

Swanson, David L. "An Analysis of the Rhetorical Design of George C. Wallace's 1968 Presidential Campaign." Master's thesis, University of Kansas, 1969.

SPEECH TEXTS

Johnson, Lyndon B. "Special Message to Congress, March 15, 1965." In *Public Papers of the Presidents of the United States, Lyndon B. Johnson.* Vol. 1, 281–287. Washington, D.C.: United States Government Printing Office, 1965.

Kennedy, John Fitzgerald. "Radio and Television Report to the American People on Civil Rights, The White House, June 11, 1963." In *Papers of the Presidents of the United States, John F. Kennedy: Containing the Messages, Speeches, and Statements of the President, 1961–1963,* 468–471. Washington, D.C.: United States Printing Office, 1962.

Wallace, George. "Speech at Madison Square Garden, October 24, 1968." In *History of U.S. Political Parties,* ed. Arthur M. Schlesinger, Jr., 4:3491–3497. New York: Chelsea House Publishers, 1973.

———. "Speech in Cleveland, Ohio, October 3, 1968." In *The Rhetorical Dialogue: Contemporary Concepts and Cases,* ed. John J. Makay and William R. Brown, 244–249. Dubuque, Iowa: William R. Brown, 1972.

VIDEOS

Crisis: Behind a Presidential Commitment. 16 mm, 52 min. Drew Associates, Brooklyn, N.Y., 1963. First broadcast by ABC News.

Wallace: Settin' the Woods on Fire. Produced and directed by Daniel McCabe and Paul Stekler. PBS Video, Washington, D.C., 2000. Videocassette.

Index

About the Author

LLOYD ROHLER is Professor of Communication Studies, University of
North Carolina, Wilmington.

Great American Orators

Dwight D. Eisenhower: Strategic Communicator
Martin J. Medhurst

Ralph Waldo Emerson: Preacher and Lecturer
Lloyd Rohler

"In a Perilous Hour": The Public Address of John F. Kennedy
Steven R. Goldzwig and George N. Dionisopoulos

Douglas MacArthur: Warrior as Wordsmith
Bernard K. Duffy and Ronald H. Carpenter

Sojourner Truth as Orator: Wit, Story, and Song
Suzanne Pullon Fitch and Roseann M. Mandziuk

Frederick Douglass: Oratory from Slavery
David B. Chesebrough

Father Charles E. Coughlin: Surrogate Spokesperson for the Disaffected
Ronald H. Carpenter

Margaret Chase Smith: Model Public Servant
Marlene Boyd Vallin

Helen Keller, Public Speaker: Sightless but Seen, Deaf but Heard
Lois J. Einhorn

Theodore Parker: Orator of Superior Ideas
David B. Chesebrough

Phillips Brooks: Pulpit Eloquence
David B. Chesebrough

Charles G. Finney: Revivalistic Rhetoric
David B. Chesebrough